ADOLESCENT PROBLEM BEHAVIORS
Issues and Research

Edited by

Robert D. Ketterlinus
Public/Private Ventures, Philadelphia
Michael E. Lamb
National Institute of Child Health and Human Development

LEA LAWRENCE ERLBAUM ASSOCIATES, PUBLISHERS
1994   Hillsdale, New Jersey   Hove, UK

Lawrence Erlbaum Associates, Inc., Publishers
365 Broadway
Hillsdale, New Jersey 07642

Library of Congress Cataloging-in-Publication Data

Adolescent problem behaviors : issues and research / edited by Robert
    D. Ketterlinus, Michael E. Lamb.
          p.   cm.
          Papers from a conference held Apr. 1991, in Berkeley
    Springs, West Virginia.
          Includes bibliographical references and index.
          ISBN 0-8058-1156-7 (alk paper). -- ISBN 0-8058-1157-5
    (pbk. : alk. paper)
        1. Adolescent psychology. 2. Problem children. 3. Conflict
    (Psychology) in adolescence. 4. Interpersonal conflict in adoles-
    cence. 5. Risk taking (Psychology) in adolescence.
    I. Ketterlinus, Robert D. II. Lamb, Michael E., 1953–   .
    BF724.A276 1994
    305.23'5--dc20   93-40763
                                                              CIP

Books published by Lawrence Erlbaum Associates are printed
on acid-free paper, and their bindings are chosen for strength
and durability.

Printed in the United States of America
10 9 8 7 6 5 4 3 2 1

Contents

Introduction

Robert D. Ketterlinus
Public/Private Ventures, Philadelphia
Michael E. Lamb
National Institute of Child Health and Human Development

> *In all civilized lands, criminal statistics show two sad and significant facts: First, that there is a marked increase in crime at the age of twelve to fourteen, not in crimes of one but of all kinds, and that this increase continues for a number of years. While the percentage of certain grave crimes increases to mature manhood, adolescence is preeminently the criminal age when most first commitments occur and most vicious careers are begun. The second fact is that the proportion of juvenile delinquents seems to be everywhere increasing and crime is more and more precocious...the significance of these facts for ethics, sociology, genetic psychology, and for the efficiency of education and religion, as well as for the success of a form of civilization, is profound and complex.*

—G. Stanley Hall (1904)

Except, perhaps, for its reference to religion, this statement by the founder of scientific child psychology could have been made by any number of contemporary social scientists interested in youthful misbehavior and deviance. Hall was the first to recognize adolescence as the period during which delinquent and criminal behaviors were most likely to emerge, and his insight has been verified repeatedly by his distant heirs and successors in the modern fields of psychology, psychiatry, criminology, and sociology. Unfortunately for him, Hall's seminal work has been largely forgotten or ignored, in part because of its atheoretical nature, outdated assumptions, and beliefs (e.g., that "ontogeny recapitulates phylogeny," and that maturation plays a major role in development), and his moralistic tone. Hall nevertheless deserves credit for being the first to identify the well-established relationship between age and problem behavior, and the negative effects of adolescent problem behavior on society. Indeed, the awareness of adolescent problem behaviors is now so great that thousands of scientific papers have been written in the past several decades, while countless policymakers and theorists have pondered mechanisms for prevention, intervention, and basic research (Smith, 1988). This book selectively surveys our current understanding of adolescent problem behaviors; contributors provide a variety of theoretical and empirical perspectives on the ontogeny, correlates, consequences, and treatment of adolescent problem behaviors.

In April 1991, a group of scholars gathered in Berkeley Springs, West Virginia, to present and discuss their recent research and theoretical attempts to explain the antecedents, correlates, and consequences of adolescent problem behaviors. Although many publications dealing with the problems of youth have appeared in recent years (e.g., Feldman & Elliott, 1990; Leone, 1990; Millstein, Petersen, & Nightingale, 1992; Rogers & Ginzberg 1992; Task Force, 1989), no other publication has presented as wide a variety of perspectives on adolescent problem behaviors as did the Berkeley Springs conference. In organizing this conference and editing this volume, our goals were to promote communication among representatives of the different disciplines—sociology, developmental, clinical, and social psychology, criminology, psychiatry, epidemiology, and history—concerned with adolescent problem behavior and allow scientists to explain, compare, and discuss commonalities and differences in their perspectives, and in the implications of their work for research, intervention, and public policy. To maximize cross-disciplinary integration, we asked each of the contributing authors to discuss in their chapters two broad themes that cut across disciplinary and theoretical boundaries: gender differences and prevention or intervention strategies. Boys are consistently more likely than girls to engage in problem behavior, yet little attention has been paid either to the origins and interpretation of these gender differences or to an examination of the distinctive problems that girls manifest. The preoccupation with the behaviors displayed by males has in turn led to a biased perception that offenders are typically male and that intervention should be focused on males. Many of the contributors discuss these issues in their chapters. In addition, most also offer their theoretical and empirical insights into the design and focus of intervention programs to help prevent involvement in problem behaviors and ameliorate the adverse consequences of such involvement.

OUTLINE OF THE BOOK

In the remainder of this introduction, we provide a chapter-by-chapter "road map" of the book. A wide range of perspectives is offered in this volume, and the chapters are arranged so that the broadest perspectives are presented first, followed by those offering a narrower perspective. In chapter 1, therefore, Moran and Vinovskis review the history of "Troubled Youth," whereas in chapter 10 Andrews and

Dishion describe ongoing research designed to specify the social learning process whereby problem behaviors are developed and maintained.

In order to be understood, adolescence in general, and adolescent problem behaviors in particular, must be placed in sociohistorical context. One implication is that the definitions of problematic behaviors and appropriate responses to them are socially constructed by individuals, sociopolitical organizations, and professional associations, all of whom have a vested interest in defining the "problem" and providing a "solution" (Burnham, 1960; Gilbert, 1986; Hilgartner & Bosk, 1988; Nathanson, 1991). Although the U. S. government did not recognize adolescents as a distinct group requiring government attention until 1972 (President's Commission on Population Growth and the American Future, 1972), Moran and Vinovskis note in chapter 1 that adolescence has been viewed since the mid-19th century as a part of the life span during which societal concern and intervention is warranted. For example, the first U. S. reformatory for *delinquent* or *dependent* children (terms used interchangeably from the antebellum through the Progressive eras) opened (in Elmira, New York) in 1824 and although the first juvenile court was not founded until 1899, the Chicago criminal courts began treating juveniles and adults differently as early as 1861 (Levine & Levine, 1992). Moran and Vinovskis argue that the contemporary concern with "troubling and troubled youth" (Leone, 1990) is neither historically nor culturally unique. Rather, such concerns were evident in precolonial England, colonial Chesapeake and New England, and in 19th-century America. In the course of their historical survey, Moran and Vinovskis examine and ultimately reject the common assumption that "youth" was not viewed as a distinct phase of life before modern times.

Before scholars can begin to understand the causes and correlates of adolescent problem behaviors in the contemporary era, we must be clear about the definition and prevalence of the behaviors concerned. As explained by Robert Ketterlinus and his colleagues in chapter 2, the primary problems faced by modern U. S. youth include delinquency, violence, alcohol and other illicit drug use, sexually transmitted diseases, and premature pregnancy/parenthood. As Ketterlinus et al. point out, however, these diverse problems have typically been the unique focus of interest or disciplinary groups with vested public and professional interests. Because these diverse behaviors and problems tend to co-occur, however, both researchers and youth themselves might be served better if the prevailing categorical approach was replaced by awareness of the interrelated correlates and causes of adolescent problem behavior. In their chapter, Ketterlinus et al. also attempt to integrate two generally distinct research traditions, one concerned with sociological (and to a lesser degree, psychological) research on delinquency, drug use, school-related problem behaviors, and the other concerned with sexual risk taking and its correlates—sexually transmitted disease, pregnancy, and parenthood.

In chapter 3, Michael Gottfredson and Travis Hirschi summarize their "general theory of adolescent problem behavior": an attempt to integrate, and go beyond, narrowly focused explanations of problem behavior. As in their earlier book (Gottfredson & Hirschi, 1990), the authors suggest that adolescent problem behavior can be attributable to a characteristic or trait that they label *low self-control.* This theory has important implications for prevention, and these are discussed by Gottfredson and Hirschi, as are some of the major issues that arise when any general explanation of behavior is developed.

"Divergent paths of influence" on the development of deviant behavior are portrayed from two perspectives in the next two chapters. In chapter 4, Michael Rutter and his colleagues report findings from their longitudinal studies of criminality and affective disorders showing that, despite the statistical "comorbidity" of conduct disorders and depressive symptomatology in adolescence, these conditions do not reflect common underlying causal factors. These highly correlated disorders actually have distinct long-term sequelae: adolescent conduct disorders leading to adult criminality and ubiquitous social malfunctioning, whereas adolescent depression presages a constellation of adult affective disorders.

Different research strategies and theoretical perspectives are then offered by David Magnusson and his colleagues in chapter 5. These researchers identify two groups of individuals: those who exhibit antisocial behavior only as adolescents, and those who are persistent offenders. Using both "variable" and "person" approaches to their data, Magnusson and his colleagues identify distinct biological antecedents of behavior problems in these distinct groups of juvenile and persistent offenders. Specifically, persistent offenders manifest low levels of adrenal activity, other signs of low autonomic activity/reactivity, and behavioral hyperactivity, which are all absent among juvenile offenders who do not behave antisocially as adults. Explanations of both acute and persistent adolescent problem behavior range from those that focus on innate tendencies to those that only acknowledge environmental factors.

The authors of the next two chapters focus even more explicitly on biological and genetic factors in the etiology of problem behaviors than do Magnusson et al. In chapter 6, Richard Udry sketches his "biosocial" theory of adolescent problem behavior, in which both social and biological factors are assigned formative roles in the origins of adolescent problem behaviors. He then compares the results of several cross-sectional and panel studies testing either additive, intermediate, or interactional models of biological and social processes before concluding that biologically based predispositions—primarily temperament—may play a more fundamental role in the etiology of problem behaviors than the environmental factors that act to shape the manifestation of these predispositions. Udry also presents some tantalizing preliminary data from a longitudinal study of 350 women who were born in the 1960s and who have been studied since the prenatal period. Personality differences among these women at the age of 5 predicted differences in the extent of their involvement in problem behaviors in adolescence. Efforts are now being made to further test and refine the biosocial model by relating levels of adolescent problem behavior to measures of biological functioning in the early years.

Although his data are consistent with Udry's model, David Rowe (chapter 7) places much greater emphasis than Udry does on the genetic determinants of involvement in adolescent problem behaviors. After discussing the genetic and cultural transmission of behavioral phenotypes, Rowe focuses on two models of adolescent problem behaviors—the sibling effects model, and the model of epi-

PROTECTION FROM RISK

One of the most positive and hopeful discussions centered around the potential for understanding the real-life and fantasy experiences of an adolescent and the protective factors that can be designed and introduced to help prevent behavior problems and risk taking behavior.

At the Berkeley Springs conference, Jessor was especially prominent in his appeal for us to regard adolescent behavior as a manifestation of an ongoing life. His work centers around attempting to understand the problems and behaviors as perceived by the adolescent, attempting to analyze the meaning and purpose of the behavior itself, what is going on in the individual considering each of these factors in terms of the social context, and most important, being able to conceptualize the adolescent as a whole person, not as a series of appropriate or inappropriate expressions of behavior (Jessor, 1992).

As we know, risk behavior involves certain costs to the individual and to society. But, it can also have certain positive effects for survival and protection. In that sense, risk behavior should be differentiated from risk-taking behavior, which is more apt to be involved with such factors as personality and deviance. From interrelated conceptual domains, Jessor postulated the risk factors and the protective factors that exist in the biological/genetic components, the social environment, the perceived environment, and the personality/behavior components.

Such risk factors as poverty, deviant behavior, and low self-esteem are rather easily identified, but difficult to study. Whereas, such protective factors as quality schools, cohesive family, neighborhood resources, invested adults, models of conventional behavior, high controls against deviant behavior, value on achievement, and value on healthy lifestyle are factors that we already know a lot about, have a positive "spin," and could serve as a forceful intervention strategy.

Attempting to change the environment, the schools, the family, involving committed adults, and promoting positive role models may be more difficult and costly than attempting to study the problems and risk factors of adolescence. However, the participants at the conference expressed the view that it could also have a long-term effect that would be very positive and would be of much greater value to society and to our future relationships with adolescents.

CRITICAL METHODOLOGY ISSUES

Validity. Much of our data gathering in studying the problems of adolescence and risk-taking behavior has been acquired through the responses of adolescents to surveys and questionnaires. Although we make every attempt to refine and revise each question so that it can be clearly understood, we rarely make any attempt to validate the understanding, the meaning of the response, the context within which the respondent considered the question and the answer, the motivation of the respondent, and/or the "truth" of the responses we get. This is a major problem with most surveys, not just those directed at adolescents.

It is not that respondents lie. Often it is just that there is a fine line between the absolute truth and the level of disclosure an individual cares to express, or to what extent the responder may consider the question to be an intentional or unintentional invasion of their own privacy.

Every clinician knows that there are certain things a patient will not disclose completely, or will modify a little, for many different reasons. Most frequently this selective screening or padding, occurs with regard to questions that might be perceived by the individual as a potential invasion of their privacy or require complete disclosure. Such sensitivity often occurs with regard to sexual activity, amount of alcohol consumed per day or week, quantity or calories of food consumed in a diet, number of cigarettes smoked per day, amount of exercise, voting behavior, and income.

The instinct or sensitivity to guard against invasion of privacy is very strong and can be easily triggered, even when an individual is trying to be conscientious and cooperative. In an adolescent's mind, it may easily be more important what a peer, a doctor, a parent, or a teacher may think about you or your response, than to try to disclose everything.

The problem is that we do not really know the extent of the validity of a survey or questionnaire response. This is a methodological issue that deserves as much attention as we give to the design of the questions themselves. We should have some standard for documentation of validity, as we now have for statistical analysis. Otherwise, we risk spending a disproportional amount of time and expense with misleading data and premature conclusions, which will make our attempts to arrive at causality even more difficult.

Group and Cross-Sectional Data.   Most social and biomedical researchers have worked primarily with group and cross-sectional data, resulting in substantial worthwhile and meaningful information. On the other hand, if we follow our agreed upon principles—that each adolescent is a unique and whole person— then we must also give more attention to data that documents how individuals grow, develop, learn, react, cope, and express themselves on the basis of biobehavioral interactions influenced by multiple and different genes, hormones, conditioned neurological pathways, purposes, meanings, reactions, perceptions, motivations, and interpretations. This would mean incorporating individuals and individuality into our design in order to study individual adolescent risk behaviors.

It is important to study groups and cohorts with cross-sectional and longitudinal designs. However, we must also begin to track individuals over time, situations, and contexts, otherwise we lose track of changes over time in individuals' specific behaviors.

Intraindividual Variability.   We are good at measuring variability between individuals and between groups, but we often fail to consider the variability within an individual. Behavior and skills are not as stable as was once believed. In comparing interindividual and intraindividual variability, colleagues like Nesselroade (1991) and others find more intraindividual variability over time, place, context, and motivation, especially with regard to affect, emotion, mood, and personality factors.

Examples of intraindividual variability equal to or exceeding the variability between individuals include feelings of depression, sleep restlessness, loneliness, appetite, self-concept, locus of control, temperament, teacher performance, work values, and other major personality dimensions and human abilities. The focus on intraindividual variability will become increasingly important as we attempt to study and measure individual factors and causality in adolescent behavior. It is even possible that what we sometimes refer to as "noise" or inconsistent variations in our data may be the result of unrecognized intraindividual variability.

We now recognize that physiological variables are not as stable as once believed, particularly with regard to such factors as heart rate, blood pressure, respiratory vital capacity, hormone secretions, metabolism, immune reactivity, and other bodily functions. And the answer is not to calculate an average, as is frequently done with blood pressure, but to understand that the individual variations are important data. With adolescents in particular, it is important to consider factors associated with intraindividual variability.

Problem and high risk behaviors of adolescents remain a major concern of all the behavioral sciences and biomedical sciences, as well as of society in general. We cannot afford to lose a significant portion of current and future adolescent generations. Nor can society afford to suffer the potential disorganization and distortion that could severely change the quality of life inflicted upon it by behavioral problems that we feel helpless to change or solve. It behooves us to accelerate and strengthen the research efforts and ideas outlined in this volume. Today's adolescents are our future selves and our future society.

REFERENCES

Jessor, R. (1992). Risk behavior in adolescence: A psychosocial framework for understanding and action. In D. E. Rogers & E. Ginzberg (Eds.), *Adolescents at risk: Medical and social perspectives* (pp. 19–34). Boulder, CO: Westview Press.

Nesselroade, J.R. (1991). The warp and wolf of the developmental fabric. In R. Downs, L. Liben, & D. S. Palermo (Eds.), *Visions of aesthetics, the environment, and development* (pp. 213–240). Hillsdale, NJ: Lawrence Erlbaum Associates.

Author Index

Subject Index

demic transmission—representing vertical transmission (parent–child) and horizontal transmission (peer–peer), respectively. The results of Rowe's analyses lead him to the controversial contention that parental behavior has little influence on children's long-term development because most parental influences are genetically mediated. Rowe thus suggests that social scientists need to replace parent-centered models of the transmission of problem behavior with more general models that attribute a larger role to genetic factors.

In the next three chapters, by contrast, nonbiological factors take center stage. In chapter 8, Cathy Spatz Widom reviews research on the intergenerational "Cycle of Violence." Widom's prospective studies of abused and neglected children suggest strong links between childhood victimization (abuse and neglect) and adolescent delinquency, violence, runaway, sexual promiscuity, pregnancy, alcohol and drug abuse, self-destructive behaviors, depression, and suicide. Although causal explanations of these links are not yet available, Widom lays solid groundwork for future research by describing mechanisms that may link childhood victimization and later problem behaviors, as well as protective factors that may explain individual differences in the manifestation of problem behavior among children who experience abuse and neglect.

In chapter 9, Joseph Pleck and his colleagues use data from a nationally representative survey sample of adolescent males to evaluate a sociopsychological explanation for adolescent problem behavior among males. Pleck et al. report that males who hold traditional ideas about the male role are at increased risk for 7 out of the 10 problem behaviors reported by the survey respondents, suggesting that at least among males, traditional attitudes about gender roles may place youth at risk of involvement in adolescent problem behaviors.

Whereas Pleck et al. focus on sex role theory, David Andrews and Thomas Dishion rely on social learning theory as they explore the microsocial bases of adolescent problem behaviors in chapter 10. Unlike the other contributors, Andrews and Dishion explicitly attempt to create an applied approach to intervention. Based on their work at the Oregon Social Learning Center, Andrews and Dishion conclude that adolescent problem behaviors are learned microsocial exchanges occurring in social context, and that a composite of microsocial behaviors underlie problem behavior "lifestyles." From this perspective, prevention and intervention programs should begin with analyses of the microsocial exchanges and the contexts in which they occur. Social policy measures alone may influence adolescents' contexts, but cannot readily change microsocial behavioral exchanges. Such changes demand that applied social scientists take the lead in attempting to change patterns of problem behavior among adolescents.

In the concluding chapter (chapter 11), Evan Pattishall reviews the preceding chapters from the perspective of a social and medical scientist who has learned over the last several decades that narrowly focused, categorical approaches to human problems are counterintuitive, inefficient, and ineffective. Like Pattishall, we hope that the chapters included in this book will stimulate researchers, clinicians, and policymakers to address the many individual and societal problems associated with adolescent problem behaviors in a comprehensive manner.

REFERENCES

Burnham, J. C. (1960). Psychiatry, psychology, and the progressive movement. *American Quarterly, 12*, 457-465.

Feldman, S. S., & Elliott, G. R. (1990). *At the threshold: The developing adolescent.* Cambridge, MA: Harvard University Press.

Gilbert, J. (1986). *A cycle of outrage: America's reaction to the juvenile delinquent in the 1950's.* New York: Oxford University Press.

Gottfredson, M. R., & Hirschi, T. (1990). *A general theory of crime.* Stanford, CA: Stanford University Press.

Hall, G. S. (1904). *Adolescence* (Vol.1–2). New York: Appleton-Century-Crofts.

Hilgartner, S., & Bosk, C. L. (1988). The rise and fall of social problems: A public arenas model. *American Journal of Sociology, 94*, 53-78.

Leone, P. E. (Ed.). (1990). *Understanding troubled and troubling youth.* Newbury Park, CA: Sage.

Levine, M., & Levine, A. (1992). *Helping children: A social history* (2nd ed.). New York: Oxford University Press.

Millstein, S., Petersen, A., & Nightingale, E. (Eds.). (1992). *Adolescent health promotion.* New York: Oxford University Press.

Nathanson, C. A. (1991). *Dangerous passage: The social control of sexuality in women's adolescence.* Philadelphia: Temple University Press.

President's Commission on Population Growth and the American Future. (1972). *Population and the American future.* Washington, DC: U.S. Department of Health, Education, and Welfare.

Rogers, D. E., & Ginzberg, E. (1992). *Adolescents at risk: Medical and social perspectives.* Boulder, CO: Westview Press.

Smith, C. J. (1988). *Public problems: The management of urban distress.* New York: Guilford Press.

Task Force on Education of Young Adolescents. (1989). *Turning points: Preparing American youth for the 21st century.* Washington, DC: Carnegie Council on Adolescent Development.

1

Troubled Youth: Children at Risk in Early Modern England, Colonial America, and 19th-Century America

Gerald F. Moran
University of Michigan, Dearborn
Maris A. Vinovskis
University of Michigan, Ann Arbor

Contemporary America is preoccupied with the issue of troubled youth. Unfortunately, contemporary perceptions of troubled youth, however sophisticated, lack historical vision. Most recent analyses of the issue portray it as being uniquely contemporary, implying that earlier times lacked comparable problems, or that they were handled more effectively. As a result, there is little understanding of the problems of youth in the past and of the strategies devised by adults to handle them. This chapter takes a first step toward providing an historical context for an understanding of contemporary problems of youth at risk. Although an understanding of the history of defining and dealing with troubled youth does not necessarily lend itself to any direct or immediate answers for coping with the problems of adolescents today, it does provide us with a broader framework and perspective by which to assess our current efforts. It also alerts us to the constant need to be aware of how much our own youth policies and programs are a reflection of the particular structural and ideological context of life in the United States today.

To appreciate the importance of a history of troubled youth, it is first necessary to overcome prejudice regarding the absence of a concept of youth in the past. Many scholars (Manning, 1983; Matter, 1984; Proefrock, 1981; Teeter, 1988) continue to accept the idea, first proposed and popularized by Aries (1962), that western society in premodern times lacked a notion of youth, treating the age-group simply as "miniature adults" rather than as a distinct segment of the population. As historians continue to investigate the history of the life course, however, evidence

1

continues to mount in support of a contrary hypothesis, that western youth has a long and venerable history, reaching as far back as the medieval period, and perhaps beyond (Hanawalt, 1986). This does not imply, however, that England or other western societies possessed a modernlike concept of adolescence. In fact, we believe that it is anachronistic to use the word *adolescence* when discussing premodern youth, because it was rarely used in England and America until the 20th century. Not once, for example, was the word employed by William Shakespeare, even though his work is suffused with the presence of youth.

Although the word *adolescence* was generally not included in premodern life-course vocabularies, early modern English and Americans nevertheless had clear and concise ideas about the life stage which they termed *youth*. They, like us, believed that the teenage years and early 20s comprised a discrete, transitional period in the development of an individual, one that involved abrupt alterations in human growth patterns, sexuality, social behavior, and work.

Not only did premodern Westerners have a clear conception of youth, but they were sometimes as deeply preoccupied by youth as we are today. Such was the case in early modern England, where policymakers and reformers were deeply concerned about the problems of youth. Such a preoccupation stemmed in part from anxieties over youth's natural propensities for vice and rebellion. It also flowed from socioeconomic changes that stimulated public awareness and concern over troubled youth. Among the most important changes were population growth and urbanization, which severely disrupted the lives of vulnerable youth wherever they lived.

This chapter explores the history of troubled youth in several premodern societies: early modern England, the colonial Chesapeake and New England, and 19th-century America. Elizabethan and Caroline England offers a striking example of how policymakers and reformers identified and addressed the problems of troubled youth in premodern times. In the colonial Chesapeake the situation was quite different; there, leaders generally ignored youth who suffered severe trauma. In New England, however, youth sustained less trauma than their southern counterparts, but commanded far more interest from adults, a disparity that reveals the influence of religious ideology on attitudes toward children. Finally, 19th-century America, a period of rapid socioeconomic change, produced increasing interest in and concern about troubled youth, paving the way for the emergence of modern adolescence and the scientific study of its manifestations.

YOUTH IN MEDIEVAL AND EARLY MODERN ENGLAND

Early modern English preoccupation with youth stemmed largely from profound demographic, economic, and social changes that significantly altered the contexts of their everyday lives, placing them increasingly at risk. The English population, which grew from 3 to 5 million people from 1550 to 1700 (Wrigley & Schofield, 1981), experienced rapid commercial growth and field enclosures resulting in disastrous socioeconomic effects, including dispossession and dislocation of the peasantry, increased unemployment, wage deflation, geographical mobility, and urbanization (Brigden, 1982). These changes created new and dangerous conditions for English youth, ripping them from home and hearth and placing them in environments that exposed them to delinquency, crime, incarceration, and death.

As early as the mid-16th century, the English state responded to worsening social conditions by enacting social legislation pertaining to crime that was less rehabilitative than punitive. The state, for example, sought to cure vagrancy (caused by unemployment) by criminalizing it. Although vagrancy legislation dates from the 14th century, it achieved its fullest development during the 16th and 17th centuries, when growing numbers of able bodied but idle poor compelled government to expand vagrancy law in defense of orderliness and stability. The 'Statute of Artificers of 1563, for example, subjected laborers who refused agricultural work to arrest and incarceration.

Although vagrancy legislation was directed at a number of groups, "the young were a special worry and were singled out in numerous statutes" (Beier, 1985, p.10). The primary purpose of legislation passed in 1576 establishing houses of correction, for example, was that "youth may be accustomed and brought up in Labour and work" (Beier, 1985, p.10). Recent demographic analyses reveal "that vagrancy was mainly a young person's crime" (Beier, 1985, p.54), insofar as youth were apprehended and incarcerated on vagrancy charges more frequently than other age groups. A list of vagrants imprisoned in Bridewell in 1602 shows that 97% of the vagrants were under the age of 21 and 54% under age 16; in Norwich in 1595–1609, 72% were under age 21 and 52% were under age 16; and in Crompton in 1597, 75% were under 21 and 50% under 16. Although vagabonds in smaller towns and rural villages were older, 50% were under 21, and 33% were under 16 (Beier, 1985).

Aside from punishment and incarceration, the primary cure for youthful vagrancy and delinquency was work; "young people" had to "be found jobs and masters to keep them under control" (Youings, 1984, p. 293; Morgan, 1975, p.65). The authority of masters and local law-enforcement officials was strengthened, so that justices of the peace, for example, were empowered to draft idle hands for field labor, "on pain, for refusal, of two days and one night in the stocks" (Youings, 1984, p. 293). Hospitals and houses of correction, furthermore, were charged to care for troubled youth and to put them to work. Thus, as early as 1522, Bridewell of London began to admit not only idle adults but also young people "found unapt for learning" and for whom no service for the moment could be found (Youings, 1984, p. 286).

In addition to the state, moralists and religious reformers, especially the Puritans, became deeply troubled by youth. Whereas Tudor and Stuart policymakers focused on the criminality and dangerousness of delinquent youth, Puritans were more concerned with their sinfulness and religious deviance. Aroused by the torrent of youthful nonconformity unleashed by the Reformation, and by local epidemics of immorality (including drunkenness, fornication, and blasphemy) allegedly produced by the weakening of family authority, the reformers mounted a moral campaign. Its primary goals were the restoration of the traditional order and also the salvation of youthful souls, to be achieved by mobilization of ecclesiastical courts against vice and expansion of education and literacy. Puritans, furthermore, employed clerical proselytization of youth, who were viewed as peculiarly prone to immorality, and thus especially in need of admonition and religious indoctrination.

The ascension of Puritanism in the period 1560 to 1640 led to an increase in clerical injunctions against the sins of youth, reflecting less concern with the outward social misbehavior of youth than with their inward sinfulness. Puritan's anxiety about youth, furthermore, tended to transcend the imperatives of particular social contexts, reflecting their belief that all youth were innately sinful.

YOUTH IN COLONIAL AMERICA

In America, transplanted Englishmen hoped to establish stable societies bereft of the social chaos that had plagued youth and distracted English authorities. Outside of New England, where Puritans managed to maintain social harmony for a generation, the social reality in colonial America fell far short of immigrant expectations. Although colonial communities were less chaotic than those the migrants had left, they were still often beset by demographic, social, and economic changes that disrupted the lives of youth. Although colonial leaders were generally less preoccupied with youth than were their English counterparts, some of them were nevertheless deeply concerned with the problems of youth.

In the 17th-century South, indentured servitude dominated the lives of immigrant youth. Although the system, as advertised, held out to English youth the opportunity to acquire land in return for 5 to 7 years of service, this promise was rarely kept. Separated from parents, kin, and neighbors, and from the protection of English labor laws and customs, immigrant youth were continuously at risk of physical abuse, labor exploitation, disease, and death. More than half of all indentured servants died before their term of service had expired. In addition, terms of service were under constant pressure to expand; youthful servants in their early teens were continuously at risk of laboring for exploitative masters until adulthood (Galenson, 1981).

Among the native-born population, whose size continued to increase relative to that of the immigrant population, high adult mortality rates played havoc with the lives of youth well into the 18th century. By the time most native-born children became teenagers, they had either lost a parent or had become orphaned. In one county of 17th-century Virginia, 73% of children had lost at least one parent before they reached age 21 or married (whichever came first; Rutman & Rutman, 1979). Although most native-born children were cared for by at least one of their natural parents, most Creole youth were not.

Southern communities were thus forced to assume responsibilities carried on traditionally by the family. Neighborhoods and kin networks were mobilized to provide support, supervision, and education for orphaned youth, whereas county courts were empowered to appoint guardians to manage properties inherited by youthful minors, and to oversee the treatment of orphaned youth bound out to labor until their majority. That orphan courts often felt compelled to scrutinize the activities of guardians and masters suggests widespread abuse of the system (Walsh, 1979). Despite the frequency of such complaints, there is no evidence to suggest that adults in the colonial South had anything but a passing interest in youth and their problems. Although southern courts sought to protect youth, especially those with property, from exploitation or physical abuse, there was no concerted effort on the part of colonial leaders to intervene on their behalf. Rather, age-specific issues, even when recognized as such, took a back seat to problems related to labor, class, and, in time, race.

The history of youth in colonial New England differs dramatically from that of the South, which is due in large part to demographic and religious differences. Low mortality rates and the group nature of the Puritan exodus to America combined to produce stable family life in first-generation New England. Even orphaned youth or unattached servants were raised within patriarchal households, a circumstance dictated by New England legislation. In contrast to the South, strong, viable churches existed to buttress the authority of the family and to help supervise the rearing of children and youth.

In cases of parental neglect or abuse of youth, the state or church was quick to intervene. If there were youth at risk in early New England, they were to be found primarily among Amerindian societies, whose populations were succumbing rapidly to European disease and war. Age-related conflict in Puritan communities primarily involved disputes between sons who desired autonomy, and fathers who attempted to withhold it from them, primarily through the retention of land ownership. Such conflict was rarely collective in nature because most Puritan youth were content with the delayed achievement of adulthood, marriage, public service, and property inheritance (Beales, 1975).

Yet early New England was far more intellectually preoccupied with youth than was the colonial South, a paradox attributable to Puritanism. To the extent that they succeeded in reproducing old-world Puritanism in the new world, New Englanders created old-world anxieties about youth, notwithstanding the stable new world contexts. New England's institutions reflected, and in turn reinforced, traditional Puritan preoccupation with youth. State supported churches and ministries, which were established primarily to perpetuate the faith, also served as media for the transmission of age-related anxieties about the survival of the faith. Thus, the Puritan system instituted mechanisms for indoctrinating youth, including youth-specific catechisms, private religious societies, catechetical exercises, lectures, and covenant renewals (in which groups of youth were assembled on the Sabbath to renew their parents' covenant).

When such measures appeared ineffective, Puritan leaders invoked traditional, English caveats against the dangers and sins of youth. Starting in the 1660s and 1670s, Puritan presses and pulpits produced a steady stream of Jeremiads lamenting the sins of the rising generation. Like their English predecessors, such Jeremiads focused on the age-specific, developmental nature of sin. The Reverend Thomas Foxcroft of Massachusetts observed in 1719, for example, that "the different ages of men have their diverse lusts and various corruptions. The impure streams run in distinct channels agreeing to the different complexions of men in several stages of life." Childhood, therefore, was marred by "stubborness" and "falseness," whereas middle age was stained by "ambition" and old age by "covetousness." There were two sins that seemed to "hang upon youth and dogg that season of life more than any other," said Foxcroft, and these were "pride" and "sensuality" (Hiner, 1975, p. 261).

Although adult preoccupation with youthful sensuality existed throughout New England's history, it seems to have increased over time, as reflected in court records of the period. New England courts prosecuted crimes against order and morals much more vigorously than their southern counterparts, and the number of prosecutions increased dramatically over time, especially against fornication and bastardy. Between 1651 and 1680 in Essex County, Massachusetts, for example, 16.8% of all prosecutions for crime were for bastardy and fornication, and a century later, the percentage had increased threefold. Between 1760 and 1774 in Middlesex County, Massachusetts, 57.6% of all prosecutions were for bastardy and fornication (Hindus, 1980).

The rise of prosecutions for sexual misconduct matched a concurrent rise in premarital pregnancy rates. By the time the Massachusetts court was vigorously prosecuting sex offenders, nearly half of all Massachusetts brides were pregnant at marriage. Religious declension, rapid population growth, increasing geographical mobility, and the concomitant weakening of patriarchal authority, were all factors producing rising numbers of youth at risk of committing sexual and other moral crimes.

Efforts to combat youthful deviance were not confined to clerical Jeremiads or court prosecutions. In response to the pressures of social change, 18th-century ministers endeavored to protect youth from vice by converting them to faith. Ignoring the traditional Puritan aversion to youthful religious conversion, ministers promoted a new view of the young that stressed the capacity for saving grace over the capacity for committing sin.

Clerical evangelicalism touched a responsive chord among many of New England's youth. During the 1740s, the era of the Great Awakening, many teens and young adults experienced conversion and entered communion, dominating, for the first time in the region's history, the admission rolls of the Established Church (Stout, 1986). Once converted, however, the young did not submit to the authority of the church. Instead, the revival deflected youthful piety into unorthodox channels—including lay exhortation and separatism—thus rekindling old anxieties about youthful religious deviance. While the opponents of the Awakening, the Old Lights, felt most threatened by such deviance, even the New Lights were troubled by the radical turn of events. In the wake of the revival, the old animus against youthful piety returned, and churches closed their doors to the young. For the remainder of the colonial period, religious leaders harped upon the traditional theme of troubled, sinful youth.

The Great Awakening, therefore, produced no new commentary on troubled youth, even though its constituency included the poorer youth of inland market towns and coastal seaports who were particularly vulnerable to the dislocations of war and raid commercialization (Heyrman, 1984; Nash, 1979). Despite their radical rhetoric, New Lights were generally oblivious to the plight of indigent, transient youth, whose numbers were growing rapidly. Even in ports outside of New England, such as New York and Philadelphia, where the religious system was weaker, the Awakening failed to produce any commentary on the social changes that helped to produce it. Instead, the poor, young and old alike, "were labelled as deviants and treated as such," and were placed indiscriminately in private homes or workhouses, or were run out of town (Withey, 1984). Not until the late 18th century did Americans begin to distinguish between the "idle" and "industrious poor," and to single out youth for special treatment and care (Alexander, 1980). Although an occasional reference was made to the problems of urban youth, little effort was undertaken on their behalf. Like their English and early New England ancestors, late 18th-century Americans viewed troubled youth as prisoners of sin and threats to the social order.

YOUTH AND CRIME IN THE 19TH CENTURY

The 19th century witnessed an increase in concern about youth and crime. In part, this was due to a nervous public response to increased urban and industrial development that weakened the traditional sources of social control by the family and local community. It also reflected a growing recognition of youth as a specific stage of the life course that was especially susceptible to deviance. In the more economically developed cities of the northeast, furthermore, new age-segregated institutions intended to deal with troubled youth further contributed to the age grouping of youth. By the end of the 19th century, contemporary observers such as G. Stanley Hall (1904) described early adolescence as an unsettling and stormy phase of the life course.

Nineteenth-century reformers usually associated youth crime with large cities and the growing urbanization of the country (Hawes, 1971; Pickett, 1969). Only 5.1% of the population in 1790 lived in communities with 2,500 or more inhabitants, but on the eve of the Civil War nearly 1 out of 5 people lived in such towns. By 1900 the proportion living in such communities rose to 39.7%. More significantly, in 1790 there were no cities with 50,000 inhabitants in the United States; by 1860 nearly 1 out of 10 people lived in these larger cities (and 37.7% lived in them in 1900) (calculated from U.S. Bureau of Census, 1975).

The growth of public schools, and the concomitant age grouping that resulted, prompted increased public concern about youth. Although some private or public primary schools were established in a few 17th-century New England towns, most parents either taught their own children or shared in the paying for a temporary private school teacher (Moran & Vinovskis, 1986). By the early 19th century, however, primary schools were established in many northeast towns, and by the mid-19th century most communities in that region had well-developed public common school systems. In the South, however, few public schools were created, so that as late as 1900 large numbers of children received little formal education (Kaestle, 1983). African-American children, furthermore, were denied equal access to schooling throughout the 19th century in most communities (Anderson, 1988; Webber, 1978).

In rural schools, children of all ages were taught together in a one-room schoolhouse. Children from ages 3 to 20 listened to the same teacher and took turns reciting their lessons based on their level of achievement rather than their age (Fuller, 1982; Link, 1986). In the mid-19th century, as towns grew and schools became more specialized, there was a rough age grading of pupils in urban schools (Angus, Mirel, & Vinovskis, 1988). During the second half of the 19th century, the age segregation of students increased, and, as a result, many youths in the urban northeast attended educational institutions, such as public high schools. Here, teenagers were brought together, and were taught, in addition to the skills necessary for economic advancement, the morals deemed necessary to resist the vices and temptations associated with city life (Kaestle, 1973; Schultz, 1973).

Nineteenth-century Americans frequently worried about increases in crime rates that they usually associated with cities. Few scholars have attempted to ascertain the actual level of crime in the 19th century, and each acknowledges the problems of measuring something so elusive (Hindus, 1980; Monkkonen, 1975). The most detailed and careful comparative study of antebellum crime traces developments in Massachusetts and South Carolina. Using aggregate Massachusetts statistics on total commitments, Hindus (1980) found that the rates fluctuated and peaked in the mid-1850s. Surprisingly, South Carolina's crime rates were consistently higher than that in Massachusetts, and primarily involved personal violence rather than crimes of theft or destruction of property characteristic in Massachusetts. Although assaults continued to dominate South Carolina crimes in both the 18th and 19th centuries, in Massachusetts there was a shift from crimes against morality in the colonial period to those involving property or liquor-related offenses in the 19th century. Urban areas such as Boston, Massachusetts, and Charleston, South Carolina, had higher crime rates than rural areas.

Unfortunately, few studies present data on the age of the criminals. Monkonnen's (1975) study of poverty and crime in Franklin County, Ohio from 1860 to 1885, however, does provide some age-specific information about criminals. He found that about 22% of criminals in 1870 were under age 21—a considerably smaller percentage than one would find today. Moreover, he found few overall urban-rural differences in crime rates in Ohio, and no indication that increasing urbanization led to more crime over time.

In another interesting study, Friedman and Percival (1981) discovered that serious crime declined in Alameda County, California in the late 19th century, resulting in increased police efforts at enforcing public order by attacking crimes such as drunkenness and brawling. They also found that although arrest rates were the highest for those ages 30–39, a substantial number of older teenagers were also arrested. Youthful offenders were more likely to be arrested for property crimes and ordinance violations compared to older adults who were more apt to be charged for drunkenness and moral offenses. Perhaps the most striking finding, however, was that arrest rates at all ages are much higher today than in the past, and that there has been a relative increase in the proportion of crime committed by young people.

The growing attention to youth crime was due, in part, to the feeling among some commentators that youth was a particularly important period of change. Authors of advice books for youth (e.g., Austin, 1854) did not pay much specific attention to age (cf. Chudacoff, 1989), but they generally believed that the adolescent phase of the life course was crucial in the development of proper values and behavior. Nineteenth-century Americans agreed that the period of youth was central in the formation of good character and devoted considerable resources to guide them through these years (Hawes, 1971). Teachers and school administrators, in particular, stressed the importance of moral training in the classroom, believing that such education was an essential component of efforts to help youth avoid the snares and temptations of crime (Kaestle & Vinovskis, 1980). Indeed, most 19th-century policymakers assumed that much, if not all, of youth and adult crime could be prevented with a proper moral education (Massachusetts Board of Education, 1849). Although some critics questioned the efficacy of education to prevent crime and pauperism, this continued to be one of the most widely held views among policymakers and the public throughout the period (Glenn, 1988; Hogan, 1985).

Religious leaders, furthermore, saw Sunday schools as a valuable tool for combatting vice. In the early 19th century, U.S. Sunday schools taught both literacy and morality to individuals of all ages, although they became more age graded as they focused more on youths than adults (Boylan, 1988). Although Sunday schools appeared throughout the country, they were viewed as most necessary in cities to combat the urban vices encountered by students. Whereas urban public schools in the North taught children the basics of literacy, Sunday schools concentrated more on teaching religion and morality.

Sunday schools were only one of many efforts by religious groups to guide youth in the 19th century. Bible societies wrote special tracts for youth and distributed thousands of copies throughout the nation. Furthermore, other special institutions such as the YMCA were created in the mid-19th century to help young men who were regarded as particularly vulnerable to the temptations of the city. Although initially many of these religious efforts and institutions did not target specific age groups, over time they increasingly targeted teenagers and young adults (Boyer, 1978; Holloran, 1989; Smith-Rosenberg, 1971).

Although educators and religious leaders provided children with moral training and guidance in an effort to prevent youthful crimes, others sought to work with youth who were already offenders to prevent them from becoming hardened criminals. During the antebellum period, for example, northeast reformers, who tried to overcome what they perceived were the dangers and evils of urban life, attempted to separate youth from experienced convicts by creating separate institutions for young offenders of both sexes. Although only a minority of youth were ever incarcerated in these reform schools, their construction in Northern cities and the publicity about them helped define the need for special attention for teenage offenders. Although facilities were provided for both girls and boys, most of the initial attention was focused on boys who were perceived as the largest group of offenders (Brenzel, 1983; Hawes, 1971; Mennel, 1973; Pickett, 1969; Platt, 1977; Schlossman, 1977).

Most reformers in the early 19th century employed environmental, or even racist, explanations for the causes of crime and poverty. Although they believed that all youth were at risk of misbehaving or becoming criminals, those from certain backgrounds were believed to be particularly susceptible to such dangers. So, for example, reformers regarded youthful crimes and misdeeds as manifestations of a basically flawed character—frequently the result of parental loss or neglect. Rather than relying only on specific crimes or misbehaviors to identify troubled youth, they assumed that any children from disadvantaged backgrounds or neglectful parents were at high risk of becoming societal problems (Hart, 1832).

Whereas ideas about environmental and familial causes of youthful corruption and criminal behavior continued to be accepted throughout the antebellum period, by the time of the Civil War additional nuances had appeared. For example, Charles Loring Brace, who worked closely with the so-called "dangerous classes" of New York City (Langsam, 1964; Wohl, 1969), divided the causes of crime into "preventible" and "nonpreventible." The list of preventible causes reads like a catalogue of earlier diagnoses: "ignorance, intemperance, over-crowding of population, want of work, idleness, vagrancy, the weakness of the marriage-tie, and bad legislation." Brace's discussion of the nonpreventible (or "those which cannot be entirely removed") causes, however, revealed a gradual shift in how reformers viewed youths at risk, from environment to heredity. Among Brace's list of nonpreventible causes of crime, for example, are "inheritance, the effects of emigration, orphanage, accident or misfortune, the strength of the sexual and other passions, and a natural weakness of moral and mental powers." Other early 19th-century reformers, furthermore, observed that immigrants or their children were likely to become criminals. After the great influx of Irish in the 1840s and 1850s, this theme received even more emphasis. Rather than raising questions about the lower quality of the "stock" of the immigrants, however, Brace (1872) explained the propensity of the children of immigrants to become criminals largely in social and environmental terms.

Although Brace's (1872) discussion of the inheritability of criminal traits prefigures the more deterministic views of other late 19th- and early 20th-century analysts, it is more optimistic and less rigid than might first appear. Brace believed, for example, that vice and indulgence weakened individuals' physical powers, thereby limiting their reproductive success. These inherited characteristics, Brace believed, could be overcome by interventions designed to improve the quality of a youth's home and neighborhood environment. Brace remained optimistic, furthermore, that "[t]he natural drift among the poor is towards virtue," despite his belief in the intergeneration transmission of the traits of paupers, criminals, and vagrants

Finally, Brace, like many other 19th-century observers, strongly believed that sexual passions lead to immoral behavior. One corollary of this belief is that Brace thought that wayward boys were more likely to be reformed than delinquent girls. This is most likely due to the fact that Brace viewed boys and girls as fundamentally biologically different in their tendency toward sexual passion and their ability to recover from early sexual activity. His almost romantic optimism concerning boys' situation, and his equally pessimistic views of girls, clearly reflected the application of a double standard characteristic of this period.

Although Brace retained some of the optimism and environmental orientation of many early 19th-century youth reformers, he also revealed greater attention to the ill effects of immigration, the possibility of transmission of defective traits across generations, and gender differences in the likelihood of being reformed. Like Brace, many postantebellum social commentators and citizens believed that early reform efforts could prevent youthful crimes and indiscretions, although there was a growing pessimism concerning how successful existing large-scale youth institutions could be.

By the late 19th century a new generation of analysts provided "scientific" studies of juvenile delinquency (Mennel, 1973; Platt, 1977; Schlossman, 1977). One school of thought, led by the Italian criminologist Cesare Lombrosco, argued that habitual criminals were a distinct and inferior anthropological type distinguished by highly visible physical traits. American scholars such as George Dawson (1896) and Arthur MacDonald (U.S. Congress, 1902) tried to explain juvenile delinquency on the basis of the physical characteristics of children, some of which, they claimed, reflected clear signs of degeneracy. The use of Lombroscian criminology to deal with juvenile delinquency was carried to its logical and absurd extreme by a U.S. physician, Thomas Travis (1908), who wanted to operate on children to alter the shape of their crania, jaws, and palates in order to alter their appearance, and, thus their behavior.

Other U.S. analysts emphasized the hereditary transmission of criminal behavior while accepting the thesis that deviant behavior could be avoided by altering the environment of youth at risk. Dugdale's (1877) famous work, *"The Jukes": A Study in Crime, Pauperism, Disease and Heredity*, for example, appeared to establish the familial basis of criminal behavior. Furthermore, William Douglas Morrison, among others, associated juvenile delinquency membership within immigrant groups, but unlike Brace, doubted that improved environments could completely erase the negative consequences associated with immigrants' backgrounds.

Nevertheless, despite a new emphasis on the physical and hereditary nature of crime in the late 19th century, and the questioning of the unbridled optimism of reformers 50 years earlier, most U.S. reformers continued to stress environmental explanations for delinquency. This is particularly reflected in the continuing belief that early intervention with high-risk youths could prevent or alleviate much of juvenile delinquency.

Although most analysts of juvenile delinquency focused on crime, a few started from the perspective of the adolescent as a whole. The first, and one of the most important scholars of adolescent development was G. Stanley Hall, who pioneered and popularized the idea of adolescence as a distinct and tumultuous stage of the life course. Although his two-volume study of adolescence dealt only briefly with juvenile delinquency (Hall, 1904), his views were frequently cited by other scholars, and widely publicized through the popular media.

Hall's evolutionary theory of development posited stages of human development which recapitulated historical changes in Western Civilization. He believed
that beginning at ages 12–14, adolescents were particularly prone to rapid, tumultuous, and even life-threatening changes. According to Hall, uneven individual
physical and mental development characteristic of adolescents, combined with the
strains of modern life, made adolescence a perilous development period. Not
surprisingly, Hall found that juvenile delinquency was on the rise and that crimes
were now committed at an earlier age.

Hall was rather eclectic in assembling and accepting a series of explanations,
often seemingly contradictory to each other, for adolescents' deviant behavior.
Although he rejected the extremes of Lombroso's views, he accepted the identification of crime with physical bearing:

> degenerate children are neurotic, irritable, vain, lacking in vigor, very fluctuating in
> mood, prone to show aberrant tendencies under stress, often sexually perverted at
> puberty, with extreme shyness or bravado, imitative, [and] not well controlled.... (Hall,
> 1904, I, pp. 335–336)

Hall stressed, however, alienated youths' difficulties adjusting to the demands
of modern society.

Because Hall viewed juvenile delinquency as a common experience among
adolescents in a modern, urban society that placed great temptations and stress on
all young people, he offered no hope for simple solutions. He rejected, for example,
strict and rigid punishment, and questioned the efficacy of the current educational
system to prevent juvenile delinquency. Instead, he called for the further scientific
study of juvenile delinquency—a call that was heeded by many early 20th-century
scholars, including many of his own students. By emphasizing the universality of
adolescence, its stormy nature, and the period of early adolescence, Hall helped to
reshape the ways Americans viewed children at risk.

CONCLUSION

We strongly disagree with those scholars who continue to believe that troubled
youth as a group were not a problem in early modern England or colonial America
because children were regarded as miniature adults. Although older children were
often seen as intellectually more precocious and emotionally more mature than
adolescents are regarded today, they were not viewed or treated simply as miniature
adults. In the past, furthermore, young people were neither as rigidly age segregated
nor as likely to be called *adolescents*, as they are today. Therefore, the concept of
troubled youth as a subcategory of the population often did have particular,
although often differing, meanings for people in the past.

Although the word *adolescence* existed in the English language in early modern
England, it was not frequently employed. Similarly, although occasionally one
finds mention of *adolescence* by the mid-19th century in America, it still is not as

commonly used as the word *youth*. Yet by the end of the 19th century the word *adolescence* appears with greater frequency. More importantly, the concept of adolescence as a stormy and often troubled transition from childhood to adulthood, thanks in large measure to the efforts of G. Stanley Hall and his colleagues, gained favor among U.S. social scientists and public in the early 20th century. As a result, today most Americans accept the idea of adolescence as a "normal" phase of the life course even though there appears to be growing disagreement and confusion over the exact nature of that transition.

Concern about youth has sometimes been triggered by broader demographic and economic changes. For example, in early modern England, the combination of rapid population growth with declining economic opportunities, led to increased internal migration and fears of vagrancy and youthful disorders. Similarly, the growing numbers of youths in 19th-century American cities amidst a rapidly changing economy contributed to increased anxiety about young people. These fears were heightened by the flood of immigrants into cities in the second half of the 19th century, an event that challenged the existing structures of authority and power.

Demographic and economic changes did not always precipitate fears of youth, however. In the colonial South, for example, societal anxiety about youth was lower than in either early modern England or in Puritan New England. Similarly, although there were problems with youth in the rapidly changing rural areas of 19th-century America, rural youths were not perceived as dangerous as those in the urban communities. Thus, although demographic and economic factors certainly play a key role in shaping the experiences of youth and stimulating and conditioning the general concerns of adults, they do not by themselves determine how societies view or react to troubled youths.

Although concerns about youth have varied from one time period to another during the past 500 years, factors such as race, ethnicity, class, and gender have also played a role in how particular subsets of young people were viewed and treated. African-American or immigrant youths, especially males from economically disadvantaged backgrounds, have usually been judged to be more dangerous and threatening to the dominant groups in English and American societies than children of White, native-born, middle-class parents. Moreover, troubled youth from disadvantaged backgrounds have typically received less sympathy and help than those with more privileged backgrounds. Indeed, we are struck by the extent to which children at risk, in both the past and today, have been categorized and labeled *deviant*, based on, to a large degree, their racial, ethnic, class, and gender characteristics. Sometimes, this has occurred among reformers who were genuinely trying to help these children rather than just trying to protect the rest of society from them.

One interesting difference between current reform strategies and policies and those of the past, is that today we are more likely to address the specific problems of troubled youth through separate, categorical programs rather than trying to deal with them as individuals as a whole. In other words, many, if not most, of our local, state, and federal programs designed to help adolescents focus in practice on some particular problem or difficulty such as an unintended adolescent pregnancy, drug use, school truancy, or juvenile crime. For example, although there exists a general consensus among social scientists that there is significant co-occurrence of different problem behaviors among individual youth (Elliott, in press; Osgood, 1991), programs designed to prevent, or ameliorate the effects of teenage pregnancy do not deal with the concomitant problems such as drug abuse or delinquency.

As a result of the categorical approach to prevention and treatment of youths' problem behavior, it is difficult, if not impossible, at times to view and help adolescents as an individuals rather than responding mainly to one or two of the particular difficulties she or he is experiencing. In contrast, in the past the emphasis was almost always on dealing with troubled youth as a person who had to be thoroughly and completely reformed rather than just addressing one of his or her specific problems. Reformers in early modern England and early America usually saw any deficiencies or problems as ultimately the result of an overall moral character weaknesses that had to be reformed before any real and lasting progress could be made. Therefore, for example, 19th-century reform schools focused on changing the overall character of the delinquent rather than just addressing any single shortcoming. Although the benefits of this approach was that it treated troubled youth as individuals, the danger was that children who challenged or violated any particular law or norm were often quickly and unfairly labeled as having a totally deficient or defective character.

REFERENCES

Alexander, J. K. (1980). *Render them submissive: Responses to poverty in Philadelphia, 1760–1800*. Amherst, MA: University of Massachusetts Press.

Anderson, J. D. (1988). *The education of Blacks in the South, 1860–1935*. Chapel Hill, NC: University of North Carolina Press.

Angus, D., Mirel, J., & Vinovskis, M. A. (1988). Historical development of age-stratification in schooling. *Teacher's College Record, 90*, 211–236.

Aries, P. (1962). *Centuries of childhood: A social history of family life* (R. Baldick, Trans.). New York: Vintage.

Austin, J. M. (1854). *A voice to youth addressed to young men and young ladies*. New York: Kiggins & Kellogg.

Beales, R. J. (1975). In search of the historical child: Miniature adulthood and youth in Colonial New England. *American Quarterly, 27*, 379–398.

Beier, A. L. (1985). *Masterless men: The vagrancy problem in England, 1560–1640*. London: Methuen.

Boyer, P. (1978). *Urban masses and moral order in America, 1820–1920*. Cambridge, MA: Harvard University Press.

Boylan, A. M. (1988). *Sunday school: The formation of an American institution, 1790–1880*. New Haven, CT: Yale University Press.

Brace, C. L. (1872). *The dangerous classes of New York and twenty years' work among them*. New York: Wynkoop & Hallenbeck.

Brenzel, B. M. (1983) . *Daughters of the state : A social portrait of the first reform school for girls in North America, 1856–1905*. Cambridge, MA: MIT Press.

Brigden, S. (1982). Youth and the English reformation. *Past and Present, 95*, 37–67.

Chudacoff, H. P. (1989). *How old age you? Age consciousness in American culture.* Princeton, NJ: Princeton University Press.

Dawson, G. E. (1896). A study in youthful degeneracy. *Pedagogical Seminary, 4,* 247–248.

Dugdale, R. L. (1877). *"The Jukes": A study in crime, pauperism, disease and hereditary.* New York: Putnam.

Elliott, D. S. (in press). Health enhancing and health compromising lifestyles. In S. G. Millstein, A. C. Petersen, & E. O. Nightingale (Eds.), *Adolescent health promotion.* New York: Oxford University Press.

Friedman, L. M., & Percival, R. V. (1981). *The roots of justice: Crime and punishment in Alameda County, California, 1870–1910.* Chapel Hill: University of North Carolina.

Fuller, W. E. (1982). *The old country school: The story of rural education in the middle west.* Chicago: University of Chicago Press.

Galenson, D. (1981). *White servitude in colonial America: An economic analysis.* Cambridge: Cambridge University Press.

Glenn, C. L., Jr. (1988). *The myth of the common school.* Amherst: University of Massachusetts Press.

Hall, G. S. (1904). *Adolescence: Its psychology and its relations to physiology, anthropology, sociology, sex, crime, religion, and education* (Vol. 2). New York: Appleton.

Hanawalt, B. A. (1986). *The ties that bound: Peasant families in medieval England.* New York: Oxford University Press.

Hart, N. C. (1832). *Documents relative to the house of refuge Instituted by the Society for the Reformation of Juvenile Delinquents in the City of New York in 1824.* New York: M. Day.

Hawes, J. M. (1971). *Children in urban society: Juvenile delinquency in nineteenth-century America.* New York: Oxford University Press.

Heyrman, C. L. (1984). *Commerce and culture: The maritime communities of Colonial Massachusetts, 1690–1750.* New York: Norton.

Hindus, M. S. (1980). *Prison and plantation: Crime, justice, and authority in Massachusetts and South Carolina, 1767–1878.* Chapel Hill: University of North Carolina Press.

Hiner, N. R. (1975). Adolescence in eighteenth-century America. *History of Childhood Quarterly, 3,* 253–280.

Hogan, D. J. (1985). *Class and reform: School and society in Chicago, 1880–1930.* Philadelphia: University of Pennsylvania Press.

Holloran, P. C. (1989). *Boston's wayward children: Social services for homeless children, 1830–1930.* Rutherford, NJ: Fairleigh Dickinson University Press.

Kaestle, C. F. (1983). *Pillars of the republic: Common schools and American society, 1780–1860.* New York: Hill & Wang.

Kaestle, C. F., & Vinovskis, M. A. (1980). *Education and social change in nineteenth-century Massachusetts.* Cambridge: Cambridge University Press.

Langsam, M. Z. (1964). *Children west: A history of the placing-out system of the New York Children's Aid Society, 1853–1890.* Madison: State Historical Society of Wisconsin.

Link, W. A. (1986). *A hard country and a lonely place: schooling, society, and reform in rural Virginia, 1870–1920.* Chapel Hill: University of North Carolina Press.

Manning, M. L. (1983). Three myths concerning adolescence. *Adolescence, 18,* 823–829.

Massachusetts Board of Education. (1849). *Twelfth annual report of the Board of Education.* Boston: Dutton & Wentworth.

Matter, R. M. (1984). The historical emergence of adolescence: Perspectives from developmental psychology and adolescent literature. *Adolescence, 19,* 131–142.

Mennel, R. M. (1973). *Thorns and thistles: Juvenile delinquents in the United States, 1825–1940.* Hanover, NH: University Press of New England.

Monkkonen, E. H. (1975). *The dangerous class: Crime and poverty in Columbus, Ohio, 1860–1885*. Cambridge, MA: Harvard University Press.

Moran, G. F., & Vinovskis, M. A. (1986). The great care of goldly parents: Early childhood in Puritan New England. *History and Research in Child Development, 50,* 24–37.

Morgan, E. S. (1975). *American slavery, American freedom*. New York: Norton.

Nash, G. B. (1979). *The urban crucible: Social change, political consciousness, and the origins of the American Revolution*. Cambridge, MA: Harvard University Press.

Osgood, D. W. (1991). *Covariation among health problems in adolescence*. Paper prepared for the United States Congress Office of Technology Assessments' Adolescent Health Project, Washington, DC.

Pickett, R. S. (1969). *House of refuge: Origins of juvenile reform in New York State, 1815–1857*. Syracuse, NY: Syracuse University Press.

Platt, A. M. (1977). *The child savers: The invention of delinquency* (2nd ed.). Chicago: University of Chicago Press.

Proefrock, D. W. (1981). Adolescence: Social fact and psychological concept. *Adolescence, 16,* 851–858.

Rutman, D. B., & Rutman, A. H. (1979). "Now-wives and sons-in-law": Parental death in a seventeenth-century Virginia County. In T. W. Ammerman, & D. L. Tate (Eds.), *The Chesapeake in the seventeenth century: Essays on Anglo-American society and politics* (pp. 153–182). Chapel Hill: University of North Carolina Press.

Schlossman, S. L. (1977). *Love and the American delinquent: The theory and practice of "progressive" juvenile justice, 1825–1920*. Chicago: University of Chicago Press.

Schultz, S. K. (1973). *The culture factory: Boston public schools, 1789–1860*. New York: Oxford University Press.

Smith-Rosenberg, C. (1971). *Religion and the rise of the American city: The New York City Mission Movement, 1812–1870*. Ithaca, NY: Cornell University Press.

Stout, H. S. (1986). *The New England soul: Preaching and religious culture in Colonial New England*. New York: Oxford University Press.

Teeter, R. (1988). The travails of 19th-century urban youth as a precondition to the invention of modern adolescence. *Adolescence, 23,* 15–18.

Travis, T. (1908). *The young malefactor*. New York: Thomas Y. Crowell.

U.S. Bureau of the Census. (1975). *Historical Statistics of the United States, Colonial Times to 1790, Bicentennial Edition, Part 1*. Washington, DC: U.S. Government Printing Office.

U.S. Congress, Arthur MacDonald. (1902). *A plan for the study of man, 57th Cong., 1st sess., Senate Doc. 400*. Washington, DC: U.S. Government Printing Office.

Walsh, L. S. (1979). "Till death us do part": Marriage and family in seventeenth-century Maryland. In T. W. Tate & D. L. Ammerman (Eds.), *The Chesapeake in the seventeenth century: Essays on Anglo-American society and politics* (pp. 126–152). Chapel Hill: University of North Carolina Press.

Webber, T. L. (1978). *Deep like the rivers: Education in the slave quarter community, 1831–1865*. New York: W.W. Norton.

Withey, L. (1984). *Urban growth in Colonial Rhode Island: Newport and Providence in the eighteenth century*. Albany: State University of New York Press.

Wohl, R. R. (1969). The "country boy" myth and its place in American urban culture: The nineteenth-century contribution. *Perspectives in American History, 3,* 77–156.

Wrigley, E. A., & Schofield, R. S. (1981). *The population history of England, 1541–1871: A reconstruction*. Cambridge: Cambridge University Press.

Youings, J. (1984). *Sixteenth-century England*. New York: Penguin.

2

Adolescent Nonsexual and Sex-Related Problem Behaviors: Their Prevalence, Consequences, and Co-Occurrence

Robert D. Ketterlinus
Public/Private Ventures, Philadelphia
Michael E. Lamb
National Institute of Child Health and Human Development
Katherine A. Nitz
University of Maryland

Delinquency, violence, substance abuse, sexually transmitted diseases (STDs), and premature pregnancy and parenthood are major health and social problems in contemporary U.S. society. Many social scientists agree that a variety of problem behaviors frequently co-occur, yet the vast majority of research initiatives are directed at the study of single categories of problems (Dryfoos, 1991). In particular, researchers have paid little attention to the co-occurrence of nonsexual and sex-related problem behaviors. For example, the National Institute of Child Health and Human Development (NICHD) has one extramural section that supports research on risk-taking behaviors such as drinking and driving and nonintentional injuries, and a separate extramural section concerned with population research on the demographics and correlates of teenage sexual and fertility behaviors. Other agencies, such as the National Institute of Drug Abuse (NIDA) and the National Institute of Justice (NIJ), fund categorical research on adolescent drug use, and adolescent crime or delinquency, respectively. Likewise, there are few comprehensive programs addressing the many problems displayed by adolescents. Recently, however, a consensus has emerged that prevention and intervention programs addressing specific behaviors do not efficiently prevent or ameliorate the effects of the many problems facing adolescents, especially those from poor and/or minority backgrounds (Mechanic, 1991; National Commission on Children, 1991;

Ooms & Herendeen, 1989; U.S. Congress Office of Technology Assessment, 1991). This chapter provides an overview of the prevalence, consequences, and co-occurrence of adolescent nonsexual and sex-related problem behaviors in order to guide researchers, clinicians, and policymakers in the future.

The chapter has three parts. In the first part, we describe the prevalance and consequences of selected adolescent problem behaviors, both nonsexual and sex-related, primarily by reviewing findings obtained using national samples of adolescents. We discuss three major types of nonsexual problem behaviors: delinquency (e.g., assaults on persons and property, running away), substance abuse (e.g., alcohol, marijuana, other illicit drugs), and school-related problems (e.g., behaviors that result in suspension, expulsion, or other disciplinary actions). We also discuss sex-related problem behaviors such as sexual risk-taking, young age-at-first-intercourse, and teenage pregnancy and parenthood. We have thus limited our discussion to the most prevalent types of adolescent problem behaviors, choosing not to deal with serious, but relatively rare behaviors such as murder (Busch, Zagar, Hughes, Arbit, & Bussell, 1990), rape (Davis & Leitenberg, 1987; Fehrenbach, Smith, Monastersky, & Deisher, 1986), prostitution (Sullivan, 1987), and sexual molestation (Ryan, 1986).

In the second part, we summarize research on the co-occurrence of adolescent nonsexual and sex-related problem behaviors. In some cases, the behaviors we discuss are directly measured (e.g., self-reports of alcohol use, or official records of property crimes), whereas other categories of problems (e.g., adolescent pregnancy and school suspension) are indicators of problem behaviors that are not directly measured. For example, adolescent pregnancy is related to early onset of sexual activity and inadequate contraceptive behavior, and being suspended or expelled from school reflects misbehavior in school. In this section we also illustrate this type of research by reviewing our research on the co-occurrence of nonsexual problem behaviors (delinquency, substance abuse, and school-related problems) and sex-related problem behaviors (early sexual activity, pregnancy, and parenthood).

In the third part, finally, we ask why adolescent problem behaviors have been defined since World War II in terms of single, isolated categories of behavior. We also discuss the implications for research, practice, and policy of the relationship between adolescent nonsexual and sex-related problem behaviors.

Like most of the contributors to this book, we discuss gender difference in the prevalence and consequences of adolescent problem behaviors throughout. Although a detailed analysis of gender differences is beyond the scope of this chapter (and indeed, this book), gender differences cannot be ignored in a chapter focused on problematic sexual behavior, which is often viewed as a female problem in special need of social control (Brenzel, 1983; Nathanson, 1991; Schlossman & Wallach, 1978; Solinger, 1992). By contrast, females are often ignored in research on delinquency, antisocial behavior, conduct disorder, and aggression. Fortunately, there is increasing awareness of the need to address these lacunae (Herzog, Bachman, Johnson, & O'Malley, 1987; Osgood, 1991; Tremblay, 1991; U. S. House of Representatives, 1992).

PREVALENCE AND INCIDENCE OF PROBLEM BEHAVIORS

Nonsexual Problem Behaviors

Delinquency.   In 1983, the juvenile courts processed nearly 1.25 million delinquency and status offense cases (Snyder & Finnegan, 1987), and in 1986 more than 2.3 million adolescents were arrested: 1.4 million for "nonindex" crimes such as vandalism, drug abuse, and running away, and almost 1 million for index crimes such as larceny–theft and robbery (Federal Bureau of Investigation, 1987). In 1990, 77% of adolescents under age 18 arrested were male. Females accounted for the majority of adolescent arrests in only two offense categories—running away from home and prostitution and commercialized vice—although other offenses with a relatively high proportion of female arrests included embezzlement, offenses against family and children, forgery and counterfeiting, and fraud (Office of Juvenile Justice and Delinquency Prevention, 1992).

Gender differences in offense and arrest rates partly account for the lack of attention to female crime and delinquency: The number of young males having contact with police and the judicial system is much larger than the number of young females. Cross-sectional analyses of gender differences in offense and arrest rates, however, frequently overlook secular changes in male and female rates of specific criminal and delinquent offenses. For example, arrest rates for adolescent females remained substantially lower than those for adolescent males from 1965 to 1989 (Office of Juvenile Justice and Delinquency Prevention, 1992), but there was a 17% increase from 1987 to 1989 in the number of adolescent females charged with violent personal crimes, compared with an 8% overall increase among all adolescents (Office of Juvenile Justice and Delinquency Prevention, 1992). This increase contrasts with the stereotypical description of violent adolescents as young, Black, inner-city males (frequently gang members). Despite a long history of research on adolescent and adult female crime and delinquency (see e.g., Campbell, 1984; Gilfus, 1992; Glueck & Glueck, 1934; Miller, 1986; Peacock, 1981; Rosenberg & Zimmerman, 1977), delinquent and aggressive females are generally accorded little attention by researchers, policymakers, and the media.

Illicit Drug and Alcohol Use.   In the United States, the rates of adolescent alcohol and substance use remain alarmingly high despite recent declines. In the 1980s, more than 90% of U.S. youth used alcohol at least once, and a large majority drank at least occasionally (Johnson, Bachman, & O'Malley, 1980; Thorne & DeBlassie, 1985). The percentage of high school seniors who were reported drinking alcohol in the past 30 days and the percentage of occasional heavy drinkers (five or more drinks at a sitting during the past 2 weeks) both peaked around 1978 (at approximately 72% and 41%, respectively), with a gradual decrease since then.[1] The rates of adolescent alcohol use have remained

---

[1]Critics have suggested that statistics on drug and alcohol use derived from national studies of high school students underestimate rates of drug use because many drug users drop out of school and therefore are not counted (Josephson & Rosen, 1978; Mensch & Kandel, 1988). However, Johnson, O'Malley, and Bachman (1988) concluded that failure to include dropouts and absentees does not substantially affect estimates of the prevalance and incidence of adolescent alcohol and drug use.

quite high, however. In 1987, for example, two thirds of high school seniors had drunk alcohol in the past 30 days, one third (and half of the males) occasionally engaged in heavy drinking, and one third reported that most or all of their friends got drunk at least once a week (U.S. Department of Health and Human Services, 1990). As previously noted, male adolescents are disproportionately represented among those who report frequent drinking, although state and national data document decreasing gender differences in the number of high school students who drink (Windle, 1991).

Between 1972 and 1990, the highest usage of any illicit drugs over the lifetime, in the past year, and in the past month occurred in 1979 (National Institute on Drug Abuse, 1990), whereas the rates of lifetime use in 1990 were similar to those reported in the early 1970s. In 1990, 37% of the adolescents over the age of 11 reported having used an illicit drug, 13.3% reported having done so in the past year, and 6.4% had done so in the past month. Alcohol and cigarette-use rates were 83.2% and 73.2% (lifetime), 66% and 32% (past year), and 51.2% and 26.7% (past month), respectively. These figures indicate that, regardless of how drug-use rates are assessed, alcohol and cigarettes are the drugs of choice for most adolescents and young adults.

It is often assumed that most illicit drug users are either older adolescents or young adults. Although recent national data generally confirm this assumption, younger adolescents (12- to 17-year-olds) also use drugs at alarmingly high rates (National Institute on Drug Abuse, 1990). In 1990, 22.7% of 12- to 17-year-olds had ever used drugs compared with 55.8% of the 18- to 25-year-olds. The lifetime rates of alcohol and cigarette use, however, were much greater for both age groups: 48.2% and 40.2% for adolescents aged 12 to 17, and 88.2% and 70.5% for youth aged 18 to 25, respectively. Rates of drug use in the past year and in the past month follow a similar pattern. In 1990, 15.9% of adolescents aged 12 to 17 reported using any illicit drugs (except alcohol and cigarettes) in the past year; 41% and 22.2% reported using alcohol and cigarettes, respectively. Among 18- to 25-year-olds, the respective figures were 28.7% (any illicit drugs), 80.2% (alcohol), and 39.7% (cigarettes). When asked about the past month, 8.1% of youth aged 12 to 17 reported using any illicit drugs, whereas the rates for alcohol and cigarettes were 24.5% and 11.6%, respectively. Among 18- to 25-year-olds, these figures were 14.9% for any drugs, 63.3% for alcohol, and 31.5% for cigarettes.

Some researchers have suggested that older adolescents who experiment with drugs are better adjusted than either frequent or nonusers (Kandel, Davies, Karus, & Yamaguchi, 1986; Newcomb & Bentler, 1988; Shedler & Block, 1990). Regardless of the age at which they first use drugs, however, many adolescents experience problems associated with dependence on drugs (e.g., increase in tolerance associated with increases in use, withdrawal symptoms, attempts to curtail use). For example, among adolescents who had used marijuana at least once in the past year, 40.8% reported at least one problem associated with dependence, and 60% of those adolescents who used marijuana in the past month reported at least one problem, indicating that more frequent users were more likely to report dependence problems (National Institute on Drug Abuse, 1990). Because the years from age 14 to 18 constitute the period of maximum risk for initiation into the use of alcohol, cigarettes, marijuana, and other illicit drugs (Kandel & Logan, 1984), it is noteworthy that the rates and numbers of drug dependence problems reported by younger and older adolescents were similar.

Although older surveys indicated that adolescent females used drugs as much as males did (Beschner & Treasure, 1979), more recent national statistics reveal interesting gender differences (National Institute on Drug Abuse, 1990). Except among 12- to 17-year-old adolescents, for example, rates of lifetime, past year, and past month use of marijuana, cocaine, and alcohol are greater among males than among females. Among 12- to 17-year-olds, however, the most popular drugs are used similarly by males and females. Unfortunately, gender differences in rates and consequences of drug and alcohol use have not been explored adequately.

School-Related Problem Behaviors. Recent national surveys indicate that many public schools face serious student behavior problems (e.g., alcohol and drug abuse, violence, disruptive behavior) that interfere with effective learning (National Center for Education Statistics, 1991, 1992). For example, 28% of teachers and 22% of principals reported that physical conflicts among students constituted serious to moderate problems in their schools. Many also reported serious problems with student alcohol use (teachers: 23%; principals: 11%), vandalism of school property (teachers: 22%; principals: 12%), the possession of weapons by students (teachers: 5%; principals: 3%), and verbal abuse of teachers (teachers: 29%; principals: 11%). Problems such as these precipitated many suspensions or expulsions. In the 1990–1991 school year, for example, 10 of every 100 public school students (approximately 3.9 million students) were suspended (including in-school suspensions). Approximately 60% of these disciplinary actions were motivated by alcohol or drug use, possession, or sales. This is in stark contrast to the types of school misbehavior that led to suspensions in the early 1970s. In a 1975 study, the Children's Defense Fund (cited by McCarthy & Hoge, 1987) found that children were mostly suspended for fighting, followed by truancy or tardiness, a variety of behaviors including verbal confrontations with teachers, and smoking.

School suspension, expulsion rates, and drop-out rates reflect the extent to which problem behaviors are observed in schools. For example, many pregnant adolescents drop out of school, although increasing numbers of them now return to school (Solinger, 1992). Adolescents who leave school for economic or judicial reasons are not as likely to complete their high school education, but the increasing numbers of pregnant teenagers in school may account for a decline (from 6.2% in 1980 to 4.1% in 1990) in the drop-out rates for 15- to 24-year-old students in Grades 10 to 12 (National Center for Education Statistics, 1991). Despite increases in the number of pregnant adolescents who drop out and then return to school, students in poor urban areas that are marked by high levels of crime and social disorganization still have the lowest retention rates in the country. Overall, only 71.5% of ninth graders graduated from public schools 4 years later (1988–1989) and the percentages ranged from a low of 57.7% in Washington, DC, to 88.6% in Minnesota.

Unfortunately, there has been little research on gender differences in school-related problems, and the gender of research participants is often unreported (e.g., National Center for Education Statistics, 1991, 1992; Sommer, 1985). When males and females have been compared, the rates of drop out, suspension, expulsion, and truancy appear to be comparable (Kratcoski & Kratcoski, 1975; National Center for Education Statistics, 1991). Clearly, gender differences in school-related problem behaviors deserve more attention in the future.

Sex-Related Problem Behaviors and Their Consequences

Sexual Intercourse and Contraception. Although we know little about the sexual behavior of contemporary adolescents, early, unprotected sexual activity has clear negative consequences, including teenage pregnancy, premature parenthood, and the acquisition of sexually transmitted diseases. In 1979, the average age at first intercourse was 16.2 years for females, and 15.7 years for males. On average, Black men initiated sex earlier than White men, and differences between Blacks and Whites were greater among males than among females (Zabin, Kantner, & Zelnik, 1979; Zelnik & Shah, 1983). The percentage of never-married urban females aged 15 to 19 who had ever engaged in sexual intercourse increased from 27.6% in 1971 to 46% in 1979, and then declined slightly to 42.2% in 1982 (Pratt, Mosher, Bachrach, & Horn, 1984; Zelnik & Kanter, 1980), compared with 70% of 17- to 21-year-old males.

More recently, Sonenstein, Pleck, and Ku (1991) reported an increase between 1979 and 1988 in the proportion of 17- to 19-year-old males who were sexually experienced, although fewer non-Black males had first intercourse by age 15 in the 1988 sample than in the 1979 sample. In 1988, three fifths of 15- to 19-year-old males were sexually experienced. The average reported 1.9 partners in the last 12 months and 2.7 sexual encounters in the last 4 weeks. Unfortunately, no comparable data are available for females.

Despite some indication that adolescents are more likely to use contraceptives today than in the past (Mosher, 1990; Sonenstein, Pleck, & Ku, 1989), only about half of those males who are at highest risk for STDs (IV drug users, homosexuals, etc.) used condoms (Sonenstein et al., 1989), whereas about 50% of White and 33% of Black females used contraception at first intercourse; the rate of contraceptive use 2 months later increased by less than 20% among Whites and less than 14% among Blacks (Kahn, Rindfuss, & Guilkey, 1990).

Adolescent Pregnancy and Childbearing. Among the Western industrialized countries, the United States has the highest rates of teenage pregnancy and childbirth (Hofferth & Hayes, 1987). Approximately 1 million teenagers (including 20,000 adolescents under 15 years of age) become pregnant every year, and nearly half give birth. The overall rates of teenage pregnancy peaked in the late 1950s, with a steady but moderate decline in adolescent birth rates over the next 25 years except among 10- to 14-year-old adolescents (Trussell, 1988; Vinovskis, 1988;

Wegman, 1988). For the past 15 years, 1 out of every 10 women aged 15 to 19 has become pregnant every year, with over 80% of these pregnancies unintended, and 54% out of wedlock (National Center for Health Statistics, 1991).

There are large racial disparities in adolescent pregnancy and birth rates (although see Hahn, 1992, for an analysis of problems with ethnic categories). Pregnancy rates among Blacks are nearly twice as high as among Whites, and because White women are more likely to elect abortion, the racial differential in birth rates is even greater. Recently, however, the rates of nonmarital birth have increased among White women more than among Black women (National Center for Health Statistics, 1991).

Although many researchers believe that teenage childbearing has long-term negative sequelae (Baldwin & Cain, 1980; Hamburg, 1986; Hayes, 1987; Ketterlinus & Lamb, 1991; Lamb & Ketterlinus, 1991; Lamb & Teti, 1991a, 1991b), our research suggests that maternal age per se is a poorer predictor of neonatal risk and intellectual aptitude in middle childhood than either sociodemographic status or biological factors associated with maternal health and behavior during pregnancy (Geronimus & Korneman, in press; Ketterlinus, Henderson, & Lamb, 1990, 1991).

Sexually Transmitted Diseases.   Together, the tendencies to initiate sexual activity earlier and to have multiple sex partners have led to an increase in the incidence of STDs among adolescents (Aral & Holmes, 1990; Bell & Hein, 1984). Bacterial STDs such as chlamydia trachomatis and incurable viral STDs such as genital human papillomavirus infection (HPV) are especially common among sexually active and pregnant teenagers regardless of ethnic or socioeconomic status (SES; Fischer, Rosenfeld, & Burk, 1991), and adolescents are at increased risk of developing acquired immune deficiency syndrome (AIDS). In their review of the literature on the prevalence of STDs among adolescent females, Werner and Biro (1990) reported STDs in 33% (trichomonas vaginalis; 37% had chlamydia tracomatis) to 90% (ureaplasma urealyticum) of inner-city pregnant teenagers; women 15 and 19 years of age had the highest incidence of nisseria gonorrhoea, pelvic inflammatory disease, and chlamydia tracomatis.

Although human immunodeficiency virus (HIV), the virus that causes AIDS, now occurs in all sectors of U.S. society, many public health officials believe that teenagers, because of their experimentation with drugs, sex, and other health-risk behaviors, are at increased risk of becoming infected with HIV (Center for Population Options, 1989; Hein, 1989a, 1989b). According to the Centers for Disease Control (1989), the rate of HIV infection among adolescents more than doubled since 1991. Although few adolescents currently have AIDS, it is worth noting that because there may be a 10-year latency between HIV infection and the onset of AIDS, victims in their 20s (more than one fifth of all AIDS victims) probably became infected in their teens.

The pattern of HIV infection among adolescents and adults in the United States appear to be somewhat dissimilar, furthermore. Compared with adult victims, for example, greater proportions of adolescent victims are female (14% vs. 7%), Black and Hispanic (53% vs. 38%), and were infected heterosexually (9% vs. 4%;

Goldsmith, 1988).   Rates of HIV infection are particularly high among certain groups of adolescents. Of the 1,111 homeless and runaway youth anonymously tested for evidence of HIV infection, 74 (7%) tested seropositive, and among New York City women aged 15 to 24, AIDS is the fourth most common cause of death (Center for Population Options, 1989). Even more striking are recent statistics from a large seroprevalence survey in Washington, DC that indicated that 1 in 77 adolescents tested seropositive for HIV (D'Angelo et al., 1991). Hein and Hurst (1988) expressed concern that homeless, drug-abusing, and/or poor adolescents may help spread the infection to low-risk adolescents and adults because they frequently engage in high-risk behavior with older individuals.

THE CO-OCCURRENCE OF PROBLEM BEHAVIORS

Theory

As already noted, delinquency, alcohol and drug abuse, and early sexual behavior have often been studied independently in the past. Recently, however, more researchers have focused on the co-occurrence or covariation among different categories or types of problem behaviors (Elliott, 1990; Ensminger, 1987; Osgood, 1991). In her review, Ensminger identified four general theoretical approaches— problem behavior theory, social control, socialization/social learning, and developmental—of which problem behavior theory has been the most popular.

In problem behavior theory, Jessor and Jessor (1977; e.g., Donovan & Jessor, 1985; Jessor, 1987, 1992; Jessor, Donovan, & Costa, 1991) emphasized the psychosocial and personality factors that play a role in the etiology of problem behaviors. They proposed that the co-occurrence of diverse behaviors and attitudes reflects a single behavioral "syndrome," or an underlying tendency to behave defiantly and unconventionally. In a longitudinal study concerned with behavior problems in late adolescence, for example, Osgood, Johnson, O'Malley, and Bachman (1988) found that a common factor called "deviance proneness" accounted for more of the variance and covariance in criminal behaviors than did any other factor. Many researchers have also presented evidence consistent with problem behavior theory (Barnes, 1984; Donovan & Jessor, 1985; Elliott & Morse, 1989; Elster, Ketterlinus, & Lamb, 1990; Elster, Lamb, Peters, Kahn, & Tavare, 1987; Elster, Lamb, & Tavare, 1987; Forslund, 1977; Hirsch, 1969; Hundleby, 1987; Hundleby, Carpenter, Ross, & Mercer, 1982; Jessor, Costa, Jessor, & Donovan, 1983; Jessor, Donovan, & Costa, 1991; Jessor & Jessor, 1975, 1977; Ketterlinus, Lamb, Nitz, & Elster, 1992; Levine & Singer, 1988; McCool, Vicary, & Susman, 1989; Robbins, Kaplan, & Martin, 1985).

Although problem behavior theory is cited most frequently, other explanations have been offered for the tendency of problem behaviors to co-occur (Farrington, 1978, 1986; Gottfredson & Hirschi, 1990, this volume; Kaplan, 1980; Robins, 1986; Robins & Price, 1991; Robins & Radcliff, 1978; West & Farrington, 1977; Zuckerman, 1984). Most of these researchers posit the existence of "delinquent lifestyles" (West & Farrington, 1977), or of an underlying personality trait ("sensation seeking"; Zuckerman, 1984), whereas behavior geneticists have posited that inherent differences in deviance proneness (labeled d) partly determine both sex-related and nonsexual deviance (Rogers, Billy, & Udry, 1988; Rogers & Rowe, 1988; Rowe, 1983; Rowe & Osgood, 1984; Rowe & Rogers, 1989; Rowe, Rogers, Meseck-Bushey, & St. John, 1989).

Other researchers have explored the stability of behavior problems over time (within individuals) and generations. Robins and Price (1991), for example, showed that the number of antisocial behaviors manifested in childhood predicts the number of antisocial behaviors evident in adulthood rather than that specific types of problem behaviors persist into adulthood. In addition, Rose, Rose, and Feldman (1989) found that behavior problems are as persistent over time among very young children as they are among older children. Finally, there is strong evidence for both heterotypic and homotypic continuity of adolescent problem behaviors across generations (Earls, 1987a; Elder, Caspi, & Downey, 1986; Glueck & Glueck, 1950, 1968; Huesmann, Eron, Lefkowitz, & Walder, 1984; Ketterlinus, Nitz, & Lamb, in prep.; Loeber & Stouthamer-Loeber, 1986; J. McCord, 1990a, 1990b; W. McCord & J. McCord, 1959; Meller, Rinehart, Cadoret, & Troughton, 1988; Schuckit, 1984; Tremblay et al., 1992; Wilson & Hernstein, 1985).

Co-Occurrence of Nonsexual and Sex-Related Problem Behaviors

Such findings strongly suggest that nonsexual and sex-related adolescent problem behaviors indeed co-occur, and that deviance proneness is a consequence of both genetic and environmental factors. Elliott (1990) thus concluded that

> the available evidence confirms the presence of a common set of etiological variables [...causally implicated in delinquent behavior, alcohol and illicit substance use, and adolescent sexual activity...(p. 52)] which account for the majority of the variance explained, but there are also unique causal variables which add significantly to the explanatory power of the common set for specific forms of health compromising behavior. (p. 53)

Although there is evidence of strong to moderate covariation among nonsexual problem behaviors, nonsexual and sex-related problem behaviors may be more weakly related (Elliott, 1990; Osgood, 1991). As a result, nonsexual and sex-related problem behaviors should be viewed as separate, albeit interrelated, conceptual categories. In the next section we describe our research on the co-occurrence of nonsexual and sex-related problem behaviors before discussing the implications of such research for future research and public policy.

Our Research on Adolescent Problem Behavior

Background.   Our interest in the association between adolescent nonsexual and sex-related problem behaviors is rooted in our attempt to understand the correlates and consequences of adolescent pregnancy and parenthood. Early research on this topic was largely concerned with the risks incurred by females who engaged in "premature" reproduction (Battaglia, Frazier, & Hellegers, 1963; Israel & Woutersz, 1963; see also Ketterlinus & Lamb, 1991). Researchers then turned their attention to the behavioral and psychosocial correlates and consequences of adolescent pregnancy and parenthood, especially for mothers and their children. The results of several large-sample epidemiological and intervention studies suggested that many, but not all, of the effects of early pregnancy and parenthood could be accounted for by low socioeconomic status and such correlates as inadequate prenatal care, nutrition, and social support (Baldwin & Cain, 1980; Monkus & Bancalari, 1981). Only among very young mothers (those under 16 years of age), in fact, does there appear to be a direct association between maternal age and poor perinatal and later childhood outcomes, such as low birthweight and cognitive development, respectively (Ketterlinus et al., 1990, 1991). In addition, Geronimus and Korenman (in press) argued that researchers have overestimated the socioeconomic and developmental consequences of adolescent childbearing by failing to control for unmeasured heterogeneity of family background. Although their statistical techniques, methodology, and assumptions have been questioned (Furstenburg, 1991), the debate about the consequences of adolescent pregnancy and childbearing continues to be focused on a narrow range of correlates and outcomes, primarily parental (mostly mothers') high school completion, educational attainment, poverty, and perinatal status. The relative paucity of research on the behavioral and psychosocial correlates and consequences of adolescent pregnancy and parenthood for both women and their partners (for reviews, see Elster & Lamb, 1986a, 1986b; Lamb & Ketterlinus, 1991; Lamb & Teti, 1991a, 1991b; Pirog-Good, 1988) led us to conduct a clinic-based study of over 300 pregnant adolescents and their partners (Elster, Lamb, Peters et al., 1987; Lamb, Elster, Peters, Kahn, & Tavare, 1986; Lamb, Elster, & Tavare, 1986). The results of this study suggested associations between adolescent parenthood and various problem behaviors that were later explored in a much larger national sample of adolescents.

Utah Study of Adolescent Mothers and Their Partners.   In the initial study, data were obtained from intake interviews conducted in a university-based adolescent pregnancy program in Salt Lake City, Utah. Over a 4-1/2-year period, 321 pregnant adolescents were able to identify the fathers of their children and these men were also included in the study. The majority of the subjects were White and came from middle- to lower middle-class urban family backgrounds. The mothers' average age at birth of child was 17 years (range 14 to 19 years), and the fathers' age at delivery averaged 19.7 years (range 14 to 36 years). A semi-structured interview was used to explore the adolescent mothers' and fathers' parenting attitudes and behaviors, history of judicial involvement and antisocial behavior, school performance, employment history, age at first intercourse, history of contraceptive behavior, and sociodemographic background. Further details of the study sample and design were reported by Lamb, Elster, and Tavare (1986); Lamb, Elster, Peters et al. (1986); and Elster, Lamb, Peters et al. (1987).

One of the main goals of this study was to assess factors associated with different patterns of problem behaviors among adolescent mothers and their partners. Lamb, Elster, and Tavare (1986) focused on intracouple age differences, distinguishing among couples in which (a) partners were the same age (i.e., within 1 year of each other), (b) the fathers were between 15 and 36 months older than their partners, and (c) the fathers were more than 42 months older than their partners.

The results indicated that adolescent mothers with much older partners were more likely than adolescent mothers in same-age couples to have dropped out of school, to have reported school-related problems, drinking, substance use, and smoking, and to have first had sex at an earlier age. Fathers in the older father group had performed more poorly at school, were more likely to smoke, and were more likely to have had contact with the judicial system. It thus appeared that adolescent mothers with substantially older partners were more likely to be involved in a pattern of problem behaviors, regardless of their partners' behavior. Mothers with much older partners also had more stable relationships with their partners, however. They were more likely to have planned their pregnancy, to have been married or seriously involved with their partners at conception, and to have received positive reactions to news of their pregnancies from their parents and partners.

Instead of focusing on intracouple age differences, Lamb, Elster, Peters et al. (1986) grouped couples according to the status of their relationships at the time of conception or birth. When young mothers were married at conception, both they and their partners were more likely than unmarried partners to have dropped out of school, although married fathers reported poorer school performance than unmarried fathers. There were no group differences in judicial involvement, however, and no differences between couples who got married between conception and delivery and those who were married at conception. Men who had been dating and did not marry after conception were more likely than those who did marry to have been involved in school-related problems and to have had contact with judicial authorities. Apparently, lack of relationship commitment was associated with a history of problematic behaviors. The results also suggested that men who married adolescent partners between conception and delivery are both more committed to their families, and less likely to engage in antisocial behavior, than fathers who do not marry before delivery, if at all.

These studies also suggested that contact with the criminal justice system was a common characteristic of the men involved with pregnant adolescents, but it was unclear whether they were more likely to have judicial records than males in the general population. Elster, Lamb, Peters et al. (1987) subsequently showed that partners of adolescent mothers were indeed disproportionately likely to have a history of encounters with the criminal justice system. We also found that offending fathers came from more unstable families, and were more likely to be unemployed and unmarried at the time of delivery. Fathers who reported criminal offenses also engaged in other problem behaviors more often than nonoffending fathers did. Interestingly, there appeared to be an assortative mating effect (see Rutter et al., this volume) such that partners tended to have similar histories of involvement (or noninvolvement) with the police. When there were discrepancies, however, fathers reported more serious offenses than mothers did.

Adolescent mothers and their partners clearly did not comprise a homogeneous group with respect to their involvement in problem behaviors, which tended to vary depending on the age of the male partners and their degree of commitment to one another. These data were derived from a relatively homogeneous sample of adolescents in a hospital-based program, however, which limited the generalizabilty of the results. In addition, the study did not include comparison groups of nonfathers and nongravid females. To remedy these deficiencies, therefore, we sought data from a national sample of adolescents, the National Longitudinal Survey of Youth (NLSY; Elster, Ketterlinus, & Lamb, 1990; Elster, Lamb, & Tavare, 1987; Ketterlinus et al., 1992).

National Longitudinal Survey of Youth Studies.   The NLSY was originally designed to assess the labor market behavior of U.S. youth by surveying a nationally representative sample of young men and women aged 14 to 21 in 1979. Blacks, Hispanics, and economically disadvantaged Whites were oversampled deliberately (see Center for Human Resource Research, 1990, and Frankel, McWilliams, & Spencer, 1983, for a full description of the sample and survey design). In 1980, respondents who were under 18 years of age completed a checklist indicating how often they had participated in a variety of problem behaviors. Data on fertility and sexual behavior were collected yearly, so we were able to identify the timing of adolescents' pregnancies and births, as well as the respondents' ages when they first had sex.

The main purpose of the first NLSY study (Elster, Lamb, & Tavare, 1987) was to compare the prevalence of problem behaviors in representative samples of adolescent fathers and adolescent nonfathers. The base sample consisted of 6,400 young men who were 15 to 22 years old when interviewed in 1980. The two comparison groups included 357 males (mean age = 19 years) who reported that they had fathered an infant before 19 years of age ("fathers"), and 1,000 randomly selected males (mean age = 18.75 years) who did not report fathering a child by 19 years of age ("nonfathers"). Stepwise logistic regression analyses were performed to assess the effect of fatherhood status, race, and income level on the presence or absence of five self-reported behavior and school problems in the past year: being expelled or suspended from school; shoplifting; threatening or actually hitting someone; smoking marijuana more than 50 times; using "other" illegal drugs; and ever being stopped, charged, or convicted of an illegal activity.

After controlling for race and income level, we found that fathers were more likely than nonfathers to have reported being involved in all of the problem behaviors except drug use. Interestingly, the percentage of NLSY fathers who reported contact with the police was very similar to the percentage reported by Utah fathers: Whereas 51% of Utah fathers reported police contact, more than half (50% Blacks, 52% of Hispanics, and 60% of non-Black non-Hispanic) of the NLSY fathers reported police contact. By contrast, only about one third of the nonfathers in the NLSY sample reported police contact. These findings lent strong support to the hypothesis that adolescent fathers and the partners of adolescent mothers are "troubled," as indexed by involvement in a variety of problem behaviors, particularly those that resulted in contact with the police and other legal authorities.

The results of the Utah studies also suggested that many adolescent mothers were likely to have adopted problem behavior lifestyles as well (see also Abrahamse, Morrison, & Waite, 1988; Yamaguchi & Kandel, 1987). In our next study involving the NLSY (Elster, Ketterlinus, & Lamb, 1990), therefore, we examined the relationship between nonsexual problem behaviors and adolescent childbearing. Using fertility data obtained in 1985, women were assigned to one of three parental status groups: (a) school-aged mothers (18 years of age and younger at the birth of their first child); (b) young adult mothers (19 to 21 years of age at the birth of their first child); or (c) young women who had not had a child by 21 years of age (nonmothers). Because the women in this sample were 15 to 17 years of age when interviewed in 1980, problem behavior status was assessed before most of these women became pregnant.

The results of preliminary analyses indicated that the parental status groups were ordered in risk, with school-aged mothers, on average, having engaged in the most problem behaviors, followed in turn by young adult mothers, and then by the nonmothers. Furthermore, urban (but not rural) women who had engaged in three or more problem behaviors were more likely than women who claimed no involvement in problem behaviors to later become mothers prior to 19 years of age. Subsequent analyses indicated that, when the effects of race and age were controlled, urban school-aged mothers were from 1.3 to 1.6 times more likely than young adult mothers to have been suspended, smoked marijuana, fought, and run away, and they were 1.8 to 3 more likely than nonmothers to report any of these behaviors. Rural school-aged mothers were 2.5 times more likely than young adult mothers to have used drugs (other than alcohol and marijuana), and compared with nonmothers they were more likely to have used drugs and to have been suspended (odds ratios of 3.2 and 2.1, respectively).

Like the Utah studies, therefore, the two NLSY studies suggested that young adolescents—especially males—who become pregnant or parents tend to be more involved in a variety of nonsexual problem behaviors than adolescents who do not. Might this simply reflect an association between problem behavior and early sexual activity? Ketterlinus et al. (1992) assessed the association between sexual experience or pregnancy/parental status and involvement in four types of problem behaviors—(a) school problems (suspension or expulsion), (b) theft (theft of less than $50, or shoplifting), (c) personal violence (serious fight, or hit with intent to harm), and (d) drug use (smoked marijuana, or used other drugs)—after controlling for the effects of religiosity, scholastic problems, SES, race, and age.

We found that sexually experienced adolescents were 1.5 to 4 times more likely than virgins to have been involved in every type of nonsexual problem behaviors and that getting pregnant or becoming a parent was not associated with a greater likelihood of involvement in problem behavior than was onset of sexual experience alone. In addition, among males only, the early onset of sexual activity (under 15 years old) was related to involvement in all four types of nonsexual problem behaviors.

These findings are consistent with reports that risk-taking behavior is related to the prevalence and frequency of sexual intercourse but not to contraceptive behavior (White & Johnson, 1988). Other researchers have also reported similar gender differences in risk-taking behaviors (Benson, Williams, & Johnson, 1987; Jessor & Jessor, 1977), but our studies were the first to suggest gender differences in the association between nonsexual and sex-related problem behaviors.

DISCUSSION

Society's concern with youth's misbehavior is neither context-free, ideologically neutral, nor isolated in time or place (Brenzel, 1983; Gilbert, 1986; Gillis, 1981; Moran & Vinovskis, this volume; Nathanson, 1991; Platt, 1977; Schlossman & Wallach, 1978; Sorensen, 1973; Vinovskis, 1988; Youniss, 1990). Prior to World War II, problem behaviors were largely defined in abstract, holistic, and moralistic terms (e.g., *wayward* or *delinquent* youth), by middle-class members of the "social purity" and "child-saving" movements. Not until relatively recently were adolescent problem behaviors defined by U.S. social scientists primarily by reference to categorically distinct types of behavior. Among the factors explaining this historical shift in the definition of adolescent problem behaviors, one could include the rapid growth of organized, professional groups that obtained politically powerful positions as advocates for children and unemancipated youth (e.g., The Society for Research on Child Development; see Rheingold, 1985), and parallel increases in the number, size, and roles of federal agencies concerned with specific adolescent problem behaviors (Hilgartner & Bosk, 1988). Competition among federal agencies for attention and, ultimately resources, was (and continues to be) intense, and this led many to establish data collections systems to document the extent and seriousness of the specific problem behaviors for which the respective agencies were responsible. In the 1950s, for example, the Children's Bureau and the Justice Department (in particular, J. Edgar Hoover's FBI) competed for the right to fight rising rates of juvenile delinquency (Gilbert, 1986). One unfortunate consequence of this territorality is that social scientists have come to rely on single mission agencies for most research funding, and as a result the literature on adolescent problem behaviors has been quite fragmented. Meanwhile, lobbying efforts by suppliers and consumers of social and behavioral research have tended to encourage maintenance of the status quo (Steiner, 1976).

Fortunately, social scientists have recently urged that adolescent problem behaviors be redefined in terms of the extent and nature of co-occurring problem behaviors (Rutter et al., this volume; National Institute on Alcohol Abuse and Alcoholism, 1991), for which there is strong empirical evidence (see earlier). The association between nonsexual and sex-related problem behaviors appears to be relatively weak, but far less attention has been paid to this topic than to the co-occurrence of nonsexual problem behaviors. In addition, adolescent sexual activity is not as visible as nonsexual problem behavior and is not inherently deviant nor reflective of psychopathology.

In our research, we have explored the co-occurrence of adolescent nonsexual and sex-related problem behaviors in both a clinic-based sample and a larger, more representative national sample of adolescents. In neither case did we assess competing explanations for the co-occurrence of nonsexual and sex-related behaviors. Specifically, (a) the co-occurrence of nonsexual and sex-related problem behaviors could be spurious or coincidental (b) engagement in nonsexual problem behaviors could lead to involvement in sex-related behavior or increase the severity of its effects (or vice versa); or (c) both nonsexual and sex-related problem behaviors might be caused by the same underlying factor (problem behavior theory). The third explanation has garnered the most support to date, and our own results also indicate that some adolescents and young adults exhibit a tendency to behave deviantly (Jessor & Jessor, 1977; Jessor et al., 1991), although limitations in the nature of the data (particularly, the lack of independent measures of risk-taking, deviance proneness, or sensation-seeking) preclude conclusive evaluations of the three explanations. Research designed to test these competing hypotheses could greatly assist policymakers in their attempts to change self-destructive behavior patterns.

Our research also suggested that the association between nonsexual and sex-related problem behaviors differs for males and females, but many questions remain unanswered. Why is age at first sex associated with an increased probability of involvement in nonsexual problem behaviors among boys but not among girls, for example? Perhaps parents and health professional attempt to impose stiffer sanctions on girls who become sexually active (Miller, 1986; Nathanson, 1991). Because pubertal females tend to be monitored more closely than pubertal boys, furthermore, girls may have fewer opportunities than boys to become involved in nonsexual problem behaviors. One undesirable consequence of this heightened social control of adolescent females is that females are much more likely than males to run away, become depressed, or manifest internalizing problems such as eating disorders (Earls, 1987b; Eme, 1979; Maccoby & Jacklin, 1974; Office of Juvenile Justice and Delinquency Prevention, 1992; Petersen, Sarigiani, & Kennedy, in press; Rutter, 1980). The majority of youth at risk would best be served in the future by moving away from a focus on distinct problem behaviors toward the construction of more integrative views of the development and consequences of nonsexual and sex-related problem behaviors. Although programs that address the immediate needs of adolescents who exhibit acute problem behaviors (e.g., suicide attempts, unprotected sexual intercourse) are still needed, prevention and intervention will best be served in the long run by similarly comprehensive programs.

REFERENCES

Abrahamse, A. F., Morrison, P. A., & Waite, L. J. (1988). *Beyond stereotypes: Who becomes a single teenage mother?* Santa Monica, CA: RAND.

Aral, S. O., & Holmes, K. K. (1990). Epidemiology of sexual behavior and sexually transmitted diseases. In K. K. Holmes, P-A. Mardh, P. F. Sparling, P. J. Wiesner, W. Cates,

Jr., S. M. Lemon, & W. E. Stamm (Eds.), *Sexually transmitted diseases* (2nd ed., pp. 19–36). New York: McGraw-Hill.

Baldwin, W., & Cain, V. S. (1980). The children of teenage parents. *Family Planning Perspectives, 12*, 34–43.

Barnes, G. M. (1984). Adolescent alcohol abuse and other problem behaviors: Their relationship and common parental influences. *Journal of Youth and Adolescence, 13*, 329–348.

Battaglia, F. C., Frazier, T. M., & Hellegers, A. E. (1963). Obstetric and pediatric complications of juvenile pregnancy. *Pediatric, 32*, 902–910.

Bell, T., & Hein, K. (1984). Adolescents and sexually transmitted diseases. In K. K. Holmes, P-A. Mardh, P. F. Sparling, P. J. Wiesner, W. Cates, Jr., S. M. Lemon, & W. E. Stamm (Eds.), *Sexually transmitted diseases* (1st ed., pp. 73–84). New York: McGraw-Hill.

Benson, P. L., Williams, D. L., & Johnson, A. L. (1987). *The quicksilver years: The hopes and fears of early adolescence*. San Francisco, CA: Harper & Row.

Beschner, G. M., & Treasure, K. G. (1979). Female adolescent drug use. In G. M. Beschner & A. A. Friedman (Eds.), *Youth drug abuse: Problems, issues, and treatment* (pp. 169–212). Lexington, MA: D. C. Heath.

Brenzel, B. M. (1983). *Daughters of the state: A social portrait of the first reform school for girls in North America, 1856–1905*. Cambridge, MA: MIT Press.

Busch, K. G., Zagar R., Hughes, J., Arbit, J., & Bussell, R. E. (1990). Adolescents who kill. *Journal of Clinical Psychology, 46*, 472–485.

Campbell, A. (1984). *The girls in the gang*. Oxford: Blackwell.

Center for Human Resource Research. (1990). *NLS Handbook 1990*. Columbus: The Ohio State University.

Center for Population Options. (1989, April). *Adolescents, AIDS, and the human immunodeficiency virus: The facts*. Washington, DC: Author.

Centers for Disease Control. (1989, March). *HIV/AIDS surveillance report*. Atlanta, GA: Author.

Donovan, J. E., & Jessor, R. (1985). Structure of problem behavior in adolescence and young adulthood. *Journal of Counseling and Clinical Psychology, 53*, 890–904.

Davis, G. E., & Leitenberg, H. (1987). Adolescent sexual offenders. *Psychological Bulletin, 101*, 417–427.

Dryfoos, J. G. (1991). Adolescents at risk: A summation of work in the field: Programs and policies. *Journal of Adolescent Health, 12*, 630–637.

Earls, F. (1987a). On the familial transmission of child psychiatric disorder. *Journal of Child Psychology and Psychiatry, 28*, 791–802.

Earls, F. (1987b). Sex differences in psychiatric disorders: Origins and developmental influences. *Psychiatric Developments, 1*, 1–23.

Elder, G. H., Jr., Caspi, A., & Downey, G. (1986). Problem behavior and family relationships: Life course and intergenerational themes. In A. B. Sorensen, F. E. Weinert, & L. R. Sherrod (Eds.), *Human development and the life course: Multidisciplinary perspectives* (pp. 293–340). Hillsdale, NJ: Lawrence Erlbaum Associates.

Elliott, D. S. (1990). *Health enhancing and health compromising lifestyles* (Prepared for Carnegie Corporation Council on Adolescent Health Promotion). Washington, DC: Carnegie Corp.

Elliott, D. S., & Morse, B. J. (1989). Delinquency and drug use as risk factors in teenage sexual activity. *Youth and Society, 21*, 32–60.

Elster, A. B., Ketterlinus, R. D., & Lamb, M. E. (1990). The association between parenthood and problem behavior in a national sample of adolescent women. *Pediatrics, 85*, 1044–1109.

Elster, A. B., & Lamb, M. E. (Eds.). (1986a). *Adolescent fatherhood*. Hillsdale, NJ: Lawrence Erlbaum Associates.

Elster, A. B., & Lamb, M. E. (1986b). Adolescent fathers: The understudied side of adolescent pregnancy. In J. B. Lancaster & B. A. Hamburg (Eds.), *School-age pregnancy and parenthood: Biosocial dimensions* (pp. 177–191). New York: Aldine de Gruyter.

Elster, A. B., Lamb, M. E., Peters, L., Kahn, J., & Tavare, J. (1987). Judicial involvement of and conduct problems of fathers of infants born to adolescent mothers. *Pediatrics, 79*, 230–234.

Elster, A. B., Lamb, M. E., & Tavare, J. (1987). Association between behavioral and school problems and fatherhood in a national sample of adolescent youths. *The Journal of Pediatrics, 111*, 932–936.

Eme, R.F. (1979). Sex differences in childhood psychopathology: A review. *Psychological Bulletin, 86*, 574–595.

Ensminger, M. E. (1987). Adolescent sexual behavior as it relates to other transition behaviors in youth. In S. L. Hofferth & C. D. Hayes (Eds.), *Risking the future: Adolescent sexuality, pregnancy, and childbearing* (Vol. 2, pp. 36–55). Washington, DC: National Academy Press.

Farrington, D. (1978). The family background of aggressive youths. In L. Hersov & M. Berger (Eds.), *Aggressive and antisocial behavior in childhood and adolescence* (pp. 73–93). Oxford: Pergamon.

Farrington, D. P. (1986). Stepping stones to adult criminal careers. In D. Olweus, J. Block, & M. Radke-Yarrow (Eds.), *Development of antisocial and prosocial behavior: Research, theories, and issues* (pp. 359–384). New York: Academic Press.

Federal Bureau of Investigation. (1987). *Crime in the United States: Uniform crime reports, 1986*. Washington, DC: U.S. Government Printing Office.

Fehrenbach, P. A., Smith, W., Monastersky, C., & Deisher, R. W. (1986). Adolescent sexual offenders: Offender and offense characteristics. *American Journal of Orthopsychiatry, 56*, 225–233.

Fisher, M., Rosenfeld, W. D., & Burk, R. D. (1991). Cervicovaginal human papillomavirus infection in suburban adolescents and young adults. *Journal of Pediatrics, 119*, 821–825.

Frankel, M. R., McWilliams, H. A., & Spencer, B. D. (1983, August). *National Longitudinal Survey of Labor Force Behavior, Youth Survey (NLS): Technical Sampling Report*. Chicago IL: NORC, University of Chicago.

Furstenberg, F. F. (1991). As the pendulum swings: Teenage childbearing and social concern. *Family Relations, 40*, 127–138.

Geronimus, A. T., & Korenman, S. (in press). The socioeconomic consequences of teen childbearing reconsidered. *Quarterly Journal of Economics*.

Gilbert, J. (1986). *A cycle of outrage: America's reaction to the juvenile delinquent in the 1950's*. New York: Oxford University Press.

Gilfus, M. E. (1992). From victims to survivors to offenders: Women's routes of entry and immersion into street crime. *Women and Criminal Justice, 4*, 97–105.

Gillis, J. R. (1981). *Youth and history: Tradition and change in European age relations, 1770–present* (Expanded student edition). New York: Academic Press.

Glueck, S., & Glueck, E. T. (1934). *Five hundred delinquent women*. New York: Knopf.

Glueck, S., & Glueck, E. T. (1950). *Unraveling juvenile delinquency*. Cambridge, MA: Harvard University Press.

Glueck, S., & Glueck, E. T. (1968). *Delinquents and nondelinquents in perspective*. Cambridge, MA: Harvard University Press.

Goldsmith, M. F. (1988). Stockholm speakers on adolescents and AIDS: "Catch them before they catch it." *Journal of the American Medical Association, 260*, 757–758.

Gottfredson, M. R., & Hirschi, T. (1990). *A general theory of crime*. Stanford, CA: Stanford University Press.

Hahn, R. A. (1992). The state of federal health statistics on racial and ethnic groups. *Journal of the American Medical Association, 267*, 268–271.

Hamburg, B. A. (1986). Subsets of adolescent mothers: Developmental, biomedical, and psychosocial issues. In J. B. Lancaster & B. A. Hamburg (Eds.), *School-age pregnancy and parenthood: Biosocial dimensions* (pp. 115–145). New York: Aldine De Gruyter.

Hayes, C. (1987). *Risking the future: Adolescent sexuality, pregnancy, and childbearing* (Vol. I). Washington, DC: National Academy Press.

Hein, K. (1989a). Commentary on adolescent acquired immunodeficiency syndrome: The next wave of the human immunodeficiency virus epidemic? *Journal of Pediatrics, 114*, 144–149.

Hein, K. (1989b). AIDS in adolescence: Exploring the challenge. *Journal of Adolescent Health Care, 10*, 10s–35s.

Hein, K., & Hurst, M. (1988). Human immunodeficiency virus infection in adolescence: A rationale for action. *Adolescent and Pediatric Gynecology, 1*, 73–82.

Herzog, A. R., Bachman, J. G., Johnson, L. D., & O'Malley, P. M. (1987). *Sex differences in adolescents' health-threatening behaviors: What accounts for them?* (Monitoring the Future Occasional Paper 23). Ann Arbor: Institute for Social Research, University of Michigan.

Hilgartner, S., & Bosk, C. L. (1988). The rise and fall of social problems: A public arenas model. *American Journal of Sociology, 94*, 53–78.

Hirschi, T. (1969). *Causes of delinquency*. Berkeley: University of California Press.

Hofferth, S. L., & Hayes, C. D. (Eds.). (1987). *Risking the future: Adolescent sexuality, pregnancy, and childbearing* (Vol. 2). Washington, DC: National Academy Press.

Huesmann, L. R., Eron, L. D., Lefkowitz, M., & Walder, L. O. (1984). Stability of aggression over time and generations. *Developmental Psychology, 20*, 1120–1143.

Hundleby, J. D. (1987). Adolescent drug use in a behavioral matrix: A confirmation and comparison of the sexes. *Addictive Behaviors, 12*, 103–112.

Hundleby, J. D., Carpenter, R. A., Ross, R. A. J., & Mercer, G. W. (1982). Adolescent drug use and other behaviors. *Journal of Child Psychology and Psychiatry, 23*, 61–68.

Israel, S. L., & Woutersz, T. B. (1963). Teenage obstetrics: A comparative study. *American Journal of Obstetrics and Gynecology, 83*, 659–668.

Jessor, R. (1987). Problem-behavior theory, psychosocial development, and adolescent problem drinking. *British Journal of Addiction, 82*, 331–342.

Jessor, R. (1992). Risk behavior in adolescence: A psychosocial framework for understanding and action. In D. E. Rogers & E. Ginzberg (Eds.), *Adolescents at risk: Medical and social perspectives* (pp. 19–34). Boulder, CO: Westview Press.

Jessor, R., Costa, F., Jessor, S. L., & Donovan, J. E. (1983). Time of first intercourse: A prospective study. *Journal of Personality and Social Psychology, 44*, 608–626.

Jessor, R., Donovan, J. E., & Costa, F. M. (1991). *Beyond adolescence: problem behavior and young adult development*. Cambridge, UK: Cambridge University Press.

Jessor, R., & Jessor, S. L. (1975). Transition from virginity to nonvirginity among youth: A social-psychological study over time. *Developmental Psychology, 11*, 473–484.

Jessor, R., & Jessor, S. L. (1977). *Problem behavior and psychosocial development: A longitudinal study of the young*. New York: Academic Press.

Johnson, L. D., Bachman, J. G., & O'Malley, P. M. (1980). *Highlights from student drug use in America 1975–1981*. Rockville, MD: National Institute on Drug Abuse.

Johnson, L. D., O'Malley, P. M., & Bachman, J. G. (1988). *Illicit drug use, smoking, and drinking by America's high school students, college students, and young adults, 1975–*

1987 (DHHS Pub. No. (ADM)89-1638). Rockville, MD: Alcohol, Drug Abuse, and Mental Health Administration.

Josephson, E., & Rosen, M. A. (1978). Panel loss in a high school drug study. In D. B. Kandel (Ed.), *Longitudinal research on drug use* (pp. 115–133). New York: Wiley.

Kahn, J. R., Rindfuss, R. R., & Guilkey, D. K. (1990). Adolescent contraceptive mehtod choices. *Demography, 27*, 323–335.

Kandel, D., & Logan, J. (1984). Patterns of drug use from adolescence to early adulthood: I. Periods of risk for initiation, stabilization, and decline in drug use from adolescence to early adulthood. *American Journal of Public Health, 74*, 660–666.

Kandel, D. B., Davies, M., Karus, D., & Yamaguchi, K. (1986). The consequences in young adulthood of adolescent drug involvement. *Archives of General Psychiatry, 43*, 746–754.

Kaplan, H. B. (1980). *Deviant behavior in defense of self.* New York: Academic Press.

Ketterlinus, R. D., Henderson, S., & Lamb, M. E. (1990). Maternal age, sociodemographics, prenatal health and behavior: Influences on neonatal risk status. *Journal of Adolescent Health Care, 11*, 423–431.

Ketterlinus, R. D., Henderson, S., & Lamb, M. E. (1991). The effects of maternal age-at-birth on children's cognitive development. *Journal of Research on Adolescence, 1*, 173–188.

Ketterlinus, R. D., & Lamb, M. E. (1991). Childbearing adolescent: Obstetric and filial outcomes. In R. M. Lerner, A. C. Peterson, & J. Brooks-Gunn (Eds.), *Encyclopedia of Adolescence* (Vol. 1, pp. 107–110). New York: Garland.

Ketterlinus, R. D., Lamb, M. E., Nitz, K., & Elster, A. B. (1992). Adolescent non-sexual and sex-related problem behaviors. *Journal of Adolescent Research, 7*, 431–456.

Ketterlinus, R. D., Nitz, K., & Lamb, M. E. (in prep.). *The intergenerational transmission of problem behaviors: The role of mothers' behavior during adolescence.*

Kratcoski, P. C., & Kratcoski, J. E. (1975). Changing patterns in the delinquent activities of boys and girls: A self-reported delinquency analysis. *Adolescence, 10*, 83–91.

Lamb, M. E., Elster, A. B., Peters, L. J., Kahn, J. S., & Tavare, J. (1986). Characteristics of married and unmarried adolescent mothers and their partners. *Journal of Youth and Adolescence, 15*, 487–496.

Lamb, M. E., Elster, A. B., & Tavare, J. (1986). Behavioral profiles of adolescent mothers and partners with varying intracouple age differences. *Journal of Adolescent Research, 1*, 399–408.

Lamb, M. E., & Ketterlinus, R. D. (1991). Adolescent parental behavior. In R. M. Lerner, A. C. Peterson, & J. Brooks-Gunn (Eds.), *Encyclopedia of adolescence.* New York: Garland.

Lamb, M. E., & Teti, D. M. (1991a). Adolescent childbirth and marriage: Associations with long-term marital stability. In R. M. Lerner, A. C. Peterson, & J. Brooks-Gunn (Eds.), *Encyclopedia of adolescence.* New York: Garland.

Lamb, M. E., & Teti, D. M. (1991b). Adolescent parenthood and adolescent marriage: Effects on educational and occupational attainment. In R. M. Lerner, A. C. Peterson, & J. Brooks-Gunn (Eds.), *Encyclopedia of adolescence.* New York: Garland.

Levine, M., & Singer, S. I. (1988). Delinquency, substance abuse, and risk-taking in middle-class adolescents. *Behavioral Sciences and the Law, 6*, 385–400.

Loeber, R., & Stouthamer-Loeber, M. (1986). Family factors as correlates and predictors of juvenile conduct problems and delinquency. In M. Tonry & N. Morris (Eds.), *Crime and justice: An annual review of research* (Vol. 7, pp. 29–149). Chicago, IL: University of Chicago Press.

Maccoby, E. E., & Jacklin, C. N. (1974). *The psychology of sex differences.* Stanford: Stanford University Press.

McCarthy, J. D., & Hoge, D. R. (1987). The social construction of school punishment: Racial disadvantage out of univeralistic process. *Social Forces, 65,* 1101–1120.

McCool, W. F., Vicary, J. R., & Susman, E. J. (1989, April). *Sexual activity in young adolescent males: Onset of sexual behavior in rural youth.* Paper presented to the Society for Research in Child Development, Kansas City, MO.

McCord, J. (1990a). Long-term perspectives on parental absence. In L.N. Robins & M. Rutter (Eds.), *Straight and devious pathways from childhood to adulthood* (pp. 116–134). Cambridge, England: Cambridge University Press.

McCord, J. (1990b). Problem behaviors. In S. S. Feldman & G. R. Elliott (Eds.), *At the threshold: The developing adolescent* (pp. 414–430). Cambridge, MA: Harvard University Press.

McCord, W., & McCord, J. (1959). *Origins of crime: A new evaluation of the Cambridge-Sommerville Study.* New York: Columbia University Press.

Mechanic, D. (1991). Adolescents at risk: New directions. *Journal of Adolescent Health, 12,* 638–643.

Meller, W. H., Rinehart, R., Cadoret, R. J., & Troughton, E. (1988). Specific familial transmission in substance abuse. *International Journal of Addictions, 23,* 1029–1039.

Mensch, B. S., & Kandel, D. B. (1988). Underreporting of substance use in a national longitudinal youth cohort: Individual and interviewer effects. *Public Opinion Quarterly, 52,* 100–124.

Miller, B. C., & Sneesby, K. R. (1988). Educational correlates of adolescents' sexual attitudes and behavior. *Journal of Youth and Adolescence, 17,* 521–530.

Miller, E. (1986). *Street women.* Philadelphia: Temple University Press.

Monkus, E., & Bancalari, E. (1981). Neonatal outcome. In R. G. Scott, T. Field, & E. G. Robertson (Eds.), *Teenage parents and their offspring* (pp. 131–144). New York: Grune & Stratton.

Mosher, W. D. (1990). Contraceptive practices in the United States, 1982–1988. *Family Planning Perspectives, 22,* 198–205.

Nathanson, C. A. (1991). *Dangerous passage: The social control of sexuality in women's adolescence.* Philadelphia: Temple University Press.

National Center for Education Statistics. (1991, November). *Teacher survey on safe, disciplined, and drug-free schools.* Washington, DC: U.S. Department of Education, Office of Educational Research and Improvement.

National Center for Education Statistics. (1992, February). *Public school principal survey on safe, discplined, and drug-free schools.* Washington DC: U.S. Department of Education, Office of Educational Research and Improvement.

National Center for Health Statistics. (1991). Advance report of final natality statistics, 1989. In *Monthly Vital Statistics Report, 40(8),* Suppl. Hyattsville, MD: Public Health Service.

National Commission on Children. (1991). *Beyond rhetoric: A new American agenda for children and families* (Final report of the National Commission on Children [U.S.]). Washington, DC: Superintendent of Documents, U.S. Government Printing Office.

National Institute on Alcohol Abuse and Alcoholism. (1991). Alcoholism and co-occuring disorders. *Alcohol Alert, 14 (PH 302).*

National Institute on Drug Abuse. (1990). *National Household Survey on Drug Abuse: Main findings, 1990.* Rockville, MD: National Institute on Drug Abuse, Division of Epidemiology and Prevention Research.

Newcomb, M., & Bentler, P. (1988). *Consequences of adolescent drug use: Impact on the lives of young adults.* Newbury Park, CA: Sage.

Office of Juvenile Justice and Delinquency Prevention. (1992, January). *Arrests of Youth 1990* (Office of Juvenile Justice and Delinquency Prevention Update on Statistics). Washington DC: U.S. Department of Justice, Office of Justice Programs.

Ooms, T., & Herendeen, L. (1989). *Integrated approaches to youths' health problems: Federal, state, and community roles.* Washington, DC: American Association for Marriage and Family Therapy, Research and Education Foundation.

Osgood, D. W. (1991). *Covariation among adolescent problem behaviors* (Report prepared for U.S. Office of Technology Assessment [OTA]). Washington, DC: OTA.

Osgood, D. W., Johnson, L. D., O'Malley, P. M., & Bachman, (1988). The generality of deviance in late adolescence and early adulthood. *American Sociological Review, 53,* 81–93.

Peacock, C. (1981). *Hand me down dreams.* New York: Schocken.

Petersen, A. C., Sarigiani, P. A., & Kennedy, R. E. (in press). Adolescent depression: Why more girls? *Journal of Youth and Adolescence.*

Pirog-Good, M. A. (1988). Teenage paternity, child support, and crime. *Social Science Quarterly, 69,* 527–546.

Platt, A. M. (1977). *The child savers: The invention of delinquency* (2nd ed., enlarged). Chicago: University of Chicago Press.

Pratt, W. F., Mosher, W. D., Bachrach, C. A., & Horn, M. C. (1984). Understanding United States fertility: Findings from the National Survey of Family Growth, Cycle III. *Population Bulletin, 39,* 1–42.

Rheingold, H. L. (1985). The first twenty-five years of the Society for Research in Child Development. In A. B. Smuts & J. W. Hagen (Eds.), *History and research in child development, Monographs of the Society for Research in Child Development, 50,* Serial No. 211 (pp. 126–140).

Robbins, C., Kaplan, H. B., & Martin, S. S. (1985). Antecedents of pregnancy among unmarried adolescents. *Journal of Marriage and the Family, 47,* 567–583.

Robins, L. N. (1986). Changes in conduct disorder over time. In D. C. Farran & J. D. McKinney (Eds.), *Risk in intellectual and psychosocial development* (pp. 227–259). New York: Academic Press.

Robins, L. N., & Price, R. K. (1991). Adult disorders predicted by childhood conduct problems: Results from the NIMH Epidemiological Catchment Area Project. *Psychiatry, 54,* 116–132.

Robins, L. N., & Radcliff, K. S. (1978). Risk factors in the continuation of childhood antisocial behavior into adulthood. *International Journal of Mental Health, 7,* 96–116.

Rogers, J. L., Billy, J.O.G., & Udry, J. R. (1984). A model of friendship similarity in mildly deviant behaviors. *Journal of Applied Social Psychology, 14,* 413–425.

Rogers, J. L., & Rowe, D. C. (1988). The influence of siblings on adolescent sexual behavior. *Developmental Psychology, 24,* 722–728.

Rose, S. L., Rose, S. A., & Feldman, J. F. (1989). Stability of behavior problems in very young children. *Development and Psychopathology, 1,* 5–19.

Rosenberg, D., & Zimmerman, L. (1977). *Are my dreams too much to ask for?* Tucson, AZ: New Directions for Young Women.

Rowe, D. C. (1983). Biometrical genetic models of self-reported delinquent behavior: A twin study. *Behavior Genetics, 13,* 473–489.

Rowe, D. C., & Osgood, D. W. (1984). Heredity and sociological theories of delinquency: A reconsideration. *American Sociological Review, 49,* 526–540.

Rowe, D. C., & Rogers, J. L. (1989). Behavioral genetics: Adolescent deviance, and "d": Contributions and issues. In G. R. Adams, R. Montemayor, & T. P. Gullotta (Eds.), *Biology of adolescent behavior and development* (pp. 38–67). Newbury Park, CA: Sage.

Rowe, D. C., Rogers, J. L., Meseck-Bushey, S., & St. John, C. (1989). Sexual behavior and non-sexual deviance: A sibling study of their relationship. *Developmental Psychology*, 25, 61–69.

Rutter, M. (1980). *Changing youth in a changing society: Patterns of adolescent development and disorder*. Cambridge, MA: Harvard University Press.

Ryan, G. (1986). Annotated bibliography: Adolescent perpetrators of sexual molestation of children. *Child Abuse and Neglect*, 10, 125–131.

Schedler, J., & Block, J. (1990). Adolescent drug use and psychological health. *American Psychologist*, 45, 612–630.

Schlossman, S., & Wallach, S. (1978). The crime of precocious sexuality: Female juvenile delinquency in the progressive era. *Harvard Educational Review*, 48, 65–94.

Schuckit, M. A. (1984). Subjective responses to alcohol in sons of alcoholics and controls. *Archives of General Psychiatry*, 41, 879–884.

Snyder, H. N., & Finnegan, T. A. (1987). *Delinquency in the United States*. Pittsburgh, PA: National Center for Juvenile Justice.

Solinger, R. (1992). *Wake up little Susie: Single pregnancy and race before Roe v. Wade*. New York: Routledge.

Sommer, B. (1985). Truancy in early adolescence. *Journal of Early Adolescence*, 5, 145–160.

Sonenstein, F. L., Pleck, J. H., & Ku, L. C. (1989). Sexual activitiy, condom use, and AIDS awareness among adolescent males. *Family Planning Perspectives*, 21, 152–158.

Sonenstein, F. L., Pleck, J. H., & Ku, L. C. (1991). Levels of sexual activity among adolescent males in the United states. *Family Planning Perspectives*, 23, 162–167.

Sorensen, R. E. (1973). *Adolescent sexuality in contemporary America*. New York: World Publishing.

Steiner, G. Y. (1976). *The children's cause*. Washington, DC: Brookings Institution.

Sullivan, T. (1987). Juvenile prostitution: A critical perspective. *Marriage and Family Review*, 12, 113–134.

Thorne, C. R., & DeBlassie, R. R. (1985). Adolescent substance abuse. *Adolescence*, 20, 335–347.

Tremblay, R. E. (1991). Aggression, prosocial behavior, and gender: Three magic words but no magic wand. In D. J. Pepler & K. H. Rubin (Eds.), *The development and treatment of childhood aggression* (pp. 71–78). Hillsdale, NJ: Lawrence Erlbaum Associates.

Tremblay, R. E., Masse, B., Perron, D., Leblanc, M., Schwartzman, A. E., & Ledingham, J. E. (1992). Early disruptive behavior, poor school achievement, delinquent behavior, and delinquent personality: Longitudinal analyses. *Journal of Consulting and Clinical Psychology*, 60, 62–72.

Trussell, J. (1988). Teenage pregnancy in the United States. *Family Planning Perspectives*, 20, 262–272.

U. S. Congress, Office of Technology Assessment. (1991). *Adolescent health-Vol. 1: Summary and policy options* (OTA-H-468). Washington, DC: U.S. Government Printing Office.

U. S. Department of Health and Human Services. (1990). *Seventh Special Report to the U. S. Congress on Alcohol and Health*. Rockville, MD: Alcohol, Drug Abuse, and Mental Health Administration.

U. S. House of Representatives. (1992). *Provision of services to girls and the juvenile justice system*. Hearings on the re-authorization of the Juvenile Justice and Delinquency Prevention Act of 1974, Committee on Education and Labor, Subcommittee on Human Resources, Washington DC.

Vinovskis, M. A. (1988). *An "epidemic" of adolescent pregnancy? Some historical and policy considerations*. New York: Oxford University Press.

Wegman, M. E. (1988). Annual summary of vital statistics-1987. *Pediatrics, 82,* 817–827.

Wellesley College Center for Research on Women. (1992). *The American Association of University Women Report: How schools shortchange girls.* Wellesley, MA: Center for Research on Women, Wellesley College.

Werner, M. J., & Biro, F. M. (1990). Contraception and sexually tranasmitted diseases in adolescent females. *Adolescent Pediatric Gynecology, 3,* 127–136.

West, D. J., & Farrington, D. P. (1977). *The delinquent way of life.* New York: Crane Russak.

White, H. R., & Johnson, V. (1988). Risk taking as a predictor of adolescent sexual activity and use of contraception. *Journal of Adolescent Research, 3,* 317–331.

Wilson, J. Q., & Hernstein, R. J. (1985). *Crime and human nature: The definitive study of the causes of crime.* New York: Simon & Schuster.

Windle, M. (1991). Alcohol use and abuse: Some findings from the National Adolescent Health Survey. *Alcohol Health and Research World, 15,* 5–10.

Yamaguchi, K., & Kandel, D. (1987). Drug use and other determinants of premarital pregnancy and its outcome: A dynamic analysis of competing life events. *Journal of Marriage and the Family, 49,* 257–270.

Youniss, J. (1990). Cultural forces leading to scientific developmental psychology. In C. B. Fisher & W. N. Tryon (Eds.), *Ethics in applied developmental psychology* (pp. 285–300). Norwood, NJ: Ablex.

Zabin, L. S., Kantner, J. F., & Zelnik, M. (1979). The risk of adolescent pregnancy in the first months of intercourse. *Family Planning Perspectives, 11,* 215–222.

Zelnik, M., Kantner, J. F. (1980). Sexual activity, contraceptive use and pregnancy among metropolitan-area teenagers, 1971–1979. *Family Planning Perspectives, 12,* 230–237.

Zelnik, M., & Shah, F. K. (1983). First intercourse among young Americans. *Family Planning Perspectives, 15,* 64–70.

Zuckerman, M. (1984). Sensation seeking: A comparative approach to a human trait. *The Behavioral and Brain Sciences, 7,* 413–471.

3

A General Theory of Adolescent Problem Behavior: Problems and Prospects

Michael R. Gottfredson
Travis Hirschi
University of Arizona

Recently, we advanced a general theory of crime and argued its applicability to a wide variety of delinquent, deviant, and reckless acts (Gottfredson & Hirschi, 1990). In our view, all of the topics of concern in this volume, whether school difficulties, drug use, sexual behavior, or criminal acts, are subsumed under the theory we propose. In this chapter we review the theory and the basic facts that in our view support it. We then address some of the issues raised by general theories of problem behaviors, particularly our own.

Our theory begins by examining the nature of criminal, deviant, or delinquent acts. All such acts have a characteristic property: They produce immediate benefit while running the risk of long-term cost. From this property of deviant acts we infer the nature of the *tendency* to engage in them; that is, the general characteristics of those individuals most likely to be involved. This characteristic or trait we call *low self-control.* From the empirical literature we also extract three reliable statistical properties of deviant acts: (a) their tendency to reach a peak early in life and then to decline with age; (b) the tendency of people committing any one deviant act to commit other deviant acts as well (versatility); and (c) the tendency of people relatively highly involved in problem behavior at one point in life to be relatively highly involved subsequently (stability). Taken together, these facts and the individual property underlying them have significant implications for causal explanations of adolescent problem behaviors.

THE NATURE OF ADOLESCENT PROBLEM BEHAVIORS

Most theories of delinquency begin with an image of an actor strongly motivated by social or psychological forces that require the acts in question. For example, sociological theories typically assume that strong desires for economic advancement or peer approval are behind most delinquent acts. Thus, adolescents are forced by their desire for peer approval into smoking marijuana, dropping out of school, or shaving their heads. Or, they are forced by their desire for material goods into shoplifting, burglary, and selling drugs. As must be the case, the motives behind such acts dictate the characteristics of those most likely to be involved in them. Thus, in these theories, sociable people concerned about the opinion of others are more likely than unsociable people to commit criminal and delinquent acts. Furthermore, people ambitious to get ahead in life are more likely than those satisfied with their lot to engage in deviant behavior. It is no accident, then, that those adhering to these theories avoid the idea that deviance is a general phenomenon, preferring instead the idea that each form of deviance requires its own sequence, stage, or explanation.

In other words, if we start with an image of a motivated offender, we predict deviant and criminal acts consistent with the motives we assume. Experience shows that such predictions are often contrary to the nature of deviance. Deviance is not status fulfilling—it is not even condoned, let alone prized, by important reference groups. Deviance is not profitable. It is, in fact, contrary to long-term economic interests.

Examination of deviant acts tells us that those involved in them are unusually attracted to the pleasures of the moment, to short-term solutions to their problems. Because this property is general, it follows that many adolescent problems can be explained in the same way. Sexual promiscuity, drug taking, dropping out of school, accidents, and auto theft may be characterized as offering immediate, universally recognized pleasure, at the risk of negative long-term consequences. The common element in all these events or behaviors we call *low self-control* (Gottfredson & Hirschi, 1990).

Available data support the view that delinquency and other problem behaviors require little effort and therefore no special motivation (see e.g., Gottfredson & Hirschi, 1990, chapter 2). Most delinquency, for example, occurs in close physical proximity to the offender's residence. The "burglar" typically walks to the scene of the crime, the "robber" victimizes available targets on the street, the "embezzler" steals from his or her own cash register at the fast food restaurant, the "car thief" drives away cars with keys left in the ignition. The burglar searches for an unlocked door, an open window, an unoccupied, single-story house. (Once inside, the burgler concentrates on easily portable goods of interest to him- or herself without concern for potential value in a larger market.) The reckless driver is more interested in getting somewhere quickly than in getting there safely, and cannot be bothered with alternative modes of transportation when drunk. Unconcerned with parental or school sanctions, the truant finds it easier to stay home and watch television than be bored by another day of school. The sexually promiscuous teenager finds it more satisfying to have sex than to worry about its consequences. The abusive adult gets his or her way (quieting a spouse or a child) more quickly with force than with reason. In every case, an opportunity for immediate gratification presents itself and the actor responds to the concerns of the moment. Self-control thus focuses attention on the structure of opportunities and on the development of the characteristic that shields people from the temptations of the moment.

Note that the skill, training, or learning required to engage in and hence benefit from general run-of-the-mill delinquencies is minimal. This applies to assault, rape, and homicide, as well as to drug use or property crimes. No training is necessary to see the advantages that might be gained from such acts, and their successful completion requires only the appearance of superior strength or command of instruments of force: A gun, a club, or a table lamp is often sufficient. Property crimes may require strength or dexterity, but in most cases no more than is necessary for the ordinary activities of life. Enjoying the pleasures of sex, drugs, alcohol, sleeping late, bullying to the front of the line, controlling a spouse, or ganging up on a weakling, similarly requires no training, no teaching, and no particular skill. Quite the contrary. Learning to defer pleasures of mood, to attend to obligations, to wait one's turn in line, to negotiate needs with others, to respect the rights of the weak, requires diligent training and teaching, and is usually accomplished only with the help of someone who cares about the outcome (Hirschi, 1983).

Note too that the particular form of deviant behavior the individual engages in will often be a matter of chance or circumstance. The general availability of a particular drug will have much to do with the level of its use. There will be only minimal effort on the part of drug users to obtain specific drugs before resorting to a more readily available alternative. As a result, alcohol or marijuana will often be the "drug of choice," the use of which will say little or nothing about the nature of the offender over and above the fact of drug use itself. This fact calls into question all so-called sequencing or stage models of delinquent development (e.g., Kandel, 1989), most of which can exist only so long as the number and variety of deviant acts in the model are kept at a minimum.

In sum, a valid theory of adolescent problem behaviors must see them for what they are—largely petty, typically not completed, usually of little lasting or substantial benefit to the actor, always jeopardizing long-term interests for the interests of the moment. They require nothing more than access to a target, to a willing partner, or to a mood-altering drug, and a lack of restraint. Differential levels of self-control are the source of the lack of restraint and, in part, the source of access. Self-control affects opportunity because important social institutions (schools, jobs, the military) select in part on self-control (and its correlates, like prior performance), thus providing greater opportunities to some to pursue self-interest, and because individuals self-select (into peer groups and into dating and marriage relationships), in part, on the basis of levels of self-control. Differences among groups in such things as tolerance for alcohol also help shape access variables, as do living arrangements and the general availability of goods. Thus, both access and self-control are causes of adolescent delinquency.

In our view, research tells us where to find the sources of self-control. It is generated in the early years of life, primarily through parental action (Glueck & Glueck, 1950; Hirschi, 1969, 1983; Loeber & Stouthamer-Loeber, 1986; McCord & McCord, 1959; West & Farrington, 1973). In families in which parents care about their children, monitor their actions, recognize deviant behavior, and sanction it negatively (Patterson, 1980), self-control will become a stable characteristic of the child. To some degree, the school also plays a role in the development of self-con-trol. In some environments, the child learns to care about the wishes of parents and the school, develops a commitment to the future and a strong set of values conducive to the denial of self-serving impulses costly to others. In the absence of such early training by the family and the school, the individual will be relatively low on self-control, and will as a consequence be unusually vulnerable to the pleasures of the moment.

THE MANY MANIFESTATIONS OF LOW SELF-CONTROL

Criminologists have come to speak of the versatility or generality of deviant, delinquent, and criminal behavior (see, especially, Osgood, 1990; Osgood, John-ston, O'Malley, & Bachman, 1988; Rowe, Osgood, & Nicewander, 1990). We have argued (Gottfredson & Hirschi, 1991) that the versatility of delinquency should be understood as having three implications. First, the apparent specialization in particular offenses sometimes observed is a function of opportunity and circum-stance rather than some characteristic or trait of the offender. Thus, premarital pregnancy may so dominate the problem picture for young women that its corre-lation with other problem behaviors tends to be forgotten—but this should not lead us to develop special theories for premarital pregnancy on the assumption that such women do not exhibit other problems.

Second, the versatility of offenders extends to analogous behavioral manifesta-tions of low self-control such as truancy, dropping out of school, employment instability, alcohol abuse, drug abuse, child and spouse abuse, motor vehicle accidents, and unrestrained sexual activity. Thus, in many important respects, problem behaviors are interchangeable with respect to etiological study and policy implications (cf. Mechanic, 1991, for the opposite view). This means that studies of delinquency are, in effect, studies of drug use, school misconduct, and sexual promiscuity. Separate funding of research on specific problems promotes the illusion of specific causation, but is inconsistent with the bulk of scientific evi-dence.

Third, efforts to see diverse acts as cause-and-effect pairs (e.g., drug use and friendship patterns, smoking and theft, or sexual activity and school failure) are doomed to falsification. Rather, the suggestion is that because all problem behav-iors are consequences of one underlying tendency of the individual, the correlations of all possible pairs will be positive and strong (and largely causally spurious). Such patterning is often misinterpreted as supporting hypothesized developmental stages or causal sequences of behavior, an error that occurs with particular frequency in the drug literature. Thus, the observation that adolescents use beer before marijuana, and both beer and marijuana before hard drugs, is taken by stage theorists to have some (typically unspecified) causal significance (Kandel, 1989). However, most such sequences can be completely explained by reference to age and opportunity. Beer is weaker and more easily obtained than heroin; beer use will therefore typically precede heroin use. These facts mirror those for truancy and auto theft. Truancy usually comes before auto theft. Second graders can be truant from school. Second graders cannot, however, drive cars, let alone steal them. Few would suggest that the connection between truancy and automobile theft is causal.

The evidence of delinquency versatility is overwhelming (Hindelang, 1971; Hindelang, Hirschi, & Weis, 1981; Hirschi, 1969; Petersilia, 1980; Rojek & Erickson, 1982; Wolfgang, Figlio, & Sellin, 1972), and has been reported in a variety of societies and over an extended period of time. Offenders commit a wide variety of deviant acts, with no strong inclination to pursue a specific type of act or to develop a pattern of delinquent acts. But versatility goes well beyond ordinary crime and delinquency (see especially, Osgood, 1990). "Thieves" are likely to smoke, drink, and skip school at considerably higher rates than nonthieves. Recently, Sorensen (in press) showed that criminal offenders are considerably more likely than nonoffenders to be involved in most types of automobile accidents. Furthermore, self-reported offenders are more likely to be victims of crime and to be included among those who set household fires (Gottfredson, 1984), and those who are arrested for driving while intoxicated are considerably more likely to have arrest records for other, nontraffic offenses (Strand & Garr, 1990). In adulthood, those most highly engaged in problem behaviors during adolescence are more likely to have difficulty in the military (and to be denied entry into the military to begin with), to suffer employment instability and marital difficulty, to abuse alcohol, and to die at an early age (Glueck & Glueck, 1968; Laub & Sampson, in press; Robbins, 1966; Sampson & Laub, 1990).

Although most delinquency researchers and theorists grant the versatility of offenders, this fact seems to have little influence on the character of research or theory in the field. Rather, we continue to treat research and theory on drug use as distinct from research and theory on homicide, and both of these as distinct from research and theory on school difficulties. Forcing our theories to come to terms with the general nature of the dependant variable, and discarding those that cannot do so, is in our view prerequisite to advancement in the field of adolescent problem behavior.

THE STABILITY OF INDIVIDUAL DIFFERENCES IN LOW SELF-CONTROL

According to virtually all reviews of developmental research on antisocial and delinquent behavior (e.g., Glueck & Glueck, 1968; Loeber & Dishion, 1983; Olweus, 1979; Sampson & Laub, 1990; West & Farrington, 1973), individual differences in antisocial behavior remain reasonably stable from the time they are first identified. Adolescent problem behavior, for example, predicts problem behavior in adulthood. It is clear that a major source of the variability in crime and deviance is determined early in life and that this variability is predictable, with reasonable accuracy for theoretical purposes, over the life course. In contrast, there is little evidence that institutional experiences late in life, including experiences with the treatment and punitive aspects of the juvenile and criminal justice systems, affect the relative ranking of individuals on the tendency to engage in crime and delinquency.

The Age Effect.   The general form of the age distribution of crime and delinquency has been examined periodically over the last 75 years (Hirschi & Gottfredson, 1983). This empirical work yields the conclusion that the age distribution of crime, whatever the type of crime and whatever the characteristics of the person, peaks in late adolescence or early adulthood (around ages 17–22) and declines sharply and continuously from the peak. Such distributions are found for all techniques of measurement, for every group in society, and for every society for which reliable data exist. The ubiquity of the age effect led us to conclude that age has a direct effect on crime.

Our characterization of the distribution of crime as invariant over demographic, cultural, and crime categories has proved controversial. Although the search for a subgroup of the offending population that deviates from this direct effect hypothesis continues, no one has reliably reported more than trivial variation in mode or the commonly observed, but minor, crime type differences we first reported (Hirschi & Gottfredson, 1983). In fact, those who have taken the hypothesis seriously (rather than simply rummaging through hundreds of distributions looking for statistical outliers) have provided impressive support for the age invariance idea (Britt, 1990; Greenberg, 1991; Osgood, O'Malley, Bachman, & Johnston, 1989).

It is important to stress that the age distribution of crime also characterizes the age distribution of other problem behaviors. In fact, the similarity of the distributions for crime and auto accidents first led us to the idea that something more than the tendency to commit crime was at issue (Hirschi & Gottfredson, 1983; see also Sorensen, in press).

OBJECTIONS TO A GENERAL THEORY OF PROBLEM BEHAVIOR[1]

Having outlined the general features of our theory of adolescent problem behaviors, we are in position to describe and to respond to several concerns raised by others concerning our theory. The first concern with our theory is that it conceptually lumps together serious (homicide, gang violence, etc.) and trivial (truancy, smok-

---

[1]We have elsewhere (Hirschi & Gottfredson, 1990) described how the disciplines themselves impede the discovery of general theory by insisting on the rules of "substantive positivism" rather than on the legitimate rules of science.

ing, etc.) problem behaviors. Second, our theory has been criticized for its inability to explain why different problem behaviors exhibit different developmental trajectories over the life course. Third, it is said that control theories ignore motivation. The fourth concern addresses our assumption that stability and age effects co-occur, when many believe they are in fact incompatible. A fifth concern is that observed social variability in problem behaviors cannot be explained by a trait theory such as ours. For example, some argue that vastly different rates of adolescent misbehavior across cultures cannot be explained by differences in characteristics of individuals. The sixth concern is that theories like ours that posit stability in underlying traits are overly deterministic and thus are too pessimistic about prospects for effective intervention.

Making Serious Behavior Trivial (and Vice Versa)

Our study of the nature of problem behavior acts suggests that they share a common element. This element, which explains why they covary, is that each entails negative long-term consequences. Common delinquencies (theft and assault), serious crimes (burglary and murder), reckless behaviors (speeding), school and employment difficulties (truancy, tardiness, unruliness, job instability), promiscuous sexual behavior, drug use, and family violence (spouse abuse or child abuse), all have negative long-term consequences. However, insofar as no special motivation for any of these acts is assumed, all provide immediate, obvious benefits to the actor (as, indeed, do all purposeful acts). What ties them together, therefore, is that they are performed by individuals who have little regard for the long-term consequences of their actions.

What separates these acts is a perception of the seriousness of their actual long-term consequences. From the perspective of the offender, all of these acts may have social or natural consequences of great moment: Murder may result in the death penalty; truancy may reduce prospects for further schooling and ruin employment opportunities; drugs may result in seriously impaired health. From the perspective of society, they differ greatly among themselves in their apparent seriousness. No one else is obviously seriously hurt by truancy, smoking, or shoplifting; others are, however, severely damaged by homicide, forcible rape, burglary, and child abuse.

It is this variability *in the consequences for others* that drives current theory to distinguish between serious and trivial acts, and results in dissatisfaction with our theory, which sees these acts as equivalent in that they are all potentially damaging to the long-term interests of the actor. The question is this: Should we expect the actor's behavior to be driven by the personal consequences of his or her acts or by their consequences for others?

Obviously, those little concerned for their own future will be even less concerned for the welfare of others. Therefore, it seems to us that we are on solid ground theoretically when we lump together acts that differ immensely in their consequences for victims. The great virtue of this kind of conception of deviance is that it explains versatility (Gottfredson & Hirschi, 1990; Hirschi, 1969; Kornhauser, 1978).

Because many will continue to see difficulty in describing acts that have very serious consequences for victims, and often for perpetrators, as being the product of ordinary desires, or as being uncomplicated and easy, let us pursue this issue further. How can child abuse, forcible rape, and employment instability be said to result from the same cause?

Such questions assume that serious acts must have serious or strong motives or that serious acts must be highly profitable (otherwise why have greater penalties in the interest of deterrence for their commission?). But the nature of deviant acts considered serious belies these assumptions.

Perhaps the most generally "serious" crime is homicide. The motives for homicide, however, are not necessarily more serious than the motives for other crimes. Killing someone because they will not give up the money or because they will not shut up is no more profound than bullying one's way to the front of the line or taking an item from a store without paying for it. Indeed, after the act, many homicide offenders cannot explain why they did it, and often report being overcome by momentary impulse or the influence of alcohol.

Another serious crime that suggests serious motivation is forcible rape. Some argue that such a horrible act can only result from powerful psychological or social pressures—from desires to dominate or demean the victim. These analysts see rape as a crime with a unique set of causes incapable of explanation in the same terms as school truancy or smoking marijuana. There are several ways to dispute these accounts of the rapist's motivation. For one, rapists are versatile offenders in that only a small portion of their offenses are sex offenses, and rape is quite often committed in concert with other offenses, offenses that have no meaningful connection to this explanation of rape. Furthermore, rape appears to be heavily situationally dependent, to be conditioned by the availability of victims and appropriate physical circumstances. But most importantly, the consequences of the act to the victim are clearly of no concern to the offender, a person focused exclusively on his own benefits of the moment.

One further comment on the seriousness of the motive behind serious crimes: Serious crimes do not differ appreciably from nonserious crimes in terms of the effort or difficulty entailed by their commission. Homicide takes only a moment, and usually little or no skill. The same may be said for heroin or cocaine use, robbery, burglary, or auto theft. No deep motive or sustained plan is involved in these crimes, and theories that presume persistent, powerful, or unique motivation for them cannot accommodate the evidence.

Researchers are constantly admonished, by the criminal justice community, by funding agencies, and by their disciplines, to focus on "serious" problems. Important public policy can only attend to important public problems, thus the emphasis on "serious, repetitive, chronic, career" delinquents, on urban street gangs, and on heavy drug users, and the deemphasis on "status offenses," on school problems, on vandalism and graffiti. But evidence that we should not be persuaded by this bias in constructing our dependant variable is readily available. Adolescent sexual behavior is today serious because the potential long-term consequences have changed, not because the motives for engaging in it have changed. Smoking cigarettes is today regarded as serious, not because the satisfactions of smoking have changed, but because the health risks are now more certain. According to our theory, those influenced by long-term consequences would be expected to change their behavior as a result of new information. Those not influenced by long-term consequences will not attend to such information, and will continue to enjoy the immediate benefits of the acts in question.

We suspect that one objection to our approach stems more from our equation of trivial acts (truancy, smoking, driving too fast) with serious acts (like homicide) than from the reverse equation. Many people, researchers and theorists included, have smoked, many occasionally drink too much, some even drive while legally under the influence, and most are nervous about what they perceive as unwarranted state interference in the lives of ordinary citizens. They are therefore concerned that equating currently noncriminal acts with serious criminal acts implies something about public policy. We think the equation does say something about current policy, but not that it implies the need for greater state intervention. Those unconcerned with long-term consequences are unconcerned with long-term consequences imposed by the state. Therefore, our analysis highlights the impotence of state sanctions for the control of deviant behaviors, whether they be serious or trivial.

Finally, all objections to equating behaviors differing greatly in seriousness must face the fact that those who engage in serious acts are more likely to engage in trivial acts, and vice versa.

Different Developmental Trajectories: The Correlation of Self-Control With Causal Variables of Other Theories

Hypothesizing a stability effect raises profound difficulties for both research and theory about adolescent problem behavior. We have elsewhere discussed the theoretical issues, therefore we concentrate here on the concerns for appropriate research. The stability effect suggests to us that standard longitudinal designs are likely to be misleading, as well as inefficient and ineffective for a number of reasons, including the overwhelming problems associated with self- and institutional selection that are highly correlated with levels of self-control (Gottfredson & Hirschi, 1987). Thus, subsequent to early individual variations in self-control, individuals differentially choose peer groups, school attendance patterns, spousal relations, and patterns of employment. These choices affect the composition of virtually every social, institutional and cultural category of interest to policy and theory. Absent random assignment into these categories, and absent a compelling theory of the relevant trait, adequately operationalized with sufficiently large samples, the passive longitudinal design cannot hope to settle important theoretical disputes.[2]

---

[2]Additionally, the stability effect suggests that very little substantive benefit can accrue to the study of individuals over the life course because, apart from opportunity considerations, the causes change so little. The costs of these designs, in sample attrition, repeated measurement bias, and in simple financial terms are seldom small enough to compensate for the small gains achieved.

Unfortunately for underlying trait theories, the effects of this relentless selection will almost always suggest the operation of powerful institutional, social, or cultural forces. In delinquency research, the hallmark of this problem is the "peer" influence variable, but it pertains to the "effects" of employment, marriage, and school failure as well.

Resolution of this dispute, in our view, cannot come from longitudinal research alone. Absent a clear theoretical perspective, such research will continue to suggest that different developmental trajectories characterize various types of problem behaviors. What is needed, then, is a clear specification of the hypothesized institutional effect *in advance of data collection*, and of the effects of the underlying trait. These specifications will of course also require clear operationalization of the dependent variables. As indicated, the dependent variable in our model is not the dependent variable found in traditional career models. For us, school failure, peer group membership, as well as crime, drug use, and other problem behaviors are consequences of low self-control. As such, they cannot cause one another, or form meaningful developmental patterns. If these behaviors do not occur together in individuals, our perspective would look for differences in opportunity or circumstance, not for differences in propensity. This view thus strongly implies survey research based on large samples, careful measurement of self-control, variability in opportunity, and deliberate exploitation of natural experiments (e.g., differential school programs and drug availability policies).

Control Theories Ignore Motivational Differences Among Behaviors

This ostensible problem with our theory is essentially another version of the typological argument encountered earlier with respect to the seriousness debate. The general argument has become, in fact, a characteristic argument of substantive positivism (Hirschi & Gottfredson, 1990). For example, aggression researchers posit two orthogonal forms of aggression, instrumental, used to get one's way, and expressive, which is more difficult to define. Delinquency theorists, furthermore, argue that acts caused by status-seeking behavior or the approval of peers involve different motivational bases than acts caused by the frustration caused by inequality.

We have already noted our agreement with the idea that the motives behind deviant acts are numerous. In fact, we believe that these motives are so numerous that efforts to catalogue them as specific causes for specific acts are not useful. But perhaps the most straightforward response to this criticism is empirical: Using the common methods of discriminate and convergent validity, it is easy to show that instrumental and expressive aggression (and theft, drug use, and sexual promiscuity) converge across individuals, and it is nearly impossible to show substantial evidence of discriminate validity for such concepts (Gottfredson & Hirschi, 1993).

Concern That the Stability and Age Effects are Incompatible

A consistent concern of those examining our position is that the stability argument is inconsistent with the age-invariance argument. How can crime ubiquitously decline with age when the propensity to engage in crime is stable over the life course? Scholars continue to fault our age thesis by pointing to differences in crime rates among different groups (e.g., men and women, Whites and Blacks, Americans and Japanese), and of course the stability thesis is routinely challenged by people who recall youthful indiscretions now unthinkable to them.

In fact, however, the age and stability arguments imply one another. If differences in crime rates were not stable across groups, the age effect could not be invariant. Similarly, if age did not affect all groups similarly, differences between groups could not remain constant over the life course. Figure 3.1 illustrates these principles. The deviant behavior of both the high rate and low rate groups declines similarly. The rate differences between the two groups persist at all ages.

The age and stability effects also imply versatility. Given the different situations or opportunities that prevail from one stage of life to another, it must be that different forms of deviant behavior are functionally equivalent (i.e., simply different manifestations of low self-control); otherwise, the age effect would not be invariant nor would differences across groups be maintained.

The significance of the *compatibility* of these phenomena is hard to overstate. Because each may be derived from the others, and each is confirmed by research on any one of them, it follows that research need not simultaneously consider all of them. Thus, given what we know, we need not reaffirm the age effect in every study of crime. Furthermore, given what we know, we need not study all manifestations of low self-control to know that we are studying the source of problem behavior. Given what we know, if we isolate a difference at one age we can assume that it existed earlier and will exist at later ages. Taken together, these facts are extremely liberating for research on deviant behavior. They make claims for the

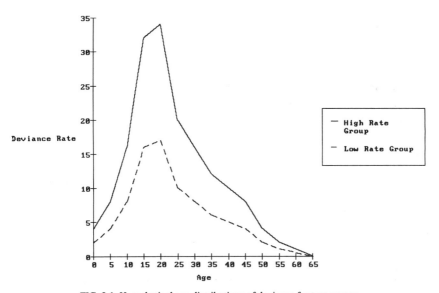

FIG. 3.1. Hypothetical age distributions of deviance for two groups.

superiority of particular research designs based on denial of one or another problem behaviors (or on purely "methodological" considerations) indefensible.

Trait Theories Ignore Social Variability

Much of the concern about our theory may be traced to the belief that only clearly social theories can account for the wide variability in rates of deviant behavior from one society to another, or from time to time in the same society (Hirschi & Gottfredson, 1990). We grant that social, moral, and natural sanctions vary from society to society, and from time to time, and that opportunities for crime vary over time and space. Therefore, we see no inconsistency between a trait theory such as ours and macrosociological variation in rates of deviance.

Our point of view requires only that, whatever the situation or social circumstance, those low on self-control have a higher rate of deviance than those high on self-control. Thus, when there are many opportunities to engage in a particular deviant act, rate differences between individuals high and low on self-control should be pronounced. When opportunities are limited, the effects of variability in self-control will be obscured. Because the production of self-control and opportunities for deviance are not independent, opportunities for deviant behavior will tend to be limited in those very groups that also produce high self-control.

Theories Based on a Trait Established Early in Life
Have Limited Policy Value

Although this critique of the scientific validity of a general theory is not as persuasive as those presented earlier, the concern that such theories are deterministic and hence void of acceptable policy implications is frequently expressed. We believe our theory is in fact optimistic about the prospects for effective and enlightened public policy, and have addressed these issues in some detail elsewhere (Gottfredson & Hirschi, 1990). However, this too is one of those issues that refuses to go away.

Our theory leads to the conclusion that government policies that focus on problems identified in late adolescence (e.g., incapacitation and rehabilitation) will be ineffective and inefficient because they violate the age effect and the fact that self-control is generated early in life. These policies waste resources by incarcerating adults unlikely to have high crime rates and by attempting to change individuals long after the optimal time for intervention (for evidence see, Gottfredson & Hirschi, 1986, 1988; Sechrest, White, & Brown, 1979). Similarly, policies that focus on the long-term consequences of problem behavior, such as penalties by the criminal justice system or reduced employment prospects by school programs, will be ineffective and inefficient because they violate the principle of low self-control (i.e., the tendency to ignore the long-term costs of one's behavior). The large literature on general deterrence in criminology fails to substantiate an appreciable effect of legal penalties. This stands in vivid contrast to the large literature, from diverse settings, that substantiates the view that a close connection between parents and their children prevents problem behaviors (e.g., Hirschi, 1969; Junger, 1988; Junger-Tas & Block, 1988; Laub & Sampson, 1988; Riley & Shaw, 1985).

We have argued that it is wrong to believe in causal sequences of problem behaviors, such as the view that drug use causes delinquency or school problems, or that truancy causes delinquency. Thus, policies that focus on one manifestation of low self-control because it is seen to cause other aspects of low self-control misconstrue the causes of delinquency and are inefficient and ineffective. The principal examples today are the many programs that see eradication of drug use as a route to the reduction of crime and delinquency. Research has shown that the use of drugs (whether they be cigarettes, alcohol, marijuana, or cough medicine) is a correlate of other forms of delinquency. It has not shown that drug use causes delinquency (Akers, 1984; Elliott, Huizinga, & Ageton, 1985). It is, therefore, not to be expected that declines in other forms of "serious" delinquency will follow from a decline in drug use, a position apparently consistent with recent trends in adolescent drug use (down) and in crime (up).

Prevention programs that focus on the development of self-control in the early years of life, have the best chance of producing meaningful reductions in problem behaviors. Identifying and assisting those families in need of training and assistance, and supporting schools that focus on the development of self-control would appear to offer the best hope for success (Gottfredson, 1986; Hurrelmann, 1987; Junger-Tas, 1991). Similarly, programs that focus directly on problem behaviors, that create obstacles to their commission, that interfere with opportunities, and provide guardians or supervisors, can also have significant benefits. Researchers in several countries have demonstrated that important reductions in crime and delinquency can be achieved, once the nature of the offense being targeted has been understood and once the effort focuses on the opportunities for committing the offense (van Andel, 1988; Clarke, 1983;van Dijk, Steinmetz, Spickenheuer, & Docter-Schamhardt, nd; Felson, 1987; Hope, 1985; Mayhew, Clarke, Sturman, & Hough, 1976). There is thus reason to believe other problem behaviors might respond similarly to straightforward impediments to their occurrence, such as increasing the difficulty in obtaining tobacco and alcohol, in staying away from school, and in engaging in risky sexual behaviors. Such programs inevitably intrude on the liberty and convenience of others, and thus raise questions of trade-offs between private and public interests. But making crime and deviance more difficult to engage in seems to us vastly superior even on these grounds to efforts to incarcerate ever larger segments of the population.

REFERENCES

Akers, R. (1984). Delinquent behavior, drugs, and alcohol: What is the relationship? *Today's Delinquent, 3*, 19–47.
van Andel, H. (1988). *Crime prevention that works*. The Hague, Netherlands: Ministry of Justice.

Britt, C. (1990). *Crime, criminal careers, and social control.* Unpublished doctoral disser-
tation, University of Arizona, Tucson.

Clarke, R. (1983). Situational crime prevention. In M. Tonry & N. Morris (Eds.), *Crime and
justice: An annual review of research* (pp. 225–256). Chicago: University of Chicago
Press.

van Dijk, J., Steinmetz, C., Spickenheuer, H., & Docter-Schamhardt, B. (nd). *External effects
of a crime prevention program in the Hague.* The Hague, Netherlands: Ministry of
Justice.

Elliott, D., Huizinga, D., & Ageton, S. (1985). *Explaining delinquency and drug use.*
Beverly Hills, CA: Sage.

Felson, M. (1987). Routine activities and crime prevention in the developing metropolis.
Criminology, 25, 911–931.

Glueck, S., & Glueck, E. (1950). *Unraveling juvenile delinquency.* Cambridge, MA:
Harvard University Press.

Glueck, S., & Glueck, E. (1968). *Delinquents and nondelinquents in perspective.* Cambridge, MA: Harvard University Press.

Gottfredson, D. (1986). An empirical test of school-based environmental and individual
interventions to reduce the risk of delinquency behavior. *Criminology, 24,* 705–732.

Gottfredson, M. (1984). *Victims of crime.* London: HMSO.

Gottfredson, M., & Hirschi, T. (1986). The true value of lambda would appear to be zero.
Criminology, 24, 213–234.

Gottfredson, M., & Hirschi, T. (1987). The methodological adequacy of longitudinal
research on crime. *Criminology, 25,* 581–614.

Gottfredson, M., & Hirschi, T. (1988). Career criminals and selective incapacitation. In J.
Scott & T. Hirschi (Eds.), *Controversial issues in crime and justice* (pp. 199–209).
Newbury Park, CA: Sage.

Gottfredson, M., & Hirschi, T. (1990). *A general theory of crime.* Stanford, CA: Stanford
University Press.

Gottfredson, M., & Hirschi, T. (1991). Three facts and their implications for research about
crime. In G. Albrecht & H. Otto (Eds.), *Social prevention and the social sciences* (pp.
525–535). Berlin: de Gruyter.

Gottfredson, M., & Hirschi, T. (1993). A control theory interpretation of psychological
research on aggression. In R. Felson & J. Tedeschi (Eds.), *Aggression and violence:
Social interactionist perspectives* (pp. 47–68). Washington, DC: APA Monographs.

Greenberg, D. (1991). Modeling criminal careers. *Criminology, 29,* 17–46.

Hindelang, M. (1971). Age, sex, and the versatility of delinquent involvements. *Social
Problems, 18,* 522–535.

Hindelang, M., Hirschi, T., & Weis, J. (1981). *Measuring delinquency.* Beverly Hills, CA:
Sage.

Hirschi, T. (1969). *Causes of delinquency.* Berkeley: University of California Press.

Hirschi, T. (1983). Crime and the family. In J. Wilson (Ed.), *Crime and public policy* (pp.
53–68). San Francisco: ICS.

Hirschi, T., & Gottfredson, M. (1983). Age and the explanation of crime. *American Journal
of Sociology, 89,* 552–584.

Hirschi, T., & Gottfredson, M. (1990). Substantive positivism and the idea of crime.
Rationality and Society, 2, 412–428.

Hope, T. (1985). *Implementing crime prevention measures.* London: HMSO.

Hurrelmann, K. (1987). The limits and potential of social intervention in adolescence: An
exemplary analysis. In K. Hurrelmann, F. Kaufmann, & F. Losel (Eds.), *Social intervention: Potential and constraints.* Berlin: de Gruyter.

Junger, M. (1988). Social control theory versus differential association: A test on panel data. In J. Junger-Tas & R. Block (Eds.), *Juvenile delinquency in the Netherlands* (pp. 77–104). Amstelveen: Kugler.

Junger-Tas, J. (1991). School drop-out and juvenile delinquency. In G. Albrecht & H. Otto (Eds.), *Social prevention and the social sciences* (pp. 551–571). Berlin: de Gruyter.

Junger-Tas, J., & Block, R. (1988). Causal factors: Social control theory. In J. Junger-Tas & R. Block (Eds.), *Juvenile delinquency in the Netherlands* (pp. 41–75). Amstelveen: Kugler.

Kandel, D. B. (1989). Issues of sequencing of adolescent drug use and other problem behaviors. *Drugs and Society, 3,* 55–76.

Kornhauser, R. (1978). *Social sources of delinquency.* Chicago: University of Chicago Press.

Laub, J., & Sampson, R. (1988). Unraveling families and delinquency: A reanalysis of the Gluecks' data. *Criminology, 26,* 355–380.

Laub, J., & Sampson, R. (in press). Unemployment, marital discord, and deviant behavior: the long-term correlates of childhood misbehavior. In T. Hirschi & M. Gottfredson (Eds.), *The generality of deviance.* New Brunswick, NJ: Transaction.

Loeber, R., & Dishion, T. (1983). Early predictors of male delinquency. *Psychological Bulletin, 94,* 68–99.

Loeber, R., & Stouthamer-Loeber, M. (1986). Family factors as correlates and predictors of juvenile conduct problems and delinquency. In M. Tonry & N. Morris (Eds.), *Crime and justice* (pp. 29–149). Chicago: University of Chicago Press.

Mayhew, P., Clarke, R., Sturman, A., & Hough, M. (1976). *Crime as opportunity.* London: HMSO.

McCord, W., & McCord, J. (1959). *Origins of crime.* New York: Columbia University Press.

Mechanic, D. (1991). Adolescents at risk: New directions. *Journal of Adolescent Health, 12,* 638–643.

Olweus, D. (1979). Stability of aggressive reaction patterns in males. *Psychological Bulletin, 86,* 852–875.

Osgood, D. (1990). *Covariation among adolescent problem behaviors.* Paper presented at the meetings of the American Society of Criminology, Baltimore, MD.

Osgood, D., Johnston, L., O'Malley, P., & Bachman, J. (1988). The generality of deviance in late adolescence and early adulthood. *American Sociological Review, 53,* 81–93.

Osgood, D., O'Malley, P., Bachman, J., & Johnston, L. (1989). Time trends and age trends in arrest and self-reported illegal behavior. *Criminology, 27,* 389–416.

Patterson, G. (1980). Children who steal. In T. Hirschi & M. Gottfredson (Eds.), *Understanding crime* (pp. 73–90). Beverly Hills, CA: Sage.

Petersilia, J. (1980). Career criminal research. In M. Tonry & N. Morris (Eds.), *Crime and justice: An annual review of research* (Vol. 2, pp. 321–379). Chicago: University of Chicago Press.

Riley, D., & Shaw, M. (1985). *Parental supervision and juvenile delinquency.* London: HMSO.

Robbins, L. (1966). *Deviant children grown up.* Baltimore, MD: Williams & Wilkins.

Rojek, D., & Erickson, M. (1982). Delinquent careers. *Criminology, 20,* 5–28.

Rowe, D., Osgood, D., & Nicewander, W. (1990). A latent trait approach to unifying criminal careers. *Criminology, 28,* 237–270.

Sampson, R., & Laub, J. (1990). Stability and change in crime and deviance over the life course: the salience of adult social bonds. *American Sociological Review, 51,* 876–885.

Sechrest, L., White, S., & Brown, E. (1979). *The rehabilitation of criminal offenders.* Washington, DC: NAS.

Sorensen, D. (in press). Motor vehicle accidents and self-control. In T. Hirschi & M. Gottfredson (Eds.), *The generality of deviance*. New Brunswick, NJ: Transaction.

Strand, G., & Garr, M. (1990). *Drunk driving and self control*. Paper presented at the meetings of the American Society of Criminology, Baltimore, MD.

West, D., & Farrington, D. (1973). *Who becomes delinquent?* London: Heinemann.

Wolfgang, M., Figlio, R., & Sellin, T. (1972). *Delinquency in a birth cohort*. Chicago: University of Chicago Press.

4

Adult Outcome of Conduct Disorder in Childhood: Implications for Concepts and Definitions of Patterns of Psychopathology

Michael Rutter
Richard Harrington[*]
David Quinton
Andrew Pickles
MRC Child Psychiatry Unit, London

The prevailing psychiatric classifications present diagnoses in nice, neat, nonoverlapping packages. The overall impression of a tidy, well-ordered diagnostic system was much strengthened by the development of the third edition of the *Diagnostic and Statistical Manual of Mental Disorders (DSM–III)* by the American Psychiatric Association (1980). Thus, *conduct disorder* was defined as a "repetitive and persistent pattern of conduct in which either the basic rights of others or major ageappropriate societal norms or rules are violated" (p. 45). This was further specified as the presence of at least one of a list of specified behaviors (such as stealing or fighting) that had persisted for at least 6 months. The revised classification, *DSM–III–R* (American Psychiatric Association, 1987) retained the same general concept but raised the threshold, requiring at least 3 out of 13 behaviors.

The validity of the diagnosis has been shown by the consistent finding that such behaviors intercorrelate and share a factor structure separate from emotional disturbance as evidenced by fears, anxiety, and depression (Quay, 1986); by the differential pattern of correlates as compared with emotional disorders (Rutter,

[*]Richard Harrington is now at the University of Manchester, UK.

1965, 1978); and by the distinctive long-term outcome of antisocial (sociopathic) personality disorder (Robins, 1966, 1978). Robins (1966) concluded that "the symptoms follow a predictable course, beginning early in childhood with illegal behavior and discipline problems and continuing into adulthood as illegal behavior, marital instability, social isolation, poor work history, and excessive drinking. Apparently then, sociopathic personality is genuinely a psychiatric disease" (pp. 302–303). The fact that further follow-up studies of contrasting samples showed the same basic pattern (Robins, 1978) seemed to wrap up the matter.

Yet in spite of this apparently clear-cut pattern, research findings indicate a much more confusing picture in which overlap (i.e., comorbidity) is the rule, rather than the exception (Caron & Rutter, 1991). This is especially the case with the overlap between depression and conduct disorder—two relatively common forms of psychopathology during the adolescent age period. All studies, both clinical and epidemiological, have shown the very high frequency with which these two supposedly very different forms of psychopathology co-occur (Garber, Quiggle, Panak, & Dodge, 1991). The overlap, moreover, extends over time, so that the British National Child Development Study showed that emotional disturbance and conduct disturbance in childhood were almost equally good as predictors of depressive symptomatology in early adult life (Rutter, 1991). Why? Does this mean that we should move to a nondifferentiated global concept of psychopathology and abandon diagnostic distinctions? After all, the terminology of internalizing and externalizing disorders (Achenbach & Edelbrock, 1978), and the psychoanalytic concepts from which they derive, suggests that these very different forms of symptomatology may represent alternative modes of response to the same underlying conflict or disturbance.

Long-term follow-up studies extending well into adult life provide one powerful means of determining what the overlap might mean and hence to begin to test competing hypotheses on the mechanisms involved. However, if longitudinal studies are to serve this purpose, it is essential to use multiple samples differing in their risk characteristics, in order to take advantage of experiments of nature to "pull apart" variables that go together in any one sample. This is an essential requirement if naturalistic data are to be manipulated to create quasiexperiments (Rutter, 1981). In this chapter, we present some findings from two long-term follow-up studies to illustrate the potential of this research strategy and to indicate the questions that remain and the further samples and measures required to provide answers.

CONCEPTUAL/EMPIRICAL ISSUES

However, before doing so, it is necessary first to consider four basic conceptual/empirical issues that have to be taken into account in any attempt to elucidate the meaning of the category of conduct disorder. First, there is the question of whether or not a categorical approach is appropriate at all. The query arises because most young people (especially boys) show disruptive or antisocial behavior at some point in their development; and because the main variation among individuals is to be seen in the degree, frequency, and persistence of such behavior rather than the categorical distinction between its absence or presence. Belson (1975) found that 70% of youths reported stealing from a shop on a least one occasion; and Willcock (1974) reported that fewer than 3% of youths had never committed any offense. Indeed, in inner cities, about one third of boys acquire a criminal record (Rutter & Giller, 1983). Given this level of antisocial behavior in the general population, it is necessary to ask whether it is appropriate to have a qualitatively distinct "disorder" category.

Second, there is the need to consider the various possible explanations for comorbidity (Caron & Rutter, 1991) and, hence, the competing hypotheses on mechanisms that have to be examined.

Third, it is necessary to ask whether antisocial personality disorder is necessarily the only form of adult outcome for conduct disorder in childhood. If not, the query arises as to whether the form of the same basic disorder changes with age (heterotypic continuity) or, rather, whether the presence of one disorder creates a risk for some second type of dysfunction (i.e., a kind of comorbidity over time).

Fourth, there is the key topic of the possible mechanisms underlying continuities between childhood and adult life. Does the high continuity over time found for both aggressivity (Olweus, 1979) and conduct disorder (Robins, 1978) necessarily mean that this is evidence for some kind of biologically determined "constitutional" condition, or do other possible explanations have to be considered?

DIMENSIONS AND CATEGORIES

Traditionally, developmental psychologists have tended to assume that there are necessary continuities between normality and disorder. Consequently, most of their research has dealt with antisocial behavior as a continuously distributed dimension. Psychiatrists, on the other hand, have tended to assume the opposite, that psychiatric conditions are qualitatively distinct from normal variations. Their research, therefore, has largely been concerned with the category of conduct disorder. It is clear that neither assumption is safe, or likely to be generally applicable. The research perspective that has come to be termed *developmental psychopathology* has taken the issue as one of its two main foci, arguing that an understanding of mechanisms and processes requires empirical study of continuities and discontinuities across the span of behavioral variation, as well as across the span for developmental course, which constitutes the second key focus (Rutter, 1986, 1988, 1992; Rutter & Rutter, 1993).

Several conceptual and methodological issues need to be appreciated in considering whether conduct disorder is most appropriately viewed in dimensional or categorical terms.

First, the fact that a trait functions dimensionally in many respects by no means rules out the existence of qualitatively distinctive categories that are biologically discontinuous with the normally distributed dimension. The best documented illustration concerns IQ (see Plomin, Rende, & Rutter, 1991; Rutter & Gould, 1985). Intelligence clearly functions as a dimension throughout the whole of its range extending from severe retardation to superior levels, insofar as correlations with educational attainment are concerned. Nevertheless, it is known that severe retardation is biologically distinct from both normality and mild retardation in terms of its markedly reduced fecundity and life expectancy, as well as its genetic determinants. Thus, the evidence, for example, that conduct problems seem to function dimensionally with respect to their association with drug use (Robins & McEvoy, 1990) does not necessarily mean that there cannot be a qualitatively distinct category of conduct disorder as well.

Second, it must be assumed that most categories will vary in their severity and, therefore, can readily be dimensionalized. This is so even with many single major gene disorders. For example, neurofibromatosis may be manifest in just a few café au lait skin spots or in multiple gross deforming nerve tumors. Similar variations are seen with tuberose sclerosis. It may be presumed, therefore, that if there is a meaningful category of conduct disorder it will vary greatly in severity.

Third, because categories vary in severity and because most normal dimensions extend into the abnormal range, there can be no reliance on bimodal distributions for the detection of categories that are discontinuous with normality. A population may consist of two categorically defined types, affected and unaffected, but these may be measured with error on some continuous scale. As one moves up the scale, there is no increase in severity, but merely an increasing proportion of truly affected individuals. Obviously, latent class analyses (Rutter & Pickles, 1990) have advantages in examining this possibility. Also, a population could consist of a mixture of two types with a continuous distribution on some observable variable. Their means would have to differ substantially one from another before the admixture of the two populations would begin to look bimodal.

Fourth, disorders may be based on a normally distributed underlying liability but function as a category because the clinical implications change above a certain threshold. Thus, blood pressure is a continuously distributed variable with a steady increase in morbid risk as levels rise. Nevertheless, above a certain point, secondary pathological changes occur (so-called *malignant hypertension*) with a consequent dramatic increase in mortality (Sleight, 1988). Similarly, it is likely that many cases of epilepsy are based on a continuously distributed convulsive liability. Even so, treatment implications change once a person begins to suffer from recurrent convulsions. Therefore, it is useful to consider epilepsy as a categorical disorder. The evidence that severe conduct disorders have a generally poor prognosis with a substantially elevated rate of personality disorder in adult life suggests that it may be useful in practice to consider this a clinical disorder regardless of etiological continuity or discontinuity with normal variations.

Fifth, any empirical test for the presence of a distinct conduct disorder category must avoid any presumption that it should be defined solely in terms of severity. Medical analogies indicate that most categorical disorders are differentiated from their relevant parallel dimension because of some distinctive pattern of features, rather than because they fall on the extreme of the dimension. Thus, the XYY chromosomal anomaly is associated with unusual height (Evans, Hammerton, & Robinson, 1991). In the Edinburgh longitudinal study, the XYY boys exceeded their fathers in height by an average of 13 cms. Nevertheless, most fell within the normal range (albeit in its top 50%). What marked out the syndrome as different (apart from the chromosome abnormality) was the pattern of communication deficits and behavioral differences associated with the above average height. The same is likely to apply within the field of conduct disorders. Magnusson and Bergman (1988), for example, found (in line with numerous other studies) that aggression in childhood predicted both adult criminality and alcohol abuse. However, they went on to show that this was accounted for by the 13% of boys with multiple problems spanning aggressiveness, motor restlessness, lack of concentration, poor educational achievement, and poor peer relationships. When this multiproblem group was removed from the sample, aggression ceased to have any link with either adult outcome. Putting together the findings from a range of studies it may be concluded that persistence of conduct disorders into adulthood is most likely when they are of unusually early onset, and when there is associated hyperactivity and inattention, poor peer relationships, educational retardation, and low autonomic reactivity (Farrington et al., 1990; Loeber, 1988; Magnusson, Klinteberg, & Stattin, 1991; Raine, Venables, & Williams, 1990; Robins, 1991; Stattin & Magnusson, 1991).

Finally, the issue cannot be the choice between a dimension or category of conduct disturbance. The finding that the great majority of young people engage in some form of disruptive or antisocial behavior clearly indicates that there must be a continuously distributed dimension. That is not the question; rather, the query is whether, in addition, there is a category of disorder that is qualitatively distinct from the extreme of that dimension.

MEANINGS OF COMORBIDITY

As noted earlier, there is a very high level of comorbidity between child psychiatric disorders that are supposedly distinct and separate (Caron & Rutter, 1991). It is apparent that this is the case within the domain of disruptive behavior disorders, as well as between these disorders and other conditions such as depression. Thus, both *DSM–III–R* (American Psychiatric Association, 1987) and *ICD–10* (World Health Organization, 1992) provide separate categories for oppositional/defiant disorders, conduct disorders, and hyperkinetic/attentional deficit disorders. Yet, empirical findings show that it is extremely common for disorders to include all three sets of symptoms. One possibility is that one symptom pattern represents an earlier stage of the same basic syndrome that is manifest somewhat differently at a later age. This seems quite likely to be the case with oppositional/defiant disorder and conduct disorder (Loeber, 1988; Loeber, Lahey, & Thomas, 1991). Oppositional/defiant problems tend to develop in early childhood with conduct problems making an appearance later. Not all children with oppositional/defiant problems show this progression but most young people with a conduct disorder exhibit oppositional defiant behavior as well. Adequate data are lacking on the etiological factors associated with the two syndromes, but they appear to be the same. At present, most of the relevant data are cross-sectional and what are needed are longitudinal studies from early childhood that can test for this behavioral change within individuals (Farrington, 1988). However, if the supposed progression from one symptom pattern to the other is confirmed, it should not be regarded as comorbidity. Rather, it is better conceptualized as earlier and later stages of the same disorder. It should be appreciated that this is not synonymous with mild and severe points on a behavioral dimension. That is because the factors involved in early stages may not be the same as those involved in later stages. Thus, for example, the study of Vietnam veterans (Robins, Davis, & Wish, 1977) showed that sociodemographic variables played quite a different role in the transition to taking heroin than in the transition from recreational use to addiction. Young inner-city African-American men were most likely to take heroin in Vietnam but older rural White men who took heroin were the ones most likely to remain addicted on return home.

The situation with respect to hyperkinetic and conduct disorders is rather different (Lilienfeld & Waldman, 1990). The former is first manifest in the preschool years, whereas the latter may have an onset at any time up to late adolescence. Accordingly, hyperkinetic disorders could constitute a precursor or early stage of conduct disorders. However, several sets of findings make this unlikely as a general explanation. Hyperkinetic and conduct disorders (especially those with a later onset) differ in their correlates (Frick, Lahey, Christ, Loeber, & Green, 1991; Taylor, Sandberg, Thorley, & Giles, 1991). Hyperactivity is associated with cognitive impairment, motor clumsiness and language delay, perinatal risk, and (possibly) hyperactivity in biological relatives. By contrast, conduct disorder is associated with family discord and with conduct or drug problems in biological relatives.

The research strategies of comparing correlates and course for comorbid disorders are crucial for the study of the possible mechanisms involved. Some of the alternatives to be considered are that the two conditions share the same risk factors, that the risk factors for each are distinct but overlap, that the comorbid pattern constitutes a meaningful syndrome in its own right, and that the one disorder creates an increased risk for the other.

RANGE OF ADULT OUTCOMES

Traditionally, trait continuities over time have usually been examined in terms of like leading to like. It is clear from numerous longitudinal studies of antisocial behavior (Robins, 1978, 1991; Rutter & Giller, 1983; Stattin & Magnusson, 1991) that such homotypic continuity in antisocial behavior is quite strong in males. For example, in the Stockholm longitudinal study (Stattin & Magnusson, 1991), three quarters of young boys who committed several underage crimes had crime records in adult life by the age of 30 (continuity was weaker for delinquency beginning in adolescence). Conversely, three quarters of adult criminals had been delinquent as juveniles. However, the proportion of the population who committed offenses as juveniles far exceeded the proportion with an adult crime record (because in many cases delinquency is a passing phase, with delinquents including many onetime offenders). It is necessary to ask whether people who showed delinquency in childhood/adolescence manifest problems in adult life when they do not have a crime record. It is not clear how nonrecidivist juvenile delinquents fare in adult life if they do not have an adult crime record.

However, both retrospective and prospective data have shown that conduct problems in childhood are associated with a much wider range of psychosocial problems in adult life than just criminality. This is most striking with respect to drug misuse (Robins & McEvoy, 1990) but several studies have also shown that conduct disorders in childhood predispose to emotional disturbance in adult life (Farrington, Gallegher, Morley, St. Ledger, & West, 1988; Robins, 1986; Rutter, 1991).

The issue of one disorder being followed by another is directly comparable with that of comorbidity. Thus, one possibility is that the heterogeneous adult outcome reflects the overlap between disorders that is already present in childhood. The British Natural Child Development Study longitudinal data (Rutter, 1991) suggest that this is unlikely to constitute an adequate explanation. Conduct disorder in childhood was associated with a two- to threefold increase in emotional disturbance at 23 years even in the absence of emotional disorder in childhood.

A second alternative is that of heterotypic continuity; that is, both the conduct problems in childhood and the emotional problems constitute varied manifestations of the same underlying disorder. It is just that the ways in which the disorder is manifest vary with age. There are several well-documented examples of this occurrence. Thus, it has been shown that the childhood precursors of schizophrenia in adult life consist of nonpsychotic social and behavioral abnormalities (Rutter & Garmezy, 1983) and that attention and habituation in infancy are the equivalent of intelligence as shown in later childhood (Sigman, Cohen, Beckwith, Asarnow, & Parmelee, 1991). However, in order to infer heterotypic continuity, it is necessary not only to show that Behavior A leads to Behavior B, but also that both show the same set of correlates and etiological factors.

A third possibility is that the childhood conduct disorder creates a risk factor for adult emotional disturbance, although the two conditions are quite distinct. Again there are several examples in medicine of just such mechanisms. For example, obesity in middle life predisposes to osteoarthritis in old age because of the joint strain that it creates and not because they represent the same disease process. The equivalent in relation to conduct disorder may be evident in the strong tendency for antisocial individuals to behave in ways that creates psychosocial stress situations. Robins (1966), for example, found that conduct disorder in childhood was associated with a marked increase in adult life of unemployment, loss of friends, marital breakdown, and lack of social support—all of which are known precipitants of depression.

Change and Stability in Behavior

Because conduct disorders show such a strong tendency to persist over time, there is a tendency to assume that this is an inevitable feature of some constitutional trait or abnormality. However, this presumption is biologically unsound for a host of different reasons (Rutter & Rutter, 1993). To begin with, development necessarily involves change as well as continuity; that is what development is all about. The major alteration in physique associated with puberty is a normal part of physical maturation. Maturation does not necessarily imply an increasing stabilization of traits (although this does occur to an important extent). Biologically speaking, both change and continuity are to be expected. Also, however, the occurrence of stability carries with it no particular expectation that the cause of the stable trait must be genetic. There are numerous examples in medicine of enduring changes that are environmentally induced; for example, immunity to infections. Rather than suppose that it is only change that requires explanation, we need to seek for mechanisms to account for both change and continuity (Rutter & Rutter, 1993).

So far as conduct disorder is concerned, several sets of findings are relevant. First, it would be seriously misleading to regard antisocial behavior per se as generally exhibiting fixity. To begin with, there have been huge changes in rates of delinquency over time and, equally, there are major geographical variations in rates of both delinquency and conduct disturbance (Rutter & Giller, 1983). Furthermore, antisocial behavior shows a marked drop in frequency in early adult life; in addition, situational influences on delinquent activities are known to be operative. Clearly, the phenomenon is open to major change even though individuals with a marked conduct disorder tend to show a persistent pattern of social malfunction.

Second, the genetic component in juvenile delinquency as a whole is very low and shared environmental influences seem quite important (DiLalla & Gottesman, 1989). Accordingly, the strong tendency for antisocial behavior to aggregate in particular families seems to be more a function of the environmental influences of family discord, disorganization, abuse, and neglect than of any heritable factor (Dodge, Bates, & Pettit, 1990; Patterson, 1982; Rutter & Giller, 1983). However, the genetic component in adult criminality and personality disorder is stronger than that in juvenile delinquency and it remains an open question whether or not the varieties of conduct disorder that persist into adult life are more genetic than the remainder.

Third, it is evident that antisocial behavior in childhood involves many features that could play a major role in their perpetuation into adult life (Quinton, Pickles, Maughan, & Rutter, 1993; Rutter, Champion, Quinton, Maughan, & Pickles, in press). Thus, we have already drawn attention to the strong tendency for antisocial individuals to behave in socially disruptive ways that tend to create stressful environments for themselves. Their tendency to quarrel and fight and behave in violent or undependable ways will mean that they have an increased likelihood of falling out with their friends, of being thrown out of their jobs, and of experiencing marital discord and break up. Stress experiences are often viewed as mechanisms of change but it is clear that in most instances they serve to accentuate preexisting traits, rather than alter them (Elder & Caspi, 1990). Also the work of Dodge et al. (1990) showed that aggressive children tend to have biased patterns of processing social information; they fail to attend to relevant social cues, they wrongly attribute hostile intentions to others, and they lack competent social problem-solving strategies. By their actions, too, they tend to elicit negative behavior from other people (Dodge, 1980). It could also be relevant that much antisocial behavior is a group activity; hence it may be perpetuated by a continuing delinquent peer group or attenuated by joining a prosocial group of friends. It seems that criminal behavior tends to become a more solo activity in early adult life (Reiss & Farrington, 1991) but that does not necessarily mean that it is not subject to social influences.

It is clear that many complex issues are involved in studying the adult outcome of conduct disorder in childhood. Equally, however, it is apparent that the research strategy of long-term follow-up studies has a rich potential for testing hypotheses on developmental and clinical processes. Together with other colleagues, we are involved in a research program comprising six longitudinal studies of contrasting samples followed from childhood to adult life, in which one key aim is to investigate the nature of conduct disturbance and the mechanisms involved in its persistence and desistance over time. In this chapter, we present some initial findings from two of these studies focusing on the questions of whether conduct disturbances and depression constitute facets of the same basic psychopathological disorder and on the nature of the adult problems that follow conduct disorders in childhood. The two samples were chosen because they represented two rather different high-risk groups: a behaviorally deviant group of young people all of whom had received psychiatric care during childhood or adolescence (Harrington, Fudge, Rutter, Pickles, & Hill, 1990, 1991) and a psychosocially deviant group of young people all of whom had been reared in group foster homes for a substantial part of their growing years (Quinton & Rutter, 1988; Rutter, Quinton, & Hill, 1990; Zoccolillo, Pickles, Quinton, & Rutter, 1992).

Follow-Up of Child Psychiatric Clinic Attenders

The first study comprised a follow-up of a sample of Maudsley Hospital child psychiatric clinic attenders in 1968–1969 (Harrington et al., 1990, 1991). The investigation was designed initially to investigate the adult outcome of depressive disorders with an onset in childhood, but it is used here to explore the meaning of the overlap between conduct and depressive problems. All of the sample had some form of psychiatric disorder in childhood. It includes all the 80 children under 16 years of age who had an operationally defined diagnosis of depressive disorder, together with a closely matched comparison group of 80 children, who showed the same symptomatology with the sole exception of the symptom of depression. The symptom matching was necessary to examine diagnosis-specific effects. About one quarter of both the depressed and non-depressed groups also showed conduct disturbance. The subjects had a mean age of 13 years at the time of initial clinic attendance, and were reexamined using standardized interview methods at a mean age of 31, with adequate outcome data on 82% of the total sample (Harrington et al., 1990).

For present purposes we concentrate on the 52 matched pairs, using a proportional hazards model. Figure 4.1 shows that the depressed children had a much higher risk for any depressive disorder in adult life—a cumulative probability of 0.6 compared with 0.27 in the comparison group (who had some nondepressive form of psychiatric disorder in childhood), the difference being highly significant. The graph indicates that, for many subjects, the first episode of depression occurred shortly after entering the observation period (the starting point being set 1 year after the childhood attendance). Because survival analyses remove subjects from the sample once the criterion outcome has occurred, a different form of comparison is needed to determine the extent to which the risk extends further into adult life.

Table 4.1 shows the relative risk separately for any depression and major depression both after 17 years and after 21 years. It is clear that the relative risk for major depressive disorders is at least as strong as that for minor depression and that the relative risk after 21 is even greater than in the late teenage years. It was, of course, necessary to check for possible artefacts and confounding variables and these more complicated multivariate analyses (using a Weibull proportional hazards model) did not materially alter the findings.

The next issue, however, was whether the markedly increased risk for depression in adult life was diagnosis-specific (Table 4.2). Perhaps, depression merely served as an index of psychopathological severity so that all common forms of psychiatric

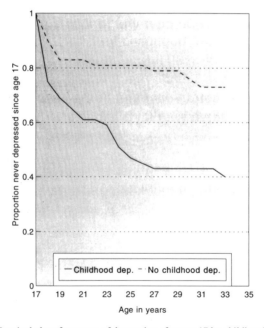

FIG. 4. 1. Survival plot of any type of depression after age 17 by childhood depression.

TABLE 4.1
Relative Risk for Depression in Adult Life for Childhood Depressives
Compared With "Other Psychiatric" Controls (from Harrington et al., 1990)

	Relative Risk
Any Depression	
After 17 years	3.9
After 21 years	5.7
Major Depression	
After 17 years	3.7
After 21 years	7.0

Note. All differences highly significant.

TABLE 4.2
Psychiatric Disorder Since 17 Years
(from Harrington et al., 1990)

	Childhood Depression %	Other Psychiatric %
Major affective disorder	16	4*
Any nonaffective psychosis	6	10
Substance abuse disorder	15	21
Anxiety disorder	38	31
Antisocial personality disorder	21	19

*$p < 0.01$. No other differences statistically significant.

disturbance would be increased in adult life for the childhood depression group. The results were unequivocal in ruling out that possibility. The only psychiatric disorders for which the risk was raised were affective disorders. Table 4.2 shows only a selection of findings for other diagnoses but the overall list examined was much greater and none showed any increase in risk for the depressed group (Harrington et al., 1990). We may conclude that the continuity between depressive disorders in childhood and adult life was both strong and highly diagnosis-specific.

The next question was whether the adult sequelae of childhood conduct disturbance were equally diagnosis-specific (Harrington et al., 1991). Again, a proportional hazards model was employed. Figure 4.2 shows that childhood conduct disorder was associated with a much increased risk for adult criminality (assessed from official crime records). It is important to note that the risk was completely unaffected by the presence or absence of depression. There was no increased risk of criminality associated with childhood depression, either on its own or in combination with conduct disturbance. As with the adult depressive outcome, not only was the raised risk very marked, but also it was syndrome-specific.

Figure 4.2 dealt with the effects (or rather the lack of effects) of depression, in relation to the criminality risks associated with childhood conduct disturbance. We need now to pose the question the other way round. The findings, as shown in Fig. 4.3, were different and striking. The overlap group who showed both

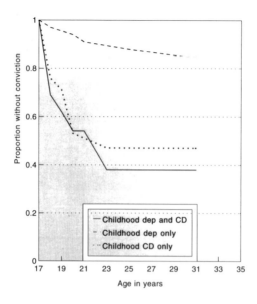

FIG. 4. 2. Survival plot of any criminal conviction by conduct disorder and depression in childhood.

conduct disturbance and depression in childhood had no increase in risk for adult depression compared with those without depression in childhood. The finding is all the more noteworthy because this overlap group was more severely disturbed than the "pure" depressed group in many respects. Yet, in spite of their generally higher level of psychopathology in childhood there was no indication of any increase in risk for adult depression. Why? The finding serves as a reminder that depression constitutes a nonspecific indicator of psychopathology (the psychiatric equivalent of "fever"), as well as the defining symptom for a specific psychiatric condition. Perhaps the depressive feelings associated with conduct disorder constitute the former and not the latter. There is some evidence that suggests that that may be so.

So far, we have dealt with the adult outcome for conduct disturbance solely in terms of criminality and the issue can be explored a little further by examining broader aspects of their social functioning. As found by other investigators, our results showed that the people who had exhibited conduct problems as children usually had a much more pervasive form of social dysfunction in adult life than those who had shown other forms of psychiatric disturbance. This pervasive dysfunction was characterized by features such as a poor employment record, marital discord, and an inability to keep friends. Table 4.3 shows that this combination often took the form described as antisocial personality disorder in psychiatric classifications. A minority showed pervasive social dysfunction of a nonantisocial type but this outcome was actually marginally more common in those without conduct disorder in childhood. The finding reminds us that acute psychiatric conditions often occur against the background of more long-standing pervasive

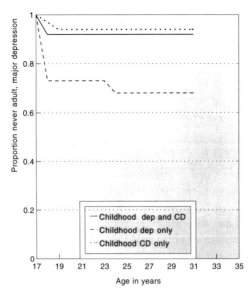

FIG. 4. 3. Survival plot of adult major depression by conduct disorder and depression in childhood.

TABLE 4.3
Conduct Disorder in Childhood and Pervasive Social Dysfunction and
Antisocial Personality Disorder in Adult Life
(Follow-up of Child Psychiatric Clinic Sample)

		Pervasive Social Dysfunction		
		Absent %	*Without Antisocial Personality* %	*With Antisocial Personality* %
Conduct Disorder	Absent	71	24	5
	Present	43	13	43

psychosocial difficulties and that recurrent mental disorders in adult life may well lead to a generalized social dysfunction.

Table 4.4 from the first follow-up study takes the matter a stage further. It focuses on all the subjects who showed pervasive social dysfunction at follow-up and subdivides them according to whether or not they showed antisocial personality disorder. The top line shows that both subgroups had a similar rate of depression in childhood. The middle line shows that the two groups were also closely comparable with respect to minor depression in adult life. It constitutes a relatively common feature associated with a whole range of problems including antisocial personality disorders. The big difference applies to major depressive disorders, as shown in the bottom line. That was

TABLE 4.4
Adult Depression in Subjects With Pervasive Social Dysfunction
According to Presence/Absence of Antisocial Personality Disorder
(Follow-up of Child Psychiatric Clinic Sample)

	Antisocial Personality Disorder		
	Absent	Present	
Depression in childhood	50%	41%	N.S.
Minor depression in childhood	18%	23%	N.S.
Major depression in childhood	46%	6%	$p < .004$

quite rare in the antisocial group but was very common in the nonantisocial group. Once again, the adult findings, like those in childhood, point to the need to differentiate between minor and major varieties of depressive disorder. Only the former are associated with antisocial personality disorder. Major depression constitutes a much more specific form of psychopathology with a high degree of consistency over time in terms of recurrence of the same form of disorder.

The findings from this follow-up of a child psychiatric disorder sample are clear-cut in showing the distinctiveness of the long-term course of depressive and conduct disorders. We may reject the hypothesis that they represent different manifestations of the same underlying psychopathology. Depression in childhood is associated with a much increased risk of depression in adult life but no increase in the risk of adult criminality. Conversely, adult criminality is predicted by conduct disorder in childhood but not by depressive conditions in early life.

The main interest with respect to the issues considered here lies in the adult outcome of the comorbid depression plus conduct disorder group. The rate of adult depressive disorder of this group was much the same as that for those without depressive disorder in childhood. The finding is incompatible with the hypothesis that the conduct disturbance is part of, or secondary to, the depressive conditions. Rather, it seems more likely that the depressive problems in childhood for this comorbid group were in some way secondary to the conduct disorder. A closer examination of the clinic case records suggested that the depressive problems tended to be somewhat atypical compared with the "pure" depressive disorders that carried a high risk of adult depression a finding in keeping with that hypothesis (Harrington et al., 1991). However, the adult follow-up data also showed the minor depressive problems in adult life were quite common in those with an antisocial personality disorder, even though major depressive conditions were distinctly uncommon. Accordingly, the question of how antisocial behavior creates an increased risk for depressive symptomatology, requires further study. Cadoret, Troughton, Merchant, and Whitters' (1990) adoptee study indicates that the risk is environmentally, rather than genetically, mediated but the precise nature of the environmental mechanisms remains to be established. The findings from other research that have already been noted provide leads on a variety of possible routes that may be involved.

Follow-Up of Institutionally Reared Children

In order to examine the adult sequelae of conduct disorder in greater detail, we need to turn to the second follow-up study—that of children reared in group foster homes (Quinton & Rutter, 1988; Rutter et al., 1990; Zoccolillo et al., 1992). This sample of 90 men and 81 women was first studied in childhood between the ages of 7 and 15 years, using parent and teacher questionnaires and official delinquency records. Subjects were followed up at a mean age of 26 years, again using standardized interview methods. A general population comparison group of 42 men and 41 women for whom similar childhood measures (apart from the parent questionnaire) were available, was studied in exactly the same way. Again a high level of follow-up was obtained. The institutionally reared group showed a high level of conduct disturbance in childhood—thus providing a good opportunity to study the adult outcome for this form of psychopathology in a group who also had severely adverse psychosocial experiences in childhood.

Figure 4.4 shows the very strong tendency for the conduct disorder boys (in both the institutionally reared and control samples) to exhibit pervasive social malfunction in adult life (as shown in the domains of work, marriage, crime, and social relationships). It is pertinent that this distinctive outcome applied only to pervasive social malfunction. Impaired functioning in just one social domain was actually

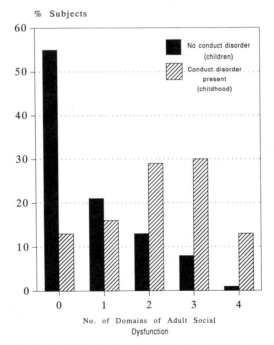

FIG. 4. 4. Conduct disorder in childhood and number of domains of adult social dysfunction (Males: institutionally reared and controls).

slightly more common in the group who did not have conduct disorder in childhood. The outcome difference between those with and without conduct disorder was highly significant.

Figure 4.5 shows the same pattern for females. Again the conduct disordered group shows a very marked increase in the rate of pervasive social malfunction, but no increase (actually a nonsignificant decrease) in isolated areas of malfunction.

The overall patterns of malfunction seen in men and women were broadly comparable, with one notable exception—namely, the lower rate of adult criminality in females (see Fig. 4.6). Crime in adult life was still strongly associated with childhood disturbance in females, as it was in males; it was just that the base rate was much lower. As a consequence, the adult outcome of conduct disorder in women was more likely to take the form of noncriminal varieties of pervasive social malfunction. Still, even in women, criminality constituted a surprisingly common part of the overall picture.

As expected, antisocial personality disorder (ASP) was the single most common outcome for definite conduct disorder in childhood. Thus, of the 35 males with such disorder, 40% were rated as showing ASP in adult life compared with only 4% of those without conduct disorder. The comparable figures for females were 35% versus 0%. However, the ASP diagnosis failed to cover the range of pervasive adult social dysfunction that followed conduct disorder in childhood (Zoccolillo et al., 1992). Thus, an additional 20% of men and a further 19% of women showed other forms of personality disorder. Sometimes these involved occasional criminal acts, but antisocial problems did not predominate.

However, even these figures did not encompass the adult sequelae. Table 4.5 summarizes the latent class model findings (Zoccolillo et al., 1992) for pervasively

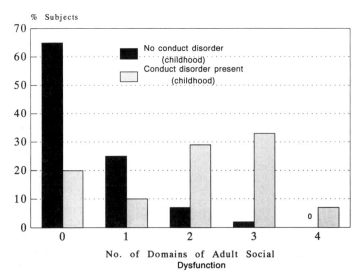

FIG. 4. 5. Conduct disorder in childhood and number of domains of adult social dysfunction (Females: institutionally reared and controls).

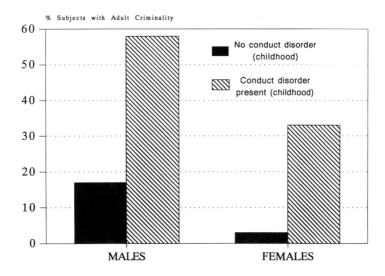

FIG. 4. 6. Childhood conduct disorder and adult criminality in males and females (institutionally reared and controls).

TABLE 4.5
Patterns of Continuity of Disorder as Shown by Frequencies
on Latent Measures (*N* = 227)
Estimated Using Latent or Underlying Child and Adult Disorders

		Adult Social Adaptation		*Adult Social Adaptation*	
		Good	*Poor*	*Good*	*Poor*
Childhood CD	No	49	5	80	0
	Yes	8	52	3	30

poor social adaptation in adult life. It is striking that the great majority of those with conduct disorder in childhood showed poor adult functioning compared with very few of those without conduct disorder.

These findings raise a number of further questions. First, both the psychiatric clinic and institutionally reared samples were deliberately chosen because they had a high risk of a poor adult outcome; the first because of their widespread psychiatric problems and the second because of their persistent psychosocial adversities. It is necessary, therefore, to ask whether or not the same outcome would apply to conduct disorders not associated with such pervasive difficulties. The rather better outcome (albeit not significantly so) for individuals with conduct disorder in our general population sample as compared with the institutionalized group (47%

vs. 24% with relatively good social functioning) suggests that the issue is an important one.

Second, it is necessary to determine the level and type of conduct disorder in childhood that carries a high risk of pervasive social malfunction in adult life. For example, does the risk apply only when there is associated hyperactivity and poor peer relationships or does it also apply in the case of the more commonly occurring varieties of oppositional/defiant disorder?

A third query concerns the nature and origins of adult criminality that has not been preceded by childhood conduct disorder. About one quarter of all cases of adult criminality in the Stockholm longitudinal study (Stattin & Magnusson, 1991), were of this type and the proportions were roughly comparable in both our follow-up studies reported here. On close inspection, the behavior of many of these individuals did show conduct problems in childhood, albeit short of the accepted diagnostic threshold for conduct disorder, but some did not. Of those who did not, a few had committed crimes closely involved with some severe mental illness or in order to obtain drugs but this did not account for all instances. We have data from a number of follow-up studies of both general population and high-risk groups that will allow all these issues to be investigated further.

In addition to these questions concerning the kinds of conduct disorder that carry a high risk of continuity to adult social malfunction, there is the further question of why the continuity over time in both males and females was so strong. Was this an intrinsic part of the disorder or was it maintained by social circumstances? To begin to provide an answer to that question, we need to return to the outcome differences between males and females (Rutter et al., 1990). Criminality was not the only contrast. The institutionally reared women with conduct disorder showed a much increased likelihood of teenage pregnancy and hasty marriages to deviant men, often from similarly disadvantaged backgrounds. This tendency was present in the men only to a trivial degree, as shown in Fig. 4.7. The figures refer to subjects who have entered the "arena" for choosing spouses, as shown by cohabitation or pregnancy and the findings refer to their circumstances at follow-up. Women, but not men, with conduct disorder in childhood showed a much increased risk of being either with a deviant spouse or without marital support.

The question that arises is whether this unfortunate assortative mating affected their outcome. The findings are graphically portrayed in the Fig. 4.8 and 4.9. Figure 4.8 deals with the findings for those who showed conduct disorder in childhood (as measured prospectively in order better to examine time relationships). The first bifurcation into dots and cross-hatching refers to a behavioral characteristic that we termed *planning*—a feature that had a strong effect on their likelihood of ending up with a nondeviant spouse. However, for present purposes we need to concentrate on the second split on the right into white (those who married deviant spouses or who were unsupported) and black (those who married nondeviant spouses). The cross-over effect illustrates the substantial protective effect of a nondeviant spouse in leading to better overall psychosocial functioning. Figure 4.9 shows a similar, but more compressed pattern, for those without conduct disturbance in childhood.

In order to sort out which variables were having which effects it was necessary to use multivariate analyses. Because we wished to make use of our multiple data sources to provide a better, error free, estimate of the latent constructs that we were seeking to study, we turned to a latent class analysis. In brief, that showed a significant assortative mating effect for females but not males and, after controlling

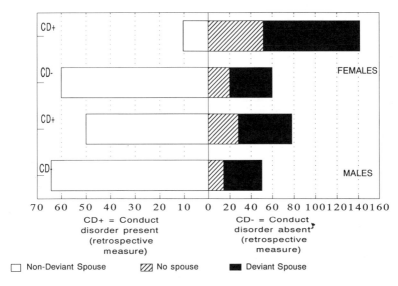

FIG. 4. 7. Assortative mating for conduct disturbance (institutionally reared subjects).

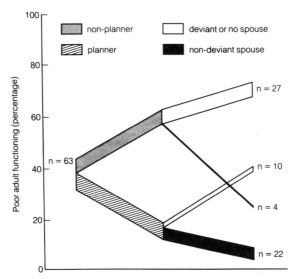

FIG. 4. 8. Adult social functioning: The impact of planning and nondeviant spouse (childhood conduct disorder group).

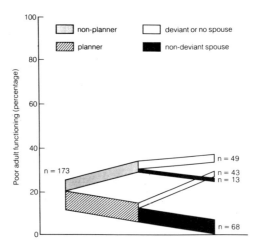

FIG. 4. 9. Adult social functioning: The impact of planning and nondeviant spouse (childhood non-conduct disorder group).

for this effect, a significant beneficial effect on outcome from a nondeviant spouse, again in females, with a lesser effect, falling short of statistical significance, in males. Both findings confirmed our earlier more straightforward analysis but also indicated that the continuity over time was likely to be substantially greater than shown by the observable variables.

CONCLUSIONS

The findings from these two long-term follow-up studies of high-risk groups give rise to four main conclusions. First, the adult outcome data provide strong validation of the distinctiveness of conduct and depressive disorders in childhood. The former leads to adult criminality and pervasive social malfunction, whereas the latter carries a much increased risk for affective disorders (but not other psychiatric conditions) in adult life. The findings are not at all compatible with the hypothesis that both represent the same underlying disorder. However, that hypothesis needs to be tested further by determining whether the two syndromes differ in familial loading and whether they are genetically distinct. The psychiatric clinic sample follow-up will provide us with the former (see Harrington et al., 1993) and our colleague, Emily Simonoff, has a longitudinal twin study extending from childhood to adult life that will provide evidence on the latter point.

Second, both in childhood and in adult life there is a strong tendency for conduct disorder to be associated with depressive symptomatology. In most instances the depressive problems do not amount to a major depressive disorder with accompanying anorexia, insomnia, and psychomotor disturbances and it is rare for there to be any bipolar element (i.e., there are no manic episodes). Nevertheless, the depressive problems may be substantial and associated with significant social impairment. It is clear that the conduct disorder is not secondary to a basic depressive condition but the findings do suggest that the depression may be secondary to the conduct disorder. Other evidence suggests that this is because conduct problems give rise to environmentally mediated psychosocial risks. The mechanisms involved have still to be investigated adequately.

Third, at least in high-risk groups, the adult outcome for conduct disorder in childhood tends to be poor. Criminality constitutes a prominent element in the adult sequelae but the social malfunction extends well beyond antisocial behavior. Thus, the characteristic outcome is a pervasive difficulty in interpersonal relationships, work and social functioning generally—often, but not always, accompanied by criminal acts. It is not yet known whether this pattern is an inherent part of a conduct disorder syndrome or a secondary feature brought about indirectly. Equally, it is not yet clear whether the poor outcome is equally characteristic of less disadvantaged and less deviant groups with conduct problems or, indeed, whether this poor outcome conduct disorder group shows a qualitative discontinuity with normality.

REFERENCES

Achenbach, T. M., & Edelbrock, C. (1978). The classification of child psychopathology: A review and analysis of empirical efforts. *Psychological Bulletin, 85,* 1275–1301.

American Psychiatric Association. (1980). *Diagnostic and statistical manual of mental disorders, DSM–III* (3rd ed.). Washington, DC: Author.

American Psychiatric Association. (1987). *Diagnostic and statistical manual of mental disorders, DSM–III–R* (3rd rev. ed.). Washington, DC: Author.

Belson, W. A. (1975). *Juvenile theft: The causal factors.* London: Harper & Row.

Cadoret, R. J., Troughton, E., Merchant, L. M., & Whitters, A. (1990). Early life psychosocial events and adult affective symptoms. In L. Robins & M. Rutter (Eds.), *Straight and devious pathways from childhood to adulthood* (pp. 300–313). Cambridge/New York: Cambridge University Press.

Caron, C., & Rutter, M. (1991). Comorbidity in child psychopathology: Concepts, issues and research strategies. *Journal of Child Psychology and Psychiatry, 32,* 1063–1080.

DiLalla, L. F., & Gottesman, I. I. (1989). Heterogeneity of causes for delinquency and criminality: Lifespan perspective. *Development and Psychopathology, 1,* 339–349.

Dodge, K. A. (1980). Social cognition and children's aggressive behavior. *Child Development, 51,* 162–172.

Dodge, K. A., Bates, J. E., & Pettit, G. S. (1990). Mechanisms in the cycle of violence. *Science, 250,* 1678–1683.

Elder, G. H. Jr., & Caspi, A. (1990). Studying lives in a changing society: Sociological and personological explorations. In A. I. Rabin, R. Zucker, S. Frank, & R. A. Emmons (Eds.), *Studying persons and lives.* New York: Springer.

Evans, J., Hammerton, J. L., & Robinson, A. (Eds.). (1991). *Children and young adults with sex chromosome aneuploidy.* New York : Wiley.

Farrington, D. P. (1988). Studying changes within individuals: The causes of offending. In M. Rutter (Ed.), *Studies of psychosocial risk : The power of longitudinal data* (pp. 158–183). Cambridge: Cambridge University Press.

Farrington, D. P., Gallagher, B., Morley, L., St. Ledger, R. J., & West D. J. (1988). Are there any successful men from criminogenic backgrounds? *Psychiatry, 50,* 116–130.

Farrington, D. P., Loeber, R., Elliott, D. S., Hawkins, J. D., Kandel, D. B., Klein, M. W., McCord, J., Rowe, D. C., & Tremblay, R. E. (1990). Advancing knowledge about the onset of delinquency and crime. In B. B. Lahey & A. E. Kazdin (Eds.), *Advances in clinical child psychology* (Vol.13, pp. 283–342). New York: Plenum.

Frick, P. J., Lahey, B. B., Christ, M. A. G., Loeber, R., & Green, S. (1991). History of childhood behavior problems in biological relatives of boys with attention-deficit hyperactivity disorder and conduct disorder. *Journal of Clinical Child Psychology, 20,* 445–451.

Garber, J., Quiggle, N. L., Panak, W., & Dodge, K. A. (1991). Aggression and depression in children: Comorbidity, specificity, and social cognitive processing. In D. Cicchetti & S. L. Toth (Eds.), *Internalizing and externalizing expressions of dysfunction : Rochester symposium on developmental psychopathology* (Vol. 2, pp. 225–264). Hillsdale, NJ: Lawrence Erlbaum Associates.

Harrington, R., Fudge, H., Rutter, M., Bredenkamp, D., Groothues, C., & Pridham, J. (1993). Child and adult depression: A test of continuities with data from a family study. *British Journal of Psychiatry, 162,* 627–633.

Harrington, R., Fudge, H., Rutter, M., Pickles, A., & Hill, J.(1990). Adult outcome of childhood and adolescent depression. I. Psychiatric status. *Archives of General Psychiatry, 47,* 465–473.

Harrington, R., Fudge, H., Rutter, M., Pickles, A., & Hill, J. (1991). Adult outcome of childhood and adolescent depression. II. Links with antisocial disorder. *Journal of the American Academy of Child and Adolescent Psychiatry, 30,* 434–439.

Lilienfeld, S. O., & Waldman, I. D. (1990). The relationship between childhood attention-deficit hyperactivity disorder and adult psychosocial behavior re-examined—the problem of heterogeneity. *Clinical Psychology Review, 10,* 699–726.

Loeber, R. (1988). Natural histories of conduct problems, delinquency, and associated substance abuse: Evidence for developmental progressions. In B. B. Lahey & A. E. Kazdin (Eds.), *Advances in clinical child psychology* (Vol.ll, pp. 73–124). New York: Plenum.

Loeber, R., Lahey, B. B., & Thomas, C. (1991). Diagnostic conundrum of oppositional defiant disorder and conduct disorder. *Journal of Abnormal Psychology, 100,* 379–390.

Magnusson, D., & Bergman, L. R. (1988). Individual and variable-based approaches to longitudinal research on early risk factors. In M. Rutter (Ed.), *Studies of psychosocial risk: The power of longitudinal data* (pp. 45–61). Cambridge: Cambridge University Press.

Magnusson, D., Klinteberg, B. af, & Stattin, H. (1991). *Autonomic activity/reactivity, behavior and crime in a longitudinal perspective* (Tech.Rep. No. 738). Stockholm: Department of Psychology, Stockholm University.

Olweus, D. (1979). Stability of aggressive reaction patterns in males: A review. *Psychological Bulletin, 86,* 852–875.

Patterson, G.R. (1982). *Coercive family process.* Eugene, OR: Castalia.

Plomin, R., Rende, R., & Rutter, M. (1991). Quantitative genetics and developmental psychopathology. In D. Cicchetti & S. L. Toth (Eds.), *Internalizing and externalizing expressions of dysfunction : Rochester symposium on developmental psychopathology* (Vol. 2, pp. 155–202). Hillsdale, NJ: Lawrence Erlbaum Associates.

Quay, H. C. (1986). Classification. In H. C. Quay & J. S. Werry (Eds.), *Psychopathological disorders of children* (3rd ed., pp. 1–34). New York: Wiley.

Quinton, D., Pickles, A., Maughan, B., & Rutter, M. (1993). Partners, peers and pathways: Assortative pairing and continuities in conduct disorder. *Development and Psychopathology, 5,* 763-783.

Quinton, D., & Rutter, M. (1988). *Parenting breakdown: The making and breaking of inter-generational links.* Aldershot: Avebury.

Raine, A., Venables, P. H., & Williams, M. (1990). Relationships between central and autonomic measures of arousal at age 15 years and criminality at age 24 years. *Archives of General Psychiatry, 47, 1003–1007.*

Reiss, A. J. Jr., & Farrington, D. P. (1991). Advancing knowledge about co-offending: Results from a prospective longitudinal survey of London males. *Journal of Criminal Law and Criminology, 82,* 360–395.

Robins, L. (1966). *Deviant children grown up.* Baltimore: Williams & Wilkins.

Robins, L. (1978). Sturdy childhood predictors of adult antisocial behaviour: Replications from longitudinal studies. *Psychological Medicine, 8,* 611–622.

Robins, L. (1986). The consequences of conduct disorder in girls. In D. Olweus, J. Block, & M. Radke-Yarrow (Eds.), *Development of antisocial and prosocial behaviour: Research, theories and issues* (pp. 385–414). New York: Academic Press.

Robins, L. (1991). Conduct disorder. *Journal of Child Psychology and Psychiatry, 32,* 193–212.

Robins, L., & McEvoy, L. (1990). Conduct problems as predictors of substance abuse. In L. Robins & M. Rutter (Eds.), *Straight and devious pathways from childhood to adulthood* (pp. 182–204). Cambridge: Cambridge University Press.

Robins, L. N., Davis, D. H., & Wish, E. (1977). Detecting predictors of rare events: Demographic, family and personal deviance as predictors of stages in the progression toward narcotic addition. In J. S. Strauss, H. M. Babigian, & M. Roff (Eds.), *The origins and course of psychopathology* (pp. 379–406). New York & London: Plenum.

Rutter, M. (1965). Classification and categorization in child psychiatry. *Journal of Child Psychology and Psychiatry, 6,* 71–83.

Rutter, M. (1978). Diagnostic validity in child psychiatry. *Advances in Biological Psychiatry, 2,* 2–22.

Rutter, M. (1981). Epidemiological/longitudinal strategies and causal research in child psychiatry. *Journal of the American Academy of Child Psychiatry, 20,* 513–544.

Rutter, M. (1986). Meyerian psychobiology, personality development and the role of life experience. *American Journal of Psychiatry, 143,* 1077–1087.

Rutter, M. (1988). Epidemiological approaches to developmental psychopathology. *Archives of General Psychiatry, 45,* 486–500.

Rutter, M. (1991). Childhood experiences and adult psychosocial functioning. In G. R. Bock & J. Whelan (Eds.), *The childhood environment and adult disease* (Ciba Foundation Symposium No. 156, pp. 189–200). Chichester: Wiley.

Rutter, M. (1992). Adolescence as a transition period: Continuities and discontinuities in conduct disorder. *Journal of Adolescent Health, 13,* 451–460.

Rutter, M., Champion, L., Quinton, D., Maughan, B., & Pickles, A. (in press). Origins of individual differences in environmental risk exposure. In P. Moen, G. Elder, & K. Luscher (Eds.), *Perspectives on the ecology of human development.* Ithaca, NY: Cornell University Press.

Rutter, M., & Garmezy, N. (1983) Developmental psychopathology. In P.H. Mussen (Series Ed.) & E. M. Hetherington (Vol. Ed.), *Handbook of child psychology: Vol. 4. Socialization, personality, and social development* (pp. 775–911). New York: Wiley.

Rutter, M., & Giller, H. (1983). *Juvenile delinquency: Trends and perspectives.* Harmondsworth, Middlesex: Penguin.

Rutter, M., & Gould, M. (1985). Classification. In M. Rutter & L. Hersov (Eds.), *Child and adolescent psychiatry : Modern approaches* (2nd ed., pp. 304–321). Oxford: Blackwell Scientific.

Rutter, M., & Pickles, A. (1990). Improving the quality of psychiatric data: Classification, cause and course. In D. Magnusson & L. R. Bergman (Eds.), *Data quality in longitudinal research* (pp 32–57). Cambridge: Cambridge University Press.

Rutter, M., Quinton, D., & Hill, J. (1990). Adult outcome of institution-reared children: Males and females compared. In L. Robins & M. Rutter (Eds.), *Straight and devious pathways from childhood to adulthood* (pp.135–157). Cambridge/New York: Cambridge University Press.

Rutter, M., & Rutter, M. (1993). *Developing minds: Challenge and continuity across the lifespan.* Harmondsworth, Middlesex: Penguin; New York: Basic Books.

Sigman, M., Cohen, S., Beckwith, L., Asarnow, R., & Parmelee, A. (1991). Continuity in cognitive abilities from infancy to 12 years of age. *Cognitive Development, 6,* 47–57.

Sleight, P. (1988). Essential hypertension. In D. J. Weatherall, J. G. G. Ledingham, & D. A. Warrell (Eds.), *Oxford textbook of medicine* (2nd ed., pp. 13.360–13.382). Oxford: Oxford University Press.

Stattin, H., & Magnusson, D. (1991). Stability and change in criminal behaviour up to age 30. *British Journal of Criminology, 31,* 327–346.

Taylor, E., Sandberg, S., Thorley, G., & Giles, S. (1991). *The epidemiology of childhood hyperactivity* (Institute of Psychiatry Maudsley Monographs No.33). Oxford: Oxford University Press.

Willcock, H.D. (1974). *Deterrents and incentives to crime among boys and young men aged 15–21* (OPCS Social Survey Division;SS 352). London: Her Majesty's Stationery Office.

World Health Organization. (1992). *The ICD-10 classification of mental and behavioural disorders: Clinical descriptions and diagnostic guidelines.* Geneva: Author.

Zoccolillo, M., Pickles, A., Quinton, D., & Rutter, M. (1992). The outcome of conduct disorder: Implications for defining adult personality disorder. *Psychological Medicine, 22,* 971–986.

5

Juvenile and Persistent Offenders: Behavioral and Physiological Characteristics

David Magnusson
Britt af Klinteberg
Håkan Stattin
Stockholm University

Research on the developmental precursors of antisocial behavior in adulthood has been focused on identifying factors in the individuals themselves and in their rearing environments. Often, the role of such factors in the developmental process has been established by estimating their predictive power with respect to later criminal activity. This raises several theoretical and methodological issues, which are addressed in this chapter. First, to what extent is it appropriate to treat those who have been convicted of crimes as one homogeneous group? Second, do developmental precursors differ depending on whether or not criminal activity co-occurs with other types of problems such as drug abuse and/or mental illness (Magnusson, 1988)? Third, to what extent do those convicted of crime at different ages differ with respect to some basic behavioral and physiological characteristics? Of particular interest here is the question of how those who commit crimes only during the teenage years might differ from those who continue their criminal activity in adulthood. This question is motivated by the observation that most of those who are convicted of crimes in adulthood have started early, whereas the predictive power of early criminality is modest (see Stattin & Magnusson, 1991).

Theoretical Framework

Our studies on the developmental background of adult antisocial behavior have indicated that hyperactivity during adolescence, reflected in motor restlessness, lack of concentration, and low autonomic reactivity, are antecedents of later behavior problems (see af Klinteberg, Magnusson, & Schalling, 1989; Magnusson, 1988). These results are in line with results presented by others. From clinical and neuro-psychological points of view, for example, early hyperactivity is recognized as a main precursor of delinquency. Although there are exceptions, results from a large number of both cross-sectional and longitudinal research studies support the connection between hyperactivity and antisocial behavior (Satterfield, 1987; cf Loeber, 1990).

For example, hyperactivity has been found to be strongly related to conduct problems in children, and a number of studies have found children with hyperactive behavior to be at excessive risk of developing antisocial behavior. Of particular interest is the finding reported by Farrington, Loeber, and Van Kammen (1990). They observed that a hyperactive–impulsivity–attention deficit measure, obtained at age 8 and 10 years, was especially predictive of future chronic offending.

The theoretical framework for our research program emphasizes the importance of biological factors for the understanding of various aspects of individual functioning. In the present study, adrenaline excretion is viewed as an indicator of autonomic reactivity in the physiological system. Many other researchers have reported a positive correlation between good social and personal adjustment and high adrenaline excretion (Bergman & Magnusson, 1979; Johansson, Frankenhaeuser, & Magnusson, 1973; Roessler, Burch, & Mufford, 1967). In agreement with these results, we have observed a negative relationship between hyperactive behavior and delinquency, on the one hand, and adrenaline excretion, on the other (see af Klinteberg & Magnusson, 1989; Magnuson, Stattin, & Dunér, 1983). A critical characteristic of earlier studies within this research domain is that they all used cross-sectional designs. To understand the role of biological factors in the development of processes underlying adult criminality, longitudinal data for individuals are needed (see, e.g., Magnusson, 1985).

Analytic Framework

Research on the developmental precursors of adult antisocial behavior is dominated by a variable approach to data analysis. The focus in a variable approach is on relations among variables, in this specific case the relation between single individual and/or environmental factors, or sets of such factors, in early life on the one hand, and measures of adult antisocial behavior, on the other. In order to more fully understand and explain the functioning of individuals as totalities, we believe that a variable approach has to be complemented with a person approach, in which individuals are studied on the basis of the patterns of variables relevant for the problem under consideration (Magnusson et al., 1983). For a more comprehensive discussion of the theoretical and methodological implications of the distinction between variable and person approaches, respectively, see Bergman and Magnusson (1983), Magnusson (1988, 1993), and Magnusson and Bergman (1990).

PRESENT STUDY

Based on the theoretical and analytic perspectives presented above, we designed a study to investigate the level of hyperactivity of boys at 10 and 13 years of age, measured as the combination of concentration difficulties and motor restlessness, and sympathetic-adrenal activity/reactivity measured by adrenaline excretion at age 13 years. We studied three categories of males: (a) Those who had not been officially recorded as having committed a crime (the *normative* group); (b) those who had been officially recorded as having committed a crime before age 18, and then conformed thereafter (the *juvenile offenders* group); and (c) those who were officially recorded as having committed a crime both during the teenage years and in adulthood (the *persistent offenders* group). Results from a combination of variable and pattern analyses will be presented, and the implications of these results for theoretical and methodological issues concerning the attempt to understand and explain the etiology of adolescent problem behaviors will be explored.

Method

Data Source. The data come from a longitudinal research project called *Individual Development and Adjustment* (IDA) that was initiated in 1965 (Magnusson, 1988; Magnusson, Dunér, & Zetterblom, 1975). The study was planned and implemented in the context of an interactional perspective, from which individual functioning is viewed as a multi-determined, stochastic process in which psychological and biological factors in the individual are hypothesized to be in constant reciprocal interaction with environmental factors (Magnusson, 1988, 1990).

Subjects. The cohort from which the data were derived consists of all third-grade boys and girls in a Swedish community. At the time of the first data collection, the subjects averaged 10 years of age, and they have been followed up to the age of 30. The study population is representative of its Swedish age cohort with respect to the incidence and prevalence of crime (Stattin, Magnusson, & Reichel, 1989).

Measures. Information about the boys' *hyperactivity* was obtained from teacher ratings. The boys were rated by their teachers at 10 and 13 years of age on their *motor restlessness* and *concentration difficulties*. The ratings were performed on 7-point scales by teachers who had known their pupils for 3 years (Magnusson et al., 1975); independent rating were made by different teachers at each age level. In the analyses presented here, the sum of ratings of motor restlessness and concentration difficulties was used as an indicator of hyperactivity. Ratings on these two variables pooled across the two age levels were summed to yield an indicator of *persistent hyperactivity*.

To measure *autonomic reactivity*, levels of urinary adrenaline were assessed in two different situations at school in a subsample of boys when they were about 13 years of age. Urine samples were collected under standardized conditions after a normal, non-stressful session (viewing a film on ore-mining), and after a stressful session (performance on an attention-demanding mental arithmetic test) (for a detailed description of the procedure, see Johansson et al., 1973).

The measure of *criminal activity* was the number of officially registered instances of law-breaking. These data were collected from national and local sources, and cover all offenses leading to public prosecution and conviction occurring before age 30 in all 540 males in the cohort.

Results

Hyperactivity and Adult Criminality.   The relationships between early hyperactivity and later criminal activity in the three categories of males are presented in Table 5.1. The figures presented in Table 5.1 show an interesting pattern. The persistent offenders had significantly higher hyperactivity scores at age 13 than the nonoffenders (normative group), and significantly higher hyperactivity scores than the juvenile offenders. Moreover, juvenile offenders had significantly higher hyperactivity scores at age 13 than the normative subjects did. The same pattern is evident when we examine levels of persistent hyperactivity, that is, motor restlessness and concentration difficulties at about 10 and 13 years of age (see Table 5.2).

These data show that persistent offenders were characterized by persistent hyperactivity in early adolescence. Persistent offenders were rated as more hyperactive than the juvenile delinquent and normative males, and had a mean score of about 5.5 on each of the four 7-point scales from which the data were pooled. Persistent offenders differed significantly from both the normative and juvenile offender groups with respect to early persistent hyperactivity.

These findings are consistent with other reports in the clinical and neuropsychological literature that hyperactivity is a risk factor for delinquency (Barcai & Rabkin, 1974; Cantwell, 1978; Robins, 1966; Satterfield, 1978, 1987; Schuckit, Petrich, & Chiles, 1978; Weiss & Hechtman, 1979; Weiss, Hechtman, Perlman,

TABLE 5.1

Mean Hyperactivity Scores (Sum of Teacher Ratings of Motor Restlessness and Concentration Difficulties) at the Age of 13 for a Group of Males Subdivided by Criminal Activity

Group	M	SE	N
(a) No criminal offenses	7.08	0.16	347
(b) Criminal offenses during adolescence only	9.40	0.33	60
(c) Criminal offenses during both adolescence and adulthood	10.78	0.36	59

Significance levels for differences: a–b: $p < .000$. b–c: $p < .005$. a–c: $p < .000$.

TABLE 5.2

Mean Hyperactivity Scores (Sum of Teacher Ratings of Motor Restlessness and Concentration Difficulties) at the Age of 10 and 13 for a Group of Males Subdivided by Criminal Activity

Group	M	SE	N
(a) No criminal offenses	13.50	0.60	46
(b) Criminal offenses during adolescence only	17.61	0.91	13
(c) Criminal offenses during both adolescence and childhood	22.18	0.86	11

Significance levels for differences: a–b: $p < .001$. b–c: $p < .001$. a–c: $p < .001$.

Hopkins, & Wenar, 1979), conduct disorder (Borland & Heckman, 1976; Loeber, 1986), antisocial behavior (Borland & Heckman, 1976; Farrington et al., 1990; Gittelman, Manuzza, Schenker, & Bonagura, 1985; Hechtman, Weiss, Perlman, & Amsel, 1984; Mendelson, Johnson, & Stewart, 1971; Menkes, Rowe, & Menkes, 1967; Nylander, 1979; Satterfield, Hoppe, & Schell, 1982; Weiss, Hinde, Werry, Douglas, & Nemeth, 1971).

Autonomic Activity/Reactivity and Criminal Activity.   Our theoretical framework also emphasizes the importance of biological factors in understanding individual functioning. In this study, adrenaline excretion was viewed as an indicator of autonomic sympathetic reactivity on the basis of earlier findings that good social and personal adjustment is associated with high adrenaline excretion (Bergman & Magnusson, 1979; Johansson et al., 1973; Lambert, Johansson, Frankenhaeuser, & Klackenberg-Larsson, 1969). To date, however, these associations have not been studied longitudinally.

In Table 5.3 we display the mean levels of adrenaline excretion under stress and at rest for the three groups of males. Of particular interest is the finding that males who commit crimes only before the age of 18 and then conform do not show lower levels of autonomic reactivity than males who have never been recorded for crime

TABLE 5.3

Mean Levels of Adrenaline Excretion (ng/min) at Rest (An) and Under Stress Condition (As) for a Group of Males Subdivided by Criminal Activity

Group	An		As		N
	M	SE	M	SE	
(a) No criminal offenses	9.47	0.91	12.11	1.06	48
(b) Criminal offenses during adolescence only	10.38	1.73	13.65	1.85	13
(c) Criminal offenses during both adolescence and adulthood	5.60	0.84	7.60	1.14	11

Significance levels for differences: a–b: An: ns; As: ns. b–c: An: $p < .03$; As: $p < .02$. a–c: An: $p < .004$; As: $p < .007$.

(normative group). On the other hand, the mean levels of adrenaline excretion by persistent offenders was significantly lower than that in the normative group in both situations.

As reported earlier, laboratory research has demonstrated a significant and sometimes high correlation between various aspects of problematic behaviors, such as aggressiveness, motor restlessness, lack of concentration, lack of school motivation, criminal activity and alcohol problems, on the one hand, and low autonomic reactivity as measured by adrenaline excretion, on the other. Until now these results have been interpreted as evidence of a systematic relationship between antisocial behavior and low autonomic reactivity. We suggest that this conclusion is incorrect. Our results instead indicate that autonomic reactivity is characteristic only of males who are persistent offenders.

The Patterning of Individual Characteristics.   A methodological consequence of our theoretical framework is that a variable approach, in which the interrelationships of variables is of most interest, has to be complemented with a person approach in which individual functioning is of central interest. In a person approach, individuals are grouped on the basis of their characteristic patterns of scores on variables relevant to the problem under consideration in order to study individual differences. The results presented in the variable approach analyses above were used as a basis for the person approach analyses presented below.

Taken together, the results presented in Tables 5.2 and 5.3 suggest that males with a persistent criminal career are characterized by high persistent hyperactivity and low adrenaline excretion, and that males without criminal records are characterized by low hyperactivity and high adrenaline excretion. For juvenile offenders, no clear pattern emerges. The extent to which these combinations characterize the three groups of males investigated here was studied in a pattern analysis.

The combination of three categories of criminality, two levels of hyperactivity, and two levels of adrenaline excretion under stress, yields 12 groupings of the 70 males for whom complete data are available. In order to test which of the 12 patterns occurred more (type) or less (anttype) often than could be expected by chance, we employed Configural Frequency Analysis (CFA; Bergman & Magnusson, 1984; Krauth & Lienert, 1982; see von Eye, 1990, for a recent introduction to CFA). The results of these analyses are presented in Table 5.4.

The results of the CFA analysis indicate that 11 of the 70 males were "persistent offenders," who had been registered for crime both before and after the age of 18. Nine of these 11 had both high levels of hyperactivity and low levels of adrenaline excretion, whereas only 1.3 would be expected by chance. Thus the 9 males shown here form a highly significant type, or pattern.

By contrast, of the 46 males without any criminal record, not one had high levels of hyperactivity and low levels of adrenaline excretion, whereas the random model predicted 5.5 males with this combination. This particular combination formed a significant antitype among the normative group.

TABLE 5.4

Observed and Expected Frequences of Patterns of (a) Belongingness to One of the Three Categories of Males, (b) Being High or Low in Hyperactivity, and (c) Being High or Low in Adrenaline Excretion in a Stressful Situation

Criminal category	Hyperact.	Adrenaline	Observed freq.	Expected freq.	p
0	0	0	25	20.2	ns
0	0	1	18	16.0	ns
0	1	0	0	5.5	< .02
0	1	1	3	4.4	ns
1	0	0	2	5.7	ns
1	0	1	8	4.5	ns
1	1	0	2	1.6	ns
1	1	1	1	1.2	ns
2	0	0	1	4.8	ns
2	0	1	1	3.8	ns
2	1	0	9	1.3	< .0000
2	1	1	0	1.0	ns

Crim: 0 — No crime record; 1 — crime record before 18; 2 — crime record both before and after the age of 18.

Hyperactivity: $0 < 20$; $1 > 20$.

Adrenaline: 0 — below average; 1 — above average.

Finally, a random model predicted that 1.6 juvenile offenders should have shown a pattern of high hyperactivity and low adrenaline excretion that was characteristic of persistent offenders: The observed frequency ($N = 2$) came close to this figure, suggesting neither a type nor an antitype.

SUMMARY AND DISCUSSION

Trait-Bound Versus Situation-Bound Criminal Activity

Overall, these results underscore the importance of distinguishing between two categories of male adolescents showing antisocial behavior in terms of registered crimes: (a) persistent offenders exhibited a persistent trait-like disposition of low autonomic activity/reactivity and high hyperactivity; and (b) juvenile offenders, who did not exhibit this disposition but who are probably more susceptible to conditions in the environment. This distinction has important implications for further research into the processes underlying antisocial behavior, and for discussions about appropriate preventive actions. The fact that the distinction has not been previously recognized may explain the incoherent results obtained in other studies examining the relationship between delinquency and autonomic arousal (see McCord, 1990). Our research indicated that persistent criminal activity in males is predicted by significantly lower levels of earlier adrenalin excretion, whereas no such pattern is evident among males who only offend as juveniles.

A Theoretical Perspective

Our results emphasize the importance of an interactional theoretical perspective on individual development and its implications for research (Magnusson, 1990). An interactional perspective regards individual functioning as an ongoing process in which psychological and biological factors in the individual interact with factors in the environment. An important implication of this view is that in order to understand the processes of individual development, researchers should strive to include all of these factors in a single overriding theoretical framework. Following this strategy in turn creates a new set of theoretical, methodological, and research issues (see Magnusson, 1988). For example, the results presented in this chapter clearly demonstrate the importance of including biological factors when striving to understand and explain antisocial behavior. Although the role of biological factors in individual functioning was emphasized almost a century or more ago by Wundt in his claim of psychology as an independent science, and by Angell in his presentation of functional psychology, until recently, one of the main characteristics of psychological research has been its neglect of such factors. It has been asserted by some of our colleagues that psychologists should not bother about the biological aspects of individual functioning.

We believe, however, that this conclusion is invalid, because knowledge about biological factors and mechanisms have contributed much to our understanding of mental and behavioral aspects of individual functioning. For example, our results demonstrate a strong, significant relationship between hyperactivity and autonomic reactivity in two independent situations. Our results also indicate that there is a strong relationship between persistent criminal activity and autonomic reactivity in early adolescence, whereas no systematic relationship was found between autonomic reactivity and criminal activity restricted to adolescence.

Our results further demonstrate the importance of including biological factors when striving to understand and explain antisocial behavior from a perceptual–cognitive perspective. For example, low autonomic reactivity might be interpreted as indicating a loss of resources for handling stressful situational demands (Frankenhaeuser, 1979), which may in turn lead to difficulties in responding adequately to environmental demands. Low adrenaline output, therefore, may be a risk factor for developing hyperactive behavior in childhood, or it might be regarded as a biochemical factor mediating between coping deficiency and criminal activity.

Implications for Research on the Developmental Background of Later Antisocial Behavior

The results of the analyses presented here lead to two conclusions concerning research on the developmental precursors of later antisocial behaviors. First, the results demonstrate the necessity of conducting longitudinal studies in order to understand and explain the process of individual social development (Magnusson, 1988; Rutter, 1988). Second, our analyses demonstrate the usefulness of combining a variable approach with an individual approach. In a variable approach, interest is directed to the interrelationships among variables primarily using linear and nonlinear regression techniques. The main focal point of a person approach, in contrast, is patterns of variables characteristic of individuals. We have spent considerable time developing and applying appropriate statistical methods (i.e., CFA; Bergman, 1988; Bergman & Magnusson, 1983; Magnusson & Bergman, 1984, 1990; see also von Eye, 1990) to apply this approach to the study of developmental issues. As demonstrated in the present study, a combination of a variable approach with a person approach is essential for progress in empirical research on individual development, including the domain of social development in general, and adolescent problem behaviors in particular.

REFERENCES

Barcai, A., & Rabkin, L. (1974). A precursor of delinquency: The hyperkinetic disorder of childhood. *Psychiatric Quarterly, 48*, 387–399.

Bergman, L. R. (1988). You can't classify all of the people all of the time. *Multivariate Behavioral Research, 23*, 425–441.

Bergman, L. R., & Magnusson, D. (1979). Overachievement and catecholamine excretion in an achievement-demanding situation. *Psychosomatic Medicine, 41*, 181–188.

Bergman, L. R., & Magnusson, D. (1983). *The development of patterns of maladjustment* (Tech. Rep. No. 50). Stockholm: Department of Psychology, University of Stockholm.

Bergman, L. R., & Magnusson, D. (1984). *Patterns of adjustment problems at age 13* (Tech. Rep. No. 620). Stockholm: Department of Psychology, University of Stockholm.

Borland, B. L., & Heckman, H. K. (1976). Hyperactive boys and their brothers. A 25 year follow-up study. *Archives of General Psychiatry, 33*, 669–675.

Cantwell, D. P. (1978). Hyperactivity and antisocial behavior. *Journal of American Academy of Child Psychiatry, 17*, 252–262.

von Eye, A. (1990). *Introduction to configural frequency analysis. The search for types and antitypes in cross-classifications.* New York: Cambridge University Press.

Farrington, D. P., Loeber, R., & Van Kammen, W. B. (1990). Long-term criminal outcomes of hyperactivity–impulsivity–attention deficit and conduct problems in childhood. In L. N. Robins & M. Rutter (Eds.), *Straight and devious pathways from childhood to adulthood* (pp. 62–81). Cambridge: Cambridge University Press.

Frankenhaeuser, M. (1979). Psychoneuroendocrine approaches to the study of emotion as related to stress and coping. In H. E. Howe & R. A. Dienstbier (Eds.), *Nebraska Symposium on Motivation* (pp. 123–161). Lincoln: University of Nebraska Press.

Gittelman, R., Mannuzza, S., Shenker, R., & Bonagura, N. (1985). Hyperactive boys almost grown up. *Archives of General Psychiatry, 42*, 45–50.

Hechtman, L., Weiss, G., Perlman, T., & Amsel, R. (1984). Hyperactives as young adults initial predictors of adult outcome. *Journal of the American Academy of Child Psychiatry, 23*, 250–260.

Johansson, G., Frankenhaeuser, M., & Magnusson, D. (1973). Catecholamine output in school children as related to performance and adjustment. *Scandinavian Journal of Psychology, 14*, 20–28.

af Klinteberg, B., & Magnusson, D. (1989). Aggressiveness and hyperactive behaviour as related to adrenaline excretion. *European Journal of Personality, 3*, 81–93.

af Klinteberg, B., Magnusson, D., & Schalling, D. (1989). Hyperactive behavior in childhood and adult impulsivity: A longitudinal study of male subjects. *Personality and Individual Differences, 1*, 43–50

Krauth, J., & Lienert, G. A. (1982). Fundamentals and modifications of configural frequency analysis (CFA). *Interdisciplinaria, 3*, 1–14.

Lambert, W. W., Johansson, G., Frankenhaeuser, M., & Klackenberg-Larsson, I. (1969). Catecholamine excretion in young children and their parents as related to behavior. *Scandinavian Journal of Psychology, 10*, 306–318.

Loeber, R., (1986). *Behavioral precursors and accelerators of delinquency.* Paper presented at the Conference Explaining Crime, University of Leiden, Holland.

Loeber, R. (1990). Development and risk factors of juvenile antisocial behavior and delinquency. *Clinical Psychology Review, 10*, 1–41.

Magnusson, D. (1985). Early conduct and biological factors in the developmental background of adult delinquency. *The British Psychological Society Newsletter, 13*, 4–17.

Magnusson, D. (1988). *Individual development from an interactional perspective.* Hillsdale, NJ: Lawrence Erlbaum Associates.

Magnusson, D. (1990). Personality development from an interactional perspective. In L. Pervin (Ed.), *Handbook of personality: Theory and research* (pp. 193–222). New York: Guilford Press.

Magnusson, D. (1993). Human ontogeny: A longitudinal perspective. In D. Magnusson & P. Casaer (Eds.), *Longitudinal research on individual development.* Cambridge: Cambridge University Press.

Magnusson, D., & Bergman, L. R. (1984). On the study of the development of adjustment problems. In L. Pulkkinen & P. Lyytinen (Eds.), *Human action and personality essays in honour of Martti Takala* (pp. 163–171). Jyväskylä, Finland: University of Jyväskylä.

Magnusson, D., & Bergman, L. R. (1990). A pattern approach to the study of pathways from childhood to adulthood. In L. N. Robins & M. Rutter (Eds.), *Straight and devious pathways from childhood to adulthood* (pp. 101–115). Cambridge: Cambridge University Press.

Magnusson, D., Dunér, A., & Zetterblom, G. (1975). *Adjustment: A longitudinal study.* Stockholm, Sweden: Almqvist & Wiksell.

Magnusson, D., Stattin, H., & Dunér, A. (1983). Aggression and criminality in a longitudinal perspective. In K. T. van Dusen & S. A. Mednick (Eds.), *Prospective studies of crime and delinquency* (pp. 277–301). Boston: Kluwer-Nijhoff.

McCord, J. (1990). Problem behaviors. In S. S. Feldman & G. R. Elliott (Eds.), *At the threshold: The developing adolescent* (pp. 414–430, 602–614). Cambridge, MA: Harvard University Press.

Mendelson, W., Johnson, N., & Stewart, M. (1971). Hyperactive children as teenagers: A follow-up study. *Journal of Nervous and Mental Disease, 153*, 272–279.

Menkes, M., Rowe, J., & Menkes, J. (1967). A twenty-five year follow-up study on the hyperkinetic child with minimal brain dysfunction. *Pediatrics, 39*, 393–399.

Nylander, I. (1979). A 20-year prospective follow-up study of 2,164 cases at the child guidance clinics in Stockholm. *Acta Pediatrica Scandinavica, 68* (Suppl. No. 276, 1–45).

Robins, L. N. (1966). *Deviant children grown up: A sociological and psychiatric study of sociopathic personality.* Baltimore, MD: Williams & Wilkins.

Roessler, R., Burch, N. R., & Mufford, R. B., Jr. (1967). Personality correlates of catecholamine excretion under stress. *Journal of Psychosomatic Research, 11*, 181–185.

Rutter, M. (1988). *Studies of psychosocial risk: The power of longitudinal data.* Cambridge: Cambridge University Press.

Satterfield, J. H. (1978). The hyperactive child syndrome: A precursor of adult psychopathy? In R. D. Hare & D. Schalling (Eds.), *Psychopathic behavior. Approaches to research* (pp. 329–346). Wiley: Chichester.

Satterfield, J. H., (1987). Childhood diagnostic and neurophysiological predictors of teenage arrest rates: An eight-year prospective study. In S. A. Mednick, T. E. Moffitt, & S. A. Stack (Eds.), *The causes of crime. New biological approaches* (pp. 146–167). Cambridge: Cambridge University Press.

Satterfield, J. H., Hoppe, C. M., & Schell, A. M. (1982). A prospective study of delinquency in 110 adolescent boys with attention deficit disorder and 88 normal adolescent boys. *American Journal of Psychiatry, 139,* 795–798.

Schuckit, M. A., Petrich, J., & Chiles, J. (1978). Hyperactivity: Diagnostic confusion. *Journal of Nervous and Mental Disease, 166,* 79–87.

Stattin, H., & Magnusson, D. (1991). Stability and change in criminal behavior up to age 30. *The British Journal of Criminology, 31,* 327–346.

Stattin, H., Magnusson, D., & Reichel, H. (1989). Criminal activity at different ages. A study based on a Swedish longitudinal research population. *The British Journal of Criminology, 29,* 368–385.

Weiss, G., & Hechtman, L. (1979). The hyperactive child syndrome. *Science, 205,* 1348–1354.

Weiss, G., Hechtman, L., Perlman, T., Hopkins, J., & Wenar, A. (1979). Hyperactives as young adults: A controlled, prospective ten year follow-up of 75 children. *Archives of General Psychiatry, 6,* 675–681.

Weiss, G., Hinde, K., Werry, J., Douglas, V., & Nemeth, E. (1971). Studies on the hyperactive child. VIII: Five year follow-up. *Archives of General Psychiatry, 24,* 409–414.

6

Integrating Biological and Sociological Models of Adolescent Problem Behaviors

J. Richard Udry
University of North Carolina at Chapel Hill

This chapter explores the foundations for a biosocial theory of adolescent problem behaviors that integrates social causation and biological models of problem behavior. In the course of reviewing empirical work derived from the integrated biosocial model, two new issues emerge: (a) Do the separate problem behaviors share a common causal model? and (b) Are problem behaviors caused by adolescent environments or by preexisting individual differences?

The history of biosocial models of behavior is short. Many psychologists and an occasional sociologist have attempted to identify biological determinants of behavior (Booth, Shelley, Mazur, Tharp, & Kittok, 1989; Zuckerman, 1984). However, the only discipline that is built on a paradigm that integrates biological and social determinants of behavior is behavior genetics (Plomin, 1986). Behavior geneticists have articulated the ways in which social and genetic biological factors can make a joint contribution to the variance in characteristics or behavior of individuals. Behavior genetic models, however, can only be used with samples in which degrees of differences in shared genes and shared environments are known. With such designs, the sources of variance among various types of genetic–environmental relationships are decomposed. Typical generic categories of variance decomposition are genetic, shared environment (environmental influences that are shared by family members), nonshared environment, gene–environment interactions, and error variance. Standard behavior genetic designs usually involve either twins or adopted children. My approach, however, does not rely on traditional behavior genetic research designs, and the questions I ask are different from those asked by most behavior geneticists. Whereas behavior geneticists allocate variance to the generic categories just listed, I attempt to discern the role of specific biological variables in explanatory models of behavior that include social determinants. In my theoretical models, I presume that biological variables cause variations in individual behavioral predispositions or motivations, and that sociological variables represent social constraints or opportunities for individuals. In the next section I compare three general biosocial models—additive, intermediate, and interaction—and demonstrate how they can be adapted for explaining adolescent risk-taking and problem behaviors.

THREE BIOSOCIAL MODELS

Additive Models

These models are based on the proposition that the effects of biological variables on behavior are independent of the effects of social variables on behavior. When combined in a model, the total variance explained is the sum of what is explained in separate biological and social models. Combining biological and social variables explains more variance than either alone, but combining the models does not involve revision of the effects of the variables within separate models.

Intermediate Variable Models

In contrast, these models are based on the proposition that the effects of biological variables on behavior are indirect, operating through the direct effects of intermediate social variables. An example of a hypothetical intermediate variable model is that variations in levels of the male hormone testosterone causes some boys to be more physically mature than others at the same age, and that more physically mature boys are expected and encouraged by others to engage in behaviors characteristic of older boys.

Interaction Models

This final group of models is based on the assumption that the effects of social factors on problem behavior predispositions will be different for individuals with different biological characteristics. A hypothetical example of an interaction model follows. First, it is assumed that boys with high testosterone levels are more sexually motivated than boys with low levels of testosterone, and that boys who go to church a lot are constrained to lower levels of sexual behavior than those who do not (Udry, 1988). An interaction model might state that whereas boys with low testosterone levels will have low levels of sexual behavior regardless of the frequency of church attendance, boys with high levels of testosterone who go to church a lot will exhibit less sexual behavior than boys with high levels of testosterone who do not attend church frequently.

Next, I illustrate these three models with previously published results from my own cross-sectional and panel studies of the effects of biological and social variables on adolescent problem behaviors.

STUDY 1

Sample

This is a cross-sectional study of about 100 adolescent males and 100 adolescent females, ages 13–16, interviewed once in 1982 (see Udry, 1988, for details). The subjects were randomly drawn from a public school roster of White students in Grades 8, 9, and 10, in Tallahassee, Florida. Interviews were done at home, and three blood samples were drawn at 15-minute intervals in the late afternoon; these blood samples were then pooled for the purpose of statistical analyses. Boys' samples were drawn on a random day, whereas girls' samples were drawn on menstrual cycle days using a narrow window in the early follicular phase, and another in the mid-luteal phase. Radioimmunoassay was done on the pooled samples for testosterone (T) and sex hormone binding globulin (SHBG), along with other hormones on which I am not reporting. The results reported here are for boys, except where otherwise indicated.

Variables

Biological independent variables included age, pubertal development (a factor score based on self-ratings on a battery of questions), and the hormone T. Because the biological availability of T is affected by the protein SHBG, I also included SHBG as an additional (inverse) measure of T. Whereas our models all involve steroid hormonal and sociological relationships to various risk behaviors, the biological variables could be nonsteroid hormones, peptides, neurotransmitters, platelet MAO, autonomic responses to stress, neural structures, or any biological variable hypothesized as altering behavioral propensities or motivations (Magnusson, af Klinteberg, & Stattin, chapter 5, this volume; Zuckerman, 1984).

We also consider age and pubertal development as possible social variables. The effects of pubertal development on behavior are thought to be through the social interpretation of development, and the residual effects of age are thought to be through age-graded norms and expectations (Udry, Billy, Morris, Groff, & Raj, 1985). Other social variables included in our considerations are socioeconomic status (SES), family structure, church attendance, and an index that I call "Good Child." The Good Child measure is an additive index of the adolescents' responses to three questions: likes to go to church; likes to do chores around the house; and likes to do homework.

The dependent variable in this study is a Problem Behavior Index consisting of several items commonly used in such indexes, including got drunk, smoked cigarettes, cut school, had sex, and used marijuana. After identifying these items through a factor analysis, we used an additive index that gave the same results as a factor score.

Theoretical Model

The easiest way to present the integrated theoretical model is through a path diagram (Fig. 6.1). Path A indicates that as individuals age, their hormone levels increase. Path B indicates that increases in hormone levels cause pubertal development. Path C indicates that age is positively correlated with stage of pubertal development. Path D indicates that hormone levels have a direct effect on problem behaviors after age and pubertal development are accounted for. Path E indicates that pubertal development has an effect on problem behavior beyond that of age and hormone levels, and may be considered an effect that works through social processes. Path F, which represents the effect of age-graded norms and opportunities, indicates that there is a residual effect of age on problem behavior after pubertal development and hormone levels are accounted for. Path G indicates that hormones may affect the extent to which individuals expose themselves to social control processes. Path H represents the effects of traditional sociological control model variables on behavior. Path I raises the possibility that the effects of social controls differ depending on the individual's hormone levels.

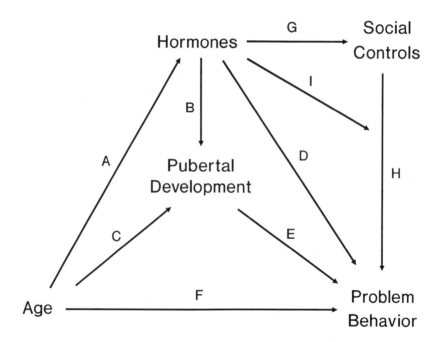

FIG. 6.1. Theoretical biosocial model of problem behavior.

In summary, the proposed model posits three ways that hormones can influence problem behavior: *directly* (Path D), through an *intermediate* variable (Paths B, E; Paths G, H), or through an *interaction* with social variables (Path I).

The theoretical roots and empirical support for elements of the model come from disparate sources. The concept of *problem behavior* emerges in the work of Jessor and Jessor (1977), who discovered that a set of age-graded norm violations of adolescence, consisting of behaviors usually not considered violations when committed by adults, tended to appear in adolescents as a group of interrelated behaviors. Social control theory (represented by Paths H and F) has ancient roots in sociology, and is ubiquitous in the literature on problem behavior. Social control theory, which was developed in detail in modern times by Hirschi (1969), states that norm violations are inhibited by emotional attachments to conventional people and institutions, commitment to conventional means of achievement, and holding conventional beliefs. The idea that biological characteristics of individuals affect their behavior is also deeply rooted in the social sciences. Glueck and Glueck (1956), for example, found strong relationships between body type and delinquency, analogous to Path E. Furthermore, the effects of T on aggressiveness, dominance, sexual behavior, and antisocial behavior (Path D) have been explored by Kreutz and Rose (1972); Olweus, Mattson, Schalling, and Low (1980); Monti, Brown, and Corriveau (1977); and Ehrenkrantz, Bliss, and Scheard (1974), among many others. Zuckerman's (1984) theory of sensation-seeking, which is conceptually and empirically closely related to the ideas of problem behavior theory, bases its approach on the concept of optimum arousal mediated by neurotransmitters in the central nervous system (e.g., Daitzman & Zuckerman, 1980, showed that testosterone was related to sensation-seeking in college males); this provides a strong theoretical foundation for Path D.

In summary, the individual elements of Fig. 6.1 are well grounded in the literature. The only thing unique about my approach is that I have integrated them into a single theoretical model to explain adolescent male problem behavior (Udry, 1990).

Results

The results of the analysis testing the simple additive social model, which omits the effects of hormones, are presented in Table 6.1 (sociological model). The results indicate that none of the socioeconomic variables are significant, pubertal development is not significant after controlling for age, and personality variables are also not significant.

The results testing the simplest biosocial model (Table 6.1, biosocial model) can best be understood through reference to the simplified path diagram presented in Fig. 6.2. The path coefficients indicate that there are strong relationships between age and hormones, between hormones and pubertal development, and between hormones and problem behavior. No direct effects of age on problem behavior remain, because the age effect works through hormones, and there are also no direct effects of pubertal development on problem behavior.

TABLE 6.1
Ordinary Least Squares Models of Problem Behaviors

| | Sociological Model | | | Biosocial Model | | |
	b*	SE	P	b*	SE	P
Testosterone				.19 (.28)	.06	.00
SHBG				− .03 (− .26)	.01	.00
Age	.64 (.29)	.20	.00			
Church attend	− .24 (− .14)	.16	.06			
Good child	− .23 (− .24)	.09	.00	− .20 (− .21)	.08	.01
Grades	− .46 (− .16)	.26	.04	− .59 (− .20)	.25	.01
R square	.24			.30		
N	101			101		

*Standardized coefficients in parentheses.

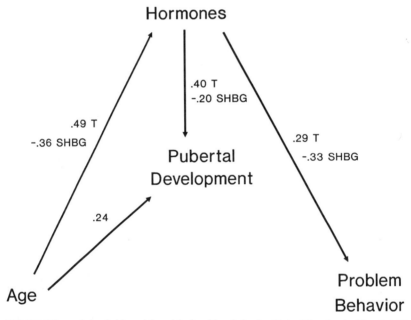

FIG. 6.2. Trimmed simple biosocial model of problem behavior (*Note*. All paths significant at .01 levels. Trimmed paths not significant at .05 level. N = 101).

Whereas the sociological model explains 24% of the variance, and a simple model of hormone effects (Path D, not shown) also explains 24% of the variance, when they are combined additively, 30% of the variance is explained, with age dropping out of the model as expected from Fig. 6.2. If the hormone effects are taken as exogenous to the social effects, we can see that the social effects add only

6% of the variance to the 24% explained by the hormones alone. The integrated model, therefore, provides a quite different view of the process than the social model alone. The fact that the social variables alone explain 24% of the variance, but add only 6% to the explained variance of the biological model, shows that the explanatory social variables are both affected by testosterone, and act as intermediate variables for testosterone effects on problem behavior.

STUDY 2

Whereas cross-sectional studies give interesting ideas about how things might work, panel studies showing the same effects in boys over time would be more convincing. Ultimately, our goal is to replicate the effects discovered earlier in panel models. Here, I present the results of a recently completed study as a first step in achieving this goal.

Sample

Subjects in this 3-year panel study consist of about 100 White boys who were selected randomly from a school district roster in Durham County, North Carolina, a county with a medium-sized city surrounded by rural areas. The average age of the boys at the first round of data collection was about 13 years old, and all were within 1 year of age of one another. They were followed for 3 years, with the first five interviews (and blood draws) spaced 6 months apart, and the sixth 1 year after the fifth.

Variables

To simplify, I only present a four-variable model. Testosterone, the independent variable, was measured in the same way as in the previous study. SHBG was eliminated from the model because it had no significant effects. Autonomy and religion were entered as intermediate variables. Autonomy was measured by an additive scale based on several items in which the respondent indicated how much independence from his parents he had in several spheres of his life. Religion was measured by a sum of scores on two items: frequency of church attendance and the importance of religion to the respondent's life. Problem behavior was measured as a summative index of 26 deviant behavior items from trivial ones like ever smoked, through vandalism, to serious crimes like robbery. The items all loaded satisfactorily on a single factor. An additive scale was used because it produced results indistinguishable from those using a factor score.

Theoretical Model

With the panel study we can put our measures in the proper causal time frames. We hypothesized 6-month time-lag effects of hormones on intermediate variables, 6-month time lags from intermediate variables to problem behavior, and 1-year time lags from hormones to problem behavior. The time lags represent time needed to learn appropriate behaviors and to develop opportunities. Simple path analysis was used to analyze the data.

Results

Results are presented in Fig. 6.3. By examining various lag structures, we find that the model closest to our theoretical expectations is one in which the hormone measures predict problem behaviors best with a 1-year lag, with 6-month lags and lags longer than 1 year producing weaker relationships. The best fitting lag for the intermediate variables is 6 months. The most interesting and troublesome finding in Fig. 6.3 is the fact that although the social/psychological variables have stable effects irrespective of which round of data we start with, the testosterone effect only appears in the first time frame, and then disappears in subsequent time frames. Moreover, the indirect effect of testosterone through autonomy is also ephemeral, weakening in subsequent time frames.

When the Problem Behavior Index is decomposed, and a similar analysis conducted, examining different lags and time frames, the models for different elements are not congruent (not shown). For example, hormonal effects on subsequent rounds of sexual behavior using Time 1 T strengthen with longer lag periods, whereas hormonal effects on most other problem behaviors weaken with longer time periods. These findings have important implications for researchers trying to replicate previous research findings. Studies at different mean ages, or with different age variances, or different developmental levels should not be expected to show the same results. At this time we can offer no firm explanation for why the hormone effects in Fig. 6.3 are only found in the first panel of the figure. We can speculate that age 13 is a critical age for testosterone effects after which the behavior becomes self-perpetuating independent of subsequent T levels. But this is little more than recapitulation of the original observation. We must ultimately consider the possibility that we are not observing T effects at all, but that T at age 13 is a marker for some more fundamental preexisting differences among individuals. In adolescence, everything is changing, and relationships found at one stage of adolescence may not be found 1 year later.

BIOSOCIAL INTERACTIONS

We now explore the biosocial interaction hypothesis, which can be stated as follows: The effects of social controls on problem behavior will be different for those with high T than for those with low T. When we tested for interactions of social variables with testosterone, we found a significant interaction between SHBG and number of siblings. We interpret this as follows: Among boys with low unbound testosterone, the number of siblings had no effect on problem behaviors. Among boys with high unbound testosterone, however, having more siblings was associated with fewer problem behaviors. It may be that the protective effect of

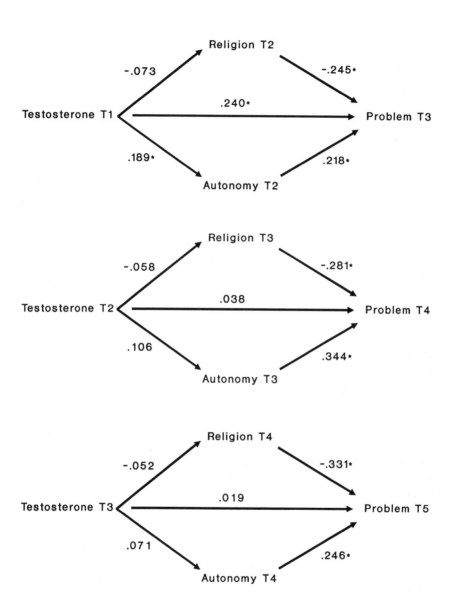

FIG. 6. 3. Sequential time-lagged path models of boys' problem behavior.

siblings was not needed among the low hormone boys, because they lacked motivation for the problem behaviors. This interaction should only be taken as illustrative because it was the only one found.

When the Problem Behavior Index was disaggregated, several interpretable interactions with hormones appeared that were not observed with the unitary index. I only cite two examples here. Using a composite factor as a measure of sexuality in my adolescent *female* cross-sectional sample, girls who were low in testosterone were low in sexuality whether they lived in a father-present or father-absent household. For girls who were high in testosterone, those who were in father-absent households were high in sexuality, whereas those in father-present households were no higher in sexuality than low testosterone girls. The interpretation is that in high T girls, father presence suppresses the effects of T on sexuality, whereas in low T girls, sexuality does not need suppressing—it is low in any case (Udry, 1988).

Boys in our cross-sectional study were asked whether they had ever been drunk. (This question is a component of the Problem Behavior Index in the models I described earlier.) In predicting "ever been drunk," I examined the effects of testosterone, SHBG, father presence, and grades in school. In the additive model, the hormone effects were significant alone, but adding the sociological variables did not make a significant improvement. However, the interactions of T and the two sociological variables were each significant. Father-absent boys were likely to get drunk regardless of testosterone levels. Father-present boys only got drunk if they had high levels of testosterone. (Father presence suppresses drinking only for low T boys.) Boys with low grades were likely to get drunk regardless of their testosterone levels. Boys with high grades were protected from getting drunk by low levels of testosterone, but got drunk anyway if they had high testosterone. These interactions were not observed when the dependent variable was the Problem Behavior Index (Udry, 1991).

Summarizing our experience in exploring biosocial interaction models, we find much support for the hypothesis that the effect of social variables on problem behaviors depends on hormone levels. We also observe that biosocial interactions are found primarily for individual problem behaviors, and less often for the Problem Behavior Indexes.

DO PROBLEM BEHAVIORS SHARE A COMMON CAUSAL STRUCTURE?

The discovery that adolescent problem behaviors constitute a strong factor in most studies (i.e., they occur in the same people), and that there are good predictors of such a factor, has led many researchers to conclude that problem behaviors share a common causal structure (cf. Kandel, 1989). My biosocial analyses, and especially those that specify biosocial interactions, lead to the rejection of this common causal structure. Purely social science models of problem behaviors have seldom hypothesized an interaction structure, but they lend themselves to such hypotheses.

For example, do boys with low grades differ in the extent to which they engage in problem behaviors depending on whether they are in father-present or father-absent households? I predict that such social science interaction models will yield different results for different problem behaviors.

The absence of a common causal structure shared by different problem behaviors is not limited to biosocial interaction models. In the boys' cross-sectional model, testosterone was independently related to each component of the Problem Behavior Index, as well as to the index as a whole. In a cross-sectional study of adolescent girls, done in parallel with our cross-sectional study of boys, we measured the same behaviors and the same hormones. We found androgenic hormonal determinants of sexual behavior for the girls that were similar to those found for boys. But neither the other individual problem behaviors observed nor the Problem Behavior Index showed any relationship to hormones among girls, yet the social model of problem behaviors was strong. This finding needs to be considered in the light of the fact that the Problem Behavior Index in girls formed just as coherent a factor as it did for boys. Because pubertal boys and girls have dramatic sex differences in hormone levels, experience their most dramatic hormone changes at different ages for each gender, and differ in their sensitivity to each hormone, it should not come as a surprise that the causal structure of problem behavior is different for each gender, and that the elements of the Problem Behavior Index respond differently to hormones in boys and girls.

Further, among the boys in the cross-sectional sample, hormones predicted the routine problem behaviors just listed, but were poor predictors of hard drug use, violent and destructive behavior, and other serious crimes. We do not know whether this is a function of the lower frequency of the more serious behaviors, of studying the behaviors at the wrong age, or the absence of a true causal relationship.

Another example of divergent causal structures for different problem behaviors emerges from a study I am conducting in which we have just finished re-interviewing a sample of 350 California women born in the San Francisco Bay area in the early 1960s. In this sample, we have data on the same women at several periods in their lives, beginning during their fetal life, and extending through their third decade. We have found that we get a clearer picture of the determinants of problem behaviors if we divide the behaviors into "ingestion" behaviors (smoke, drink alcohol, use other drugs) and other behaviors (shop-lifted, got speeding tickets, got arrested, other stealing). These two groups of behaviors show different childhood antecedents and different adult sequelae.

The finding of different causal structures for different problem behaviors does not necessarily lead us to abandon the problem behavior concept. Instead, it suggests that problem behaviors share some gross biological and social determinants and not others, and that the more we learn about the causal structure, the more we will want to disaggregate them for study.

ADOLESCENT ENVIRONMENT VERSUS INDIVIDUAL TEMPERAMENT

Our analysis of the California sample is an example of looking back into childhood for determinants of problem behaviors. Most of the sociological (and some of the psychological) research done on adolescent problem behaviors has relied on self-reports of adolescents about current environment and recent behavior. In our California study, we have discovered that those who had high Problem Behavior Indexes at adolescence were already different from other girls when they were 5 years old. For example, at 9 they had a different personality profile. Some of these factors appear to be genetic. Caspi, Lynam, and Moffitt (1990) also discovered childhood determinants of adolescent problem behaviors in their analysis of a sample of New Zealand girls. Their analysis shows that adolescent environment *interacts* with behavior patterns identified in preadolescence to determine adolescent problem behaviors.

The findings presented here suggest that typical sociological problem behavior models are identifying adolescent environmental correlates of problem behaviors that are proxies for or consequences of underlying temperamental variables, and that the more fundamental determinants of who will show problem behaviors in adolescence may be found in the individual differences in temperament as opposed to or in interaction with differences in adolescent social experiences. Block, Block, and Keyes (1988) for example, criticized research on adolescent drug use on the grounds that the researchers are preoccupied with the effects of current situational factors, and ignore childhood antecedents, the inclusion of which would give a far different picture of the causal structure. They show they can make good predictions of who will use marijuana at age 14 by personality and environmental factors measured in the same children at age 4. If the foundations for problem behavior are in temperamental variables determined genetically or at earlier ages, how is it that we find so many adolescent environmental variables predicting problem behaviors? We propose that children with different temperaments select environments congenial to their behavioral predispositions (see Scarr & McCartney, 1983).

Rowe and Osgood (1984) provided a good example of how preexisting behavior predispositions lead to selection of adolescent environments. In their twin sample, most of the variance in their delinquency measure was accounted for by genetic factors. More specifically to my point, they found that the *covariance* of friends' delinquency and own delinquency was mostly genetically explained. This implies that the "effect" of delinquent peers is primarily a function of individuals with genetic predispositions to delinquency selecting one another as friends. This is an elegant example of how the integration of biological and social models can illuminate sociological theory.

CONCLUSIONS AND IMPLICATION FOR FUTURE RESEARCH

Biosocial models have promise in illuminating and expanding social science models of problem behaviors and other risk behaviors. Hormonal and other biological factors can be integrated into social science research models for relatively small samples without changing sampling designs and within the bounds of reasonable field logistics. The theoretical foundation for integrating them is well developed. As I have demonstrated, such integrated models are likely to come to quite different conclusions than straight social science models about even the *social* foundations of problem behaviors.

The fact that the various problem behaviors co-occur in individuals, and therefore generate a stable statistical factor, has led researchers to postulate a single causal structure for the unified construct of problem behavior. There is some theoretical justification for this on the biological level, and biosocial models that are quite satisfactory can be built around the construct. Nevertheless, biosocial models built on the disaggregated elements of the construct do not produce similar results for each element, and are dissimilar from the aggregated model. This is especially true when biosocial interactions are included in the models. Such interactions are frequently present in disaggregated models, but disappear or are transformed in the aggregated models. As we learn more about the determinants of problem behaviors, future research will profit from *testing* the hypothesis that problem behaviors share a common causal model, rather than *assuming* a common causal model.

Current social science models of adolescent problem behaviors tend to focus their explanatory attention on concurrent situational and environmental variables. Recent lines of inquiry indicate that the behavioral foundations for problem behaviors are already present in childhood, and may be substantially genetic (Block et al., 1988; Rowe, this volume). When such considerations are absent from investigations of adolescent problem behaviors, situational and environmental factors in adolescence will appear to be strong determinants of problem behaviors when they are really only the intermediate pathways through which more fundamental predispositions of individuals are expressed. These conclusions lead to the overall recommendation that when we are trying to understand adolescent problem behaviors, we should learn to think of adolescents as actors with a biological and developmental history that affects their predispositions toward problem behaviors in adolescence. If we see adolescents primarily as responding to situational forces around them, we will misunderstand why some are deep into problem behaviors and some are not.

This chapter has discussed only theories and research that try to explain variance among individuals in problem behaviors. This is what biosocial models do, and also what most social science models do. If we want to address the causes of social change in the levels of various problem behaviors, biosocial models are of little use because biological factors in a population would not show secular change over the short run. But social science models of individual variance are not designed to explain social change either. Nor can the causes of social change in the incidence of problem behaviors be inferred from models explaining variance among individuals. For example, if self-esteem is inversely related to problem behaviors in individual models, it cannot logically be inferred that increases in self-esteem in the population will reduce the incidence of problem behaviors. Therefore, we should be modest about the usefulness of research on the causes of variance in problem behaviors in informing public policies and programs dealing with ameliorating the effects of environmental and social deprivation, at least in the short run. Nevertheless, models explaining variance in problem behaviors may be useful in identifying high risk individuals and groups for interventions, and in designing the interventions.

ACKNOWLEDGMENT

This research was supported by grants from the National Institute of Child Health and Human Development (Grants # HD12806 and HD23454).

REFERENCES

Block, J., Block, J. H., & Keyes, S. (1988). Longitudinal foretelling drug usage in adolescence: Early childhood personality and environmental precursors. *Child Development*, *59*, 336–355.

Booth, A., Shelley, G., Mazur, A., Tharp, G., & Kittok, R. (1989). Testosterone, winning and losing in human competition. *Hormones and Behavior*, *23*, 556–571.

Caspi, A., Lynam, D., & Moffitt, T. E. (1990). *Unraveling girls' delinquency: Biological, dispositional, and contextual contributions to adolescent misbehavior.* Unpublished manuscript.

Daitzman, R. J., & Zuckerman, M. (1980). Disinhibitory sensation seeking, personality and gonadal hormones. *Personality and Individual Differences*, *1*, 103–110.

Ehrenkrantz, J., Bliss, E., & Scheard, M.H. (1974). Plasma testosterone: Correlation with aggressive behavior and social dominance in man. *Psychosomatic Medicine*, *36*, 469–475.

Glueck, S., & Glueck, E. (Eds.). (1956). *Physique and delinquency.* New York: Harper.

Hirschi, T. (1969). *Causes of delinquency.* Berkeley: University of California Press.

Jessor, R., & Jessor, S. L. (Eds.). (1977). *Problem behavior and psychosocial development.* New York: Academic Press.

Kandel, D. B. (1989). Issues of sequencing of adolescent drug use and other problem behaviors. *Drugs and Society*, *3*, 55–76.

Kreutz, L. E., & Rose, R. M. (1972). Assessment of aggressive behavior and plasma testosterone in a young criminal population. *Psychosomatic Medicine*, *34*, 321–332.

Monti, P. M., Brown, W. A., & Corriveau, D. D. (1977). Testosterone and components of aggressive and sexual behavior in man. *American Journal of Psychiatry*, *134*, 692–694.

Olweus, D., Mattson, A., Schalling, D., & Low, H. (1980). Testosterone, aggression, physical, and personality dimensions in normal adolescent males. *Psychosomatic Medicine*, *42*, 253–269.

Plomin, R. (1986). *Development, genetics, and psychology.* Hillsdale, NJ: Lawrence Erlbaum Associates.

Rowe, D. C., & Osgood, D. W. (1984). Heredity and sociological theories of delinquency: A reconsideration. *American Sociological Review*, *49*, 526–540.

Scarr, S., & McCartney, K. (1983). How people make their own environments: A theory of genotype→environment effects. *Child Development*, *54*, 424–435.

Udry, J. R. (1988). Biological predispositions and social control in adolescent sexual behavior. *American Sociological Review*, *53*, 709–722.

Udry, J. R. (1990). Biosocial models of adolescent problem behaviors. *Social Biology*, *37*, 1–10.

Udry, J. R. (1991). Predicting alcohol use by adolescent males. *Journal of Biosocial Science*, *23*, 381–386.

Udry, J. R., Billy, J. O. G., Morris, N. M., Groff, T. R., & Raj, M. H. (1985). Serum androgenic hormones motivate sexual behavior in adolescent boys. *Fertility and Sterility*, 43, 90–94.

Zuckerman, M. (1984). Sensation seeking: A comparative approach to a human trait. *Behavioral and Brain Sciences*, *7*, 413–471.

7

Genetic and Cultural Explanations of Adolescent Risk Taking and Problem Behavior

David C. Rowe
University of Arizona

In this chapter on risk-taking behavior, I start not with an analysis of risk-taking behaviors per se, but rather, with a discussion of the genetic and cultural transmission of phenotypes (any trait or behavior measurable on individuals). I begin with a highly abstract discussion because the purpose of social science is to reach beyond narrow findings to broad generalizations; and I believe that the field is ready to take a step in this direction. Of importance for risk-taking behavior are the generalizations that (a) rearing experiences in the family have little impact on adult phenotypes, (b) social influence on risk-taking phenotypes is much more horizontal (peer to peer) rather than vertical (parent to child), and (c) current social experiences can amplify the effects of inherited trait phenotypes.

This chapter first addresses models of genetic and cultural transmission, and later applies these ideas in transmission models of particular risk-taking phenotypes. In particular, I use a "sibling effects" model to show that inherited traits, immediate social influence, and age-associated social norms can be united in one statistical model to explain variation in delinquency and sexual experience. Of particular interest is the model's demonstration that social influence amplifies the effects of a preexisting trait disposition on delinquent behavior. The second example is an "epidemic" model of smoking and sexual intercourse. In this model, genetic influences are not represented directly. Rather, the model describes the increasing prevalence of these behaviors with age as a result of social interactions between same-aged peers. Thus, the "epidemic" model is an example of purely horizontally driven social transmission process.

The kinds of risk correlates that I identify, such as social interaction with peers, family interactions (Jessor, 1992), and personality traits (Gottfredson & Hirschi, this volume), are similar to those identified in many social science models of risk-taking behavior. However, my approach fundamentally differs from most social science models in my specification of causal process—primarily because most associations with childrearing "influences" are regarded as spurious rather than causal. Although the chapter does not discuss specific biological measures, this perspective clearly complements Udry's (this volume) biosocial approach.

The terms *trait* and *trait phenotype* are used to refer to an enduring personality disposition indexed by a broad range of specific behaviors and only estimable from many behaviors aggregated over time and context. The term *behavioral phenotype* is defined as any specific behavior that is measurable on individuals and transmissible in human populations. Thus, *sociability* is a trait because it would be assessed using a multiple-item personality inventory. A particular behavior such as "wearing a tattoo" would be described as a behavioral phenotype because is measurable on individuals and socially transmissible. The term *phenotype* is meant in the broad sense of either a trait or behavioral phenotype.

Phenotype transmission may be defined as the adoption of phenotypes present in one generation by another generation. It may occur between parent and child (*vertical transmission*), between any adult in the parental generation and a child in the next (*oblique transmission*), or between peers who are close in age (*horizontal transmission*). The underlying transmission mechanisms may be genetic, cultural, or some combination of the two. The phrase *transmission model* refers to a mathematically stated model describing the likelihood and pattern of phenotype transmission between individuals in different and/or the same generation using concepts from genetics, evolution, and theories of culture (Boyd & Richerson, 1985; Cavalli-Sforza & Feldman, 1981; Eaves, Eysenck, & Martin, 1989; Eaves, Last, Young, & Martin, 1978). They are commonly used in fields of behavioral genetics, anthropology, and evolutionary biology; but my emphasis is on behavior genetic models in particular.

TRANSMISSION OF PHENOTYPES

In this section, what is known about phenotype transmission is summarized in the form of general propositions. Following the outline of the general propositions, I offer a general theory of behavioral transmission that is consistent with the propositions but also open to further refinement and change. My propositions apply to family backgrounds in the working to professional social class range and not to the worst family environments—whether rearing effects exist at environmental extremes (e.g., threshold effects), or whether particular gene by environment interactions occur at such extremes, is not presently answerable with available evidence. The propositions thus cover about 70% of the U.S. population.

Proposition 1: Personality Traits are Heritable

This result is well known and not particularly surprising in light of genetic influence on brain structure and function. About 30% of the variation in personality traits is additive genetic variation, and an additional 20% may represent genetic epistasis (i.e., interactions among gene loci; Loehlin, Willerman, & Horn, 1988; Rowe, 1987). Variation in intellectual traits is about 50% additive heredity, with some family environmental effects at young ages that appear to diminish later (Plomin, 1986). "Broad-sense" heritability refers to total genetic influence on a phenotype, including interaction effects among genes at different loci (i.e., chromosomal locations). Estimates of broad-sense heritability for IQ go as high as 70% (Loehlin et al., 1988). Nontwin adoption studies suggest that long-term changes in family environment affect IQ by about 6 points, a difference far smaller than many social scientists would have anticipated, but one that is consistent with the small IQ difference within pairs of MZ twins raised separately (Bouchard, Lykken, McGue, Segal, & Tellegen, 1990; Locurto, 1990; see also, Bouchard & Segal, 1985).

Proposition 2: Vertical Environmental Parent–Child Transmission is Negligible

Lay persons and experts alike in Western societies widely assume that the imitation of parents leads to the development of children's psychological traits—that traits are molded by parental example, discipline, and affection. But, according to a body of accumulated evidence from behavioral genetic studies, families have nearly no rearing influence over the kinds of traits children will eventually develop as adults (Plomin & Daniels, 1987; Rowe & Plomin, 1981). As stated by Scarr (1991):

> There is no evidence that family environments, except the worst, have any significant effects on the development of familial retardation, conduct disorders, psychopathy, or other common behavioral disorders. The behavior genetic evidence . . . is that differences among families' environments have little to do with differences in children's behavioral outcomes. (p. 403)

A detailed literature review is beyond the scope of this chapter. However, Table 7.1 provides an illustrative example showing findings typical for a behavioral and physical phenotype (Grilo & Pogue-Geile, 1991; Loehlin & Rowe, 1992).

The physical phenotype is body weight—and the pattern of correlations can be interpreted as showing that weight resemblances among parent and child are due to their shared genes rather than to the way in which they were reared. Even when adopted in infancy, the weight of adopted children lacks any association with the weight of their adoptive parents ($r = .04$) or with that of adoptive siblings ($r = .01$). Although the correlations for extraversion were lower than those for weight (which can be measured with nearly perfect reliability, unlike the psychological trait phenotype), the pattern was the same. Resemblance follows genetic relatedness, which is greater for MZ twins than for first degree biological relatives, but fails to

TABLE 7.1
Familial Correlations for Weight and Extraversion

	Weight	*Extraversion*
Genetic Relatedness = 1.0		
Identical (MZ) twins reared together	.80	.55
Identical (MZ) twins reared apart	.72	.38
Genetic Relatedness = 0.5		
Fraternal (DZ) twins reared together	.43	.11
Biological parent–child	.26	.16
Biological siblings	.34	.20
Genetic Relatedness = 0.0		
Adoptive parent–adopted child	.04	− .01
Unrelated siblings reared together	.01	− .06

Source. Weight correlations, Grilo and Pogue-Geile (1991); Extraversion correlations, weighted average *r*s from Loehlin and Rowe (1992, Tables 2 and 4).

appear when relatives only share rearing experiences but not genes (adoptive parent–child, $r = -.01$; biologically unrelated siblings, $r = -.06$). According to model-fitting analyses of both data sets, environmental transmission parameters can be omitted when describing the transmission of either weight or extraversion.

In other words, it would make little difference for personality development whether children were reared in the typical family environment (an overweight child with an overweight parent; an extraverted child with an extraverted parent); or whether they were reared under some other condition, because those children reared together would be no more alike environmentally than those reared in different households. If vertical parent–child transmission occurs, then significant parent–child correlations should be found in adoptive families; typically, they are not (Goldsmith, 1983; Loehlin & Rowe, 1992; Plomin & Daniels, 1987). Further, the entire pattern of resemblances for pairs of relatives of different genetic and social relatedness supports a genetic interpretation of the modest behavioral resemblance seen when pairs are biologically related to one another and live together.

Proposition 3: Childrearing Style, If Not at Pathological Extremes, Is Not an Influence on Personality Development

It is known that childrearing styles correlate with children's traits (Maccoby & Martin, 1983). Childrearing behaviors usually factor into two broad dimensions: one associated with parental control (e.g., setting rules such as a fixed bed time each night); the other with parental affection. Greater affection is associated with children's greater self-esteem and social competence. Particular combinations of rearing behaviors are associated with the "best" child outcomes. For instance, the authoritative pattern of high affection and developmentally appropriate levels of control correlates with many desirable traits in children (e.g., high intelligence, social competence). How can we reconcile these childrearing outcome associations with Proposition 3—the absence of rearing effects? The answer is that these associations would be *spurious* (i.e., noncausal) and thus their absence in transmission models is not problematic. In Sherlock Holmes' words to Doctor Watson, when you have eliminated the impossible, whatever remains, however improbable, must be the truth.

Why regard these associations as spurious ones? The first reason is reverse causality, whereby parents' behavior is responsive to children's traits but does not cause them (Bell & Harper, 1977; Lytton, 1990).

The second reason involves two observations. First, environmental measures may contain genetic variation when they assess parental behavior that is partly due to heritable trait dispositions. For example, books in the home—which do not appear there by magic, but by parental choice—reflect parental dispositions such as intellectual curiosity, reading ability, and concern for a child's welfare, while they also assess the home environment to which a child is exposed. Recent evidence from a variety of research designs—including reared-apart twins—is consistent with genetic variation in environmental measures (Plomin & Bergeman, 1991):

> ...it is remarkable that research reported to date, using diverse measures and methods, so consistently converges on the conclusion that genetic influence is significant and substantial on widely used measures of the environment ... the bottom line is that labeling a measure environmental does not make it environmental. (p. 386)

Second, if rearing measures contain genetic variation, then their association with child outcomes can be mediated genetically rather than environmentally, as the genes that favor a particular rearing behavior in the parent can find expression as a trait phenotype in the child. In the earlier example, an association of "books in the home" with a child's IQ could be mediated genetically, rather than reflecting a causal influence of home intellectual stimulation on children's IQ. Genetic mediation can be shown in a research design comparing biological and adoption families if the rearing outcome association is greater in the former (heredity plus rearing influence) than in the latter (rearing influence alone). Using this research design, genetic mediation of childrearing outcome associations has been demonstrated for young children's temperamental traits and IQ (Plomin, DeFries, & Fulker, 1988; Plomin, Loehlin, & DeFries, 1985). In summary, because rearing outcome associations in biological families are generally spurious, no conflict exists between finding them in a study of biological families and the general lack of rearing effects inferred from methodologically superior research designs.

Proposition 4: With the Exception of Current Social Contacts, Environmental Rearing Influences Shared by Siblings are Weak or Nonexistent

Although most theories of familial social influence choose to focus on trait transmission via childrearing styles, behavioral genetic models clearly distinguish two possible pathways of family social influence. The first is the parent–child pathway. The second consists of rearing influences shared by siblings, but which may be independent of parent–child social influence. As shown in the weight and extraversion examples, one might anticipate that siblings' shared-rearing effects also would be negligible. In general, this interpretation has been supported as adoptive siblings raised together are generally no more alike in personality than children raised in different families—that is, the adoptees correlate close to zero for most personality traits (Plomin & Daniels, 1987). In model-fitting analyses involving multiple kinship groups (adoptees, twins raised apart and together, biological families, uncle/aunt with niece/nephew), Loehlin and Rowe (1992) found that for some trait dimensions, a sibling environment parameter added to explained variation. Nonetheless, averaged over five trait dimensions, the average contribution of sibling shared-rearing environment was small in absolute terms (6% of total variation) and small relative to variation explained by heredity (43%) or nonfamilial environmental influences (51%; see Loehlin & Rowe, 1992, Table 7).

Proposition 5: Natural Selection Processes May Maintain Undesirable Traits in a Population

We feel intuitively that children's "undesirable" traits result from "bad" rearing conditions. From an evolutionary perspective, however, trait phenotypes may be maintained in a population because natural selection has been either relaxed or even favorable toward the genes underlying them. It is conceivable for risk taking to be adaptive, despite considerable mortality (Daly & Wilson, 1983). For example, suppose we roughly divide the population into low and high risk takers. We may discover that, although the high risk takers have a 20% mortality during their reproductive years, they average six children; whereas the low risk takers suffer 3% mortality, but average only one and one half children. We can calculate that the high risk takers have been more reproductively successful than the low risk takers (i.e., $.8 \times 6$ is greater than $.97 \times 1.5$), indicating that the genes contributing to a greater risk taking would then become more frequent in later generations.

A MODEL OF TRAIT AND BEHAVIOR TRANSMISSION

Figure 7.1 presents a model of the social transmission of a behavioral phenotype that assists our understanding of the earlier propositions. Specifically, the model is meant to display how the relative influence of parents on behavioral phenotypes becomes greatly diminished through social learning; and how learned behaviors develop associations with genetic dispositions. Concretely, the model might be thought of in terms of the acquisition of smoking behavior by a young adolescent. Smoking is a good example

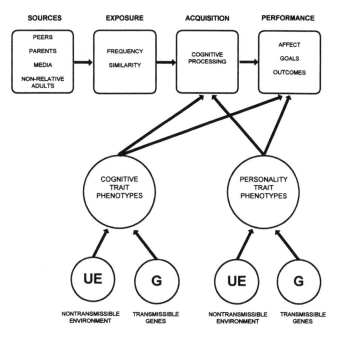

FIG. 7. 1. A model of trait transmission.

because behavioral genetic data indicate that familial resemblance is not due to rearing influence (see Eysenck, 1980).[1]

The individual clearly possesses trait phenotypes, resulting from the effects of prior experiences and genes accumulated over many years. The experiences are labeled *unshared environment* (UE) because they are environmental effects not transmissible from parent to child. That is, whatever effect UE has had on the trait phenotype of a parent, this effect cannot be replicated on that parent's own children. Genes (G) are transmissible, producing some parent–child resemblance in trait phenotypes, as noted earlier. Thus, the bottom of the diagram captures the behavior genetic component of the model.

The horizontal boxes at the top represent the immediate social learning process (Bandura, 1977). People are the sources of behavioral example—a model for smoking behavior may be children's peers, parents, unrelated adults, or the media. Whether an individual is exposed to a model depends on the proportion of potential models who present the phenotype. In addition, greater attention is often given to a model who is similar in status (age, social class) or behavioral inclinations to a target child, a standard condition in social learning theory influencing the likeli-

---

[1]Eysenck's smoking results were like those shown for extraversion. Based on twin and adoption data, rearing influences were negligible in adulthood; parent–child resemblance for regular smoking was the result of shared genes.

hood of attempting modeled behavior. Social learning theory also distinguishes between acquisition and performance—people know the "scripts" for many more behaviors than they typically perform in daily life. Whereas acquisition is dependent on cognitive processing of incoming information, performance is dependent on the emotion experienced after a behavior is tried, on the connection between the behavior and personal goals, and on whether the behavior produces psychologically favorable outcomes (see Fig. 7.1, Acquisition and Performance).

Why Parents Have Little Impact

Although parents may immediately influence children's behaviors, their long term effects are likely to be minimal. The model assumes that the human learning process is highly generalized and not tied to any particular source (see Fig. 7.1, Sources). Thus, a behavior can be learned with equal facility from a parent, sibling, peer, or nonrelative adult. In my view, parents have no special primacy in the learning process other than that created by mere opportunity, a factor that diminishes in intensity after early childhood, as children spend more time outside the home in contact with other children and adults.

In contrast, although social learning theory is consistent with this generality assumption, it has been argued that parents are especially powerful models because of the affective bond between parent and child. I assume that a powerful parent–child attachment exists, but that it does not guide or restrict the learning process in any particular way. Many social learning experiments have been conducted with nonparental adults as models, and children readily imitate them. Many of the variables manipulated in social learning experiments (such as a model's power, affection, etc.) apply equally to nonparental adults who can serve the same modeling function. Furthermore, the proportion of adult or peer models who demonstrate a behavioral phenotype may influence the probability of children's imitation more so than any single model's example (Perry & Bussey, 1979). In mathematical models of cultural transmission, population average phenotypes are often regarded as optimal (see Boyd & Richerson, 1985), as in the Japanese proverb that "a nail that sticks out is hammered in." So children should learn via the example of multiple instead of single models.

Under these assumptions, the weight of influence of a parental model would be $1/N$, where N is the total number of models sampled, including the parent. Although multiple sampling sharply reduces parental influence, the total lack of influence would be unpredictable from this condition alone, especially if the number of available models for a particular phenotype was small. A further reduction in parent–child similarity, however, results from the influence of inherited trait phenotypes on the learning process—because parent and child lack identical genetic make-up, genetic effects produce further parent–child disparities that are at a maximum when an adoptive rather than biological parent does the rearing. This second process results from genotype–environment correlation.

Genotype–Environment Correlation

Two relevant kinds of genotype–environment (G–E) correlation occur: (a) reactive G–E correlation, which refers to inherited traits eliciting responses from the social environment, for example, peer's response to inherited high or low activity levels (Saudino & Eaton, 1991); and (b) active G–E correlation, which refers to the selection of environmental opportunities that reinforce genetic dispositions, for example, high IQ children reading library books when on their own time (Plomin, DeFries, & Loehlin, 1977; Scarr & McCartney, 1983). In Fig. 7.1, the active G–E correlation is implied by the effects of inherited phenotypes on affect, goals, and outcomes. The reactive kind is not directly illustrated, but could be represented by an arrow from Sources to trait phenotypes. Figure 7.1 reflects the position of Scarr (1991), that the most influential environments are not those imposed on the child, but rather, those created through the reactive and active G–E correlation processes:

> in most respects people make their own environments, primarily through the reactions they evoke in other people and the choices they make from the array of environmental opportunities. Obviously, if people do not have opportunities to learn music, geometry, or cooking, they cannot develop those skills. . . . Given that the vast majority of children in Western societies have wide arrays of environmental opportunities, it stands to reason (supported by research) that individual differences in who develops what depend more on the person's characteristics than on differences in opportunities to learn. (p. 404)

ILLUSTRATIONS

My current work is concerned with formal models of the transmission of phenotypes through vertical and horizontal (i.e., peer group) transmission processes. These formal models can be used to illustrate how general assumptions about behavioral transmission can be built into models that can be tested with actual data. I choose as illustrations sibling effects models, and epidemic transmission models.

Sibling Effects Models

My sibling effects model began as an application of the family study research design to test the hypothesis that both delinquency (regarded here as a *trait phenotype*) and sexual experience (regarded here as a *behavioral phenotype*) were "symptoms" of some underlying personality disposition (see Gottfredson & Hirschi, 1990, this volume; Zuckerman, 1984). The stronger the disposition, the greater the probability of delinquent behavior; and the greater the probability of sexual experience as well (on a 5-item measure of sexual intimacy—from dating to sexual intercourse). Using the family design, we can ask: Does a child who inherits the underlying disposition display the various "symptoms" produced by it? This is called *comorbidity* in a family study: If a person displays one symptom, he or she should display others as well, and the disposition also should induce correlations across family members.

118   Rowe

But both phenotypes present complications. In early adolescence—the data set used in this example covers children 10–16 years old—sexual intimacy is closely associated with age. That is, older teens have more experience on the *sexual intimacy* scale, where age is a proxy for both the aged-graded social norms and opportunities and for physical maturation. After all, for 10th graders, dating and some sexual experience is to be expected—most people would approve; but disapproval attends sexual intercourse in an unmarried 12-year-old.

Delinquency also presents special complications: sibling effects. We use the term *sibling effect* to refer to either the direct influence of one sibling on another; or to the indirect effects of the peer group in which both children are embedded. Brothers can be "partners in crime," and this unfortunate cooperation is not rare (Rowe, 1985).

One structural equation model can integrate these ideas (see Fig. 7.2). Siblings' ages affect both their manifest delinquency and sexual experience (shown as squares). The latent (i.e., not directly measured) trait of the younger sibling or girl (Y/G) affects both phenotypes; as does the latent trait of the older sibling or boy (O/B). Genetic theory imposes the correlation of .50 between the siblings' latent traits. The dotted lines represent sibling effects: from younger's trait to older's delinquency and vice versa.

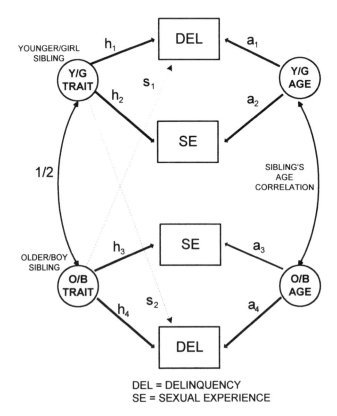

DEL = DELINQUENCY
SE = SEXUAL EXPERIENCE

FIG. 7.2. Sibling trait model.

TABLE 7.2
Completely Standardized Parameter Estimates
From Sibling Effects Model

Parameter	Latent Trait
h_1	.40
h_2	.64
h_3	.44
h_4	.57
	Age
a_1	.69
a_2	.68
a_3	.64
a_4	.48
	Siblings Effects
s_1	.36
s_2	.09

This model was fit to a sample containing 142 sister pairs, 141 mixed-sex pairs, and 135 brother pairs, nearly all 10–16 years of age.

Sibling effects do not occur for all pairs. Two variables condition sibling effects—siblings' mutual warmth and siblings' mutual friends. We used the latter to divide the sample into five groups: (a) brothers with mutual friends, (b) brothers without mutual friends, (c) sisters with mutual friends, (d) sisters without mutual friends, and (e) mixed-sex pairs. As expected, delinquency correlations were greater when siblings reported mutual friends; for example, the brothers' correlations were .49 and .08, for pairs with and without mutual friends, respectively. The model permitted sibling effects (dotted lines) only in Groups a and b. Overall, the LISREL model gave a good fit to the five groups' observed covariance matrices, yielding a chi-square equal to 47.1 (df = 48, $p > .51$).

Table 7.2 displays the parameter estimates from the completely standardized solution. Notice that the sibling effect has directionality: It is greater from the older to younger child than vice versa (0.36 vs. 0.09). Removing sibling effects and age effects, the model-estimated sibling correlations for delinquency and sexual experience were low (0.11 and 0.14, respectively), and in accord with typical estimates of familial genetic influence given their precision (i.e., heritabilities of 22% and 28%, respectively). Finally, phenotypic variance of delinquency was greater for siblings with mutual friends than those without them, as seen in the model's mathematical expectations.[2] Thus, sibling effects actually increase the proportions of youths with very

---

[2]The generalized variance expectations, for the case where $s_1 = s_2$ and $h_1 = h_2 = h_3 = h_4$, are:
1. with sibling effect
DEL var = $h^2 + a^2 + s^2(1 + .5h^2) + e^2$, and
2. without sibling effects
DEL var= $h^2 + a^2 + e^2$,
where h, a, and s are shown in Fig. 7.1 and "e" represents measurement error and unshared environment.

high and very low delinquency scores. This result shows how social environmental effects can amplify the effects of inherited traits (represented as the latent traits) on particular trait phenotypes—that is, the social environment conditions the expression of genetic dispositions.

Epidemic Trait Models

As illustrated by sibling mutual interaction, many behavioral phenotypes pass horizontally, among peers, rather than vertically from adults to children. One of the classic animal examples of cultural transmission was a Japanese macaque monkey's discovery that sand could be washed off potatoes (human-supplied provisions), an innovation that spread from this young female to other young monkeys and females. The last step in transmission was mothers demonstrating the washing procedure to their offspring. The young female's later innovation of dumping grain mixed with sand into water to separate them also spread via imitation through the monkey colony (Kummer, 1971). Another example is human childhood games such as hopscotch that spread among adjacent generations of children with little adult intervention. A characteristic of both examples is that phenotypes can both originate in and pass primarily among peers.

Epidemic Modeling

The epidemic modeling approach is an effort to describe the horizontal transmission of behavioral phenotypes in adolescent peer groups using adaptations of the mathematics in such related areas as the epidemic spread of infectious disease and the adoption of cultural innovations. The basic assumption of the epidemic approach is that a phenotype spreads in face-to-face meetings among adolescents. This assumption can be represented in the mathematical expression for the proportion of adopters in a mixing population:

$$\text{new adopters} = TP_a(1 - P_a), \tag{1}$$

where P_a is the proportion who have already adopted in generation (or age) "a", its difference from one is the fraction of the population still at risk, and T is a rate parameter. The parameter T represents both the number of contacts potentially leading to adoption and the probability that a contact is effective (leads to adoption when it occurs). Conceptually, the parameter T represents the effects of individual difference variables, such attitudes and personality traits, as well as social interaction patterns. More complicated epidemic models permit parameter studies of the influences determining T, for example, by fitting models to multiple groups where T should vary on theoretical grounds.

Implicit in the epidemic equation is the major source of risk to uninitiated adolescents—merely the number of current phenotype-positive individuals in a population. From the epidemic perspective, the greatest cause of risk to virgin adolescents is the number of current nonvirgins; the greatest cause of risk to nondrinkers, the number of current drinkers. This simple idea, and its quantitative implications for behavioral spread, is often missed by regression-based approaches to adolescent risk taking.

Epidemic models have been written for three behavioral phenotypes: sexual intercourse, drinking, and smoking (Rowe, Chassin, Presson, Edwards, & Sherman, 1992; Rowe & Rodgers, 1991a, 1991b, 1991c; Rowe, Rodgers, & Meseck-Bushey, 1989). The sexual intercourse model allows for two spread processes: (a) epidemic spread via social contacts between virgin males and nonvirgin females, and vice versa; and (b) nonepidemic spread, via social contacts between virgins. The model also includes a restriction on whether females are at risk for sexual intercourse: Only females in Tanner's stages of pubertal development 4 and 5 are permitted to move from virgin to nonvirgin status.

The model consists of recursive difference equations that predict the prevalence of sexual intercourse at different ages. Figure 7.3 compares predicted and observed values for White females and males for data collected from two school systems.

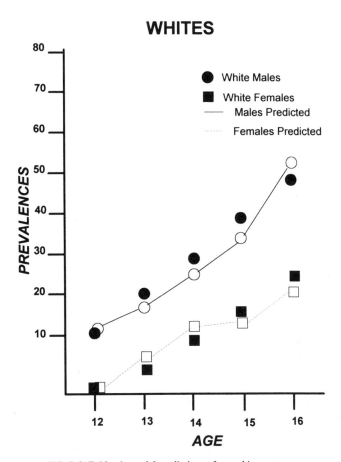

FIG. 7. 3. Epidemic model predictions of sexual intercourse.

Agreement was fairly close, although the model predicted Black intercourse rates (not shown) somewhat less accurately.

Probably the most interesting result to emerge is the possible role of pubertal maturation in producing racial differences in sexual intercourse rates. Black females mature earlier than White females, and this fact accounts for a good portion of the greater rate of sexual intercourse in Blacks. In a sense, mature girls are the rate-limiting "resource" for the spread of sexual intercourse. If there are more mature girls in the Black population at ages 9, 10, 11, and 12, then the spread of intercourse will initiate sooner there and be more rapid—and small early differences in rates culminate in disparate outcomes in middle adolesence, until later, when intercourse rates approach unity in both the Black and White populations. Although our model places more emphasis on puberty than most theories of adolescent sexuality, we do not claim that pubertal differences are the sole cause of racial differences in sexual behavior.

Another epidemic model deals with the spread of smoking in adolescent populations (see Fig. 7.4). As with the sexuality model, this model was implemented in recursive difference equations and it also predicted prevalence by age. The smoking model, however, distinguished among stages of smoking acquisition. Intermediate between nonsmoker and regular smoker is the stage of "experimental smoker," someone who has used cigarettes just a few times. The stage of "ex-smoker" occurs after regular smoker, along with the possibility of relapse.

The main concern of the smoking model was whether the transition between the various stages involved social contacts or not. A noncontact model can be written as,

$$\text{new adopters} = T(1 - P_a), \tag{2}$$

where T is the rate parameter and $(1 - P_a)$ is the proportion of the population still at risk at age "a." Note that social contacts are not implied in Equation

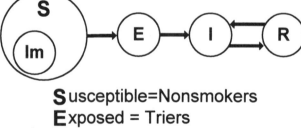

FIG. 7. 4. Permitted transitions in epidemic model of smoking cigarettes.

2—rather, a regular proportion of the population ($T < 1.0$) adopts a behavior at each transition between ages. Our smoking models were designed to compare this alternative with that of social contact transitions, as represented by Equation 1.

The best-fitting models indicated that the transition between nonsmoker and experimenter was social-contact driven, whereas that between experimenter and regular smoker was not. One interpretation of this result is that one's first cigarettes are obtained from peers, who may encourage their use, whereas regular smoking may develop as a habit depending on psychological rewards and the physiological effects of nicotine.

Although the epidemic models are intriguing, their ultimate potential will depend on incorporating more variables, and on dealing with some of their limitations. For example, personality risk factors are not explicit in the epidemic models just described. A way to deal with this in an epidemic model is to partition a population according to individual differences in risk, and then to examine the spread of behavior within each subgroup. Also, these models make many simplifying assumptions, such as homogeneous mixing, which are only approximations to reality. The violation of this mixing assumption, however, may not be as serious as one might suppose (Rowe et al., 1989). More importantly, mathematical results are compatible with a plethora of social processes, such as peer pressure versus mere opportunity. The inability of models to distinguish the immediate social process is a source of frustration for those seeking solid answers in statistical results.

SUMMARY AND CONCLUSIONS

I suggest a paradigm shift away from parent-centered models of environmental transmission to models of greater generality. In practice, this shift means that studies of biological families should not be interpreted as presenting evidence for family environmental influences. It also means that researchers should routinely adopt the practice of including adoptee and other comparison groups when investigating childrearing "influence," and that more attention should be devoted to the biological bases of behavior.

My two illustrations demonstrate how efforts can be made to move to transmission models of greater generality. In the sibling effects model, a childrearing parameter was not included because such effects are very unlikely; we assume that by adolescence, most phenotypes are innocent of rearing influence until proven guilty through behavior genetic research designs. Nonetheless, we investigated other social influences—sibling effects through the incorporation of a sibling effects parameter and the division of the sample into pairs with and without mutual friends; and social norms, through the proxy variable of age. The model leads to a subtle conclusion that siblings who interact with brothers, sisters, or peers somewhat like themselves, will increase their rate of delinquent behavior in some proportion of their interactants' dispositions. Contrary to a view often in the peer literature that social selection and social influence are opposing processes, closer phenotypic matching of friends strengthens social influence.

The second model described the epidemic-like spread of adolescent social behaviors via horizontal transmission. The primacy of the peer group is directly acknowledged here; and model parameters capture the rate of spread in a particular group. The psychosocial interpretation of model parameters is worthy of further investigation.

In the policy area, the suggestion that improving family environments other than the very worst would change trait distributions should be taken with a grain of salt—the adoption data are extremely discouraging to this presumption. In interventions, greater emphasis should be given to the current environment, and to the process of peer-to-peer horizontal transmission of deviant behaviors. Applied research using experimental designs should be encouraged—because only well-controlled experimental studies with follow-ups can reliably indicate the strength of treatment effects. Finally, social learning theorists should become cognizant of cultural/genetic transmission models to enlarge their research perspectives. In conclusion, some mix of new ideas must emerge if we are to understand the bases of behavior: a social science that is more biological, and a biology that is more cultural.

ACKNOWLEDGMENT

The National Institute of Drug Abuse (DA06287) funded the Arizona Sibling Study and supported the preparation of this chapter.

REFERENCES

Bandura, A. (1977). *Social learning theory*. Englewood Cliffs, NJ: Prentice-Hall.
Bell, R. Q., & Harper, R. V. (1977). *Child effects on parents*. Hillsdale, NJ: Lawrence Erlbaum Associates.
Bouchard, T. J., Jr., Lykken, D. T., McGue, M., Segal, N. L., & Tellegen, A. (1990). Sources of human psychological differences: The Minnesota study of twins reared apart. *Science*, *250*, 223–228.
Bouchard, T. J., & Segal, N. L. (1985). Environment and IQ. In B. J. Wolman (Ed.), *Handbook of intelligence: Theories, measurements and applications* (pp. 391–464). New York: Wiley.
Boyd, R., & Richerson, P. J. (1985). *Culture and evolutionary process*. Chicago: University of Chicago Press.
Cavalli-Sforza, L. L., & Feldman, M. W. (1981). *Cultural transmission and evolution: A quantitative approach*. Princeton, NJ: Princeton University Press.
Daly, M., & Wilson, M. (1983). *Sex, evolution, and behavior* (2nd ed.). Boston: PSW Publishers.
Eaves, L. J., Eysenck, H. J., & Margin, N. G. (1989). *Genes, culture, and personality: An empirical approach*. San Diego, CA: Academic Press.

Eaves, L. J., Last, K. A., Young, P. A., & Martin, N. G. (1978). Model-fitting approaches to the analysis of human behavior. *Heredity, 41*, 249–320.

Eysenck, H. J. (1980). *The cause and effects of smoking.* London: M.T. Smith.

Goldsmith, H. H. (1983). Genetic influences on personality from infancy to adulthood. *Child Development, 54*, 331–335.

Gottfredson, M. R., & Hirschi, T. (1990). *A general theory of crime.* Stanford, CA: Stanford University Press.

Grilo, C. M., & Pogue-Geile, M. F. (1991). The nature of environmental influences on weight and obesity: A behavior genetic analysis. *Psychological Bulletin, 110*, 520–537.

Jessor, R. (1992). Risk behavior in adolescence: A psychosocial framework for understanding and action. In D. E. Rogers & E. Ginzberg (Eds.), *Adolescents at risk: Medical and social perspectives* (pp. 19–34). Boulder, CO: Westview Press.

Kummer, H. (1971). *Primate societies: Group techniques of ecological adaptation.* Chicago: Aldine-Atherton.

Locurto, C. (1990). The malleability of IQ as judged from adoption studies. *Intelligence, 14*, 275–292.

Loehlin, J. C., & Rowe, D. C. (1992). Genes, environment, and personality. In G. Caprara & G. L. Van Heck (Eds.), *Modern personality psychology: Critical reviews and new directions* (pp. 352–370). Herts, England: Harvester-Wheatsheaf.

Loehlin, J. C., Willerman, L., & Horn, J. M. (1988). Human behavior genetics. *Annual Review of Psychology, 39*, 101–133.

Lytton, H. (1990). Child and parent effects in boys' conduct disorder: A reinterpretation. *Developmental Psychology, 26*, 683–697.

Maccoby, E. E., & Martin, J. A. (1983). Socialization in the context of the family: Parent–child interaction. In P. H. Mussen (Series Ed.) & E. M. Hetherington (Vol. Ed.), *Handbook of child psychology: Vol. 4. Socialization, personality, and social development* (4th ed., pp. 1–101). New York: Wiley.

Perry, D. G., & Bussey, K. (1979). The social learning theory of sex differences. *Journal of Social and Personality Psychology, 37*, 1699–1712.

Plomin, R. (1986). *Development, genetics, and psychology.* Hillsdale, NJ: Lawrence Erlbaum Associates.

Plomin, R., & Bergeman, C. S. (1991). The nature of nurture: Genetic influences on "environmental" measures. *Behavioral and Brain Sciences, 14*, 373–427.

Plomin, R., & Daniels, D. (1987). Why are children in the same family so different from one another? *Behavioral and Brain Sciences, 10*, 1–16.

Plomin, R., DeFries, J. C., & Fulker, D. W. (1988). *Nature and nurture during infancy and early childhood.* Cambridge, England: Cambridge University Press.

Plomin, R., DeFries, J. C., & Loehlin, J. (1977). Genotype–environment interaction and correlation in the analysis of human behavior. *Psychological Bulletin, 84*, 309–322.

Plomin, R., Loehlin, J. C., & DeFries, J. C. (1985). Genetic and environmental components of "environmental" influences. *Developmental Psychology, 21*, 391–402.

Rowe, D. C. (1985). Sibling interaction and self-reported delinquent behavior: A study of 265 twin pairs. *Criminology, 23*, 223–240.

Rowe, D. C. (1987). Resolving the person–situation debate: Invitation to an interdisciplinary dialogue. *American Psychologist, 42*, 218–227.

Rowe, D. C, Chassin, L., Presson, C. C., Edwards, D., & Sherman, S. J. (1992). An "epidemic" model of adolescent cigarette smoking. *Journal of Applied Social Psychology, 22*, 261–285.

Rowe, D. C., & Plomin, R. (1981). The importance of nonshared (E^1) environmental influences in behavioral development. *Developmental Psychology, 17*, 517–531.

Rowe, D. C., & Rodgers, J. L. (1991a). Adolescent smoking and drinking: Are they epidemics? *Journal for Studies on Alcohol, 52*, 110–117.

Rowe, D. C., & Rodgers, J. L. (1991b). *Race differences in adolescent sexual behavior: Pubertal maturation effects.* Manuscript submitted for publication.

Rowe, D. C., & Rodgers, J. L. (1991c). An "epidemic" model of adolescent sexual intercourse: Applications to national survey data. *Journal of Biosocial Sciences, 23*, 211–219.

Rowe, D. C., Rodgers, J. L., & Meseck-Bushey, S. (1989) .An "epidemic" model of sexual intercourse prevalence for Black and White adolescents. *Social Biology, 36*, 127–145.

Saudino, K. J., & Eaton, W. 0. (1991). Infant temperament and genetics: An objective twin study of motor activity level. *Child Development, 62*, 1167–1174.

Scarr, S. (1991). The construction of family reality. *Behavioral and Brain Sciences, 14*, 403–404.

Scarr, S., & McCartney, K. (1983). How people make their own environments: A theory of genotype—>environment effects. *Child Development, 54*, 424–435.

Zuckerman, M. (1984). Sensation seeking: A comparative approach to a human trait. *Behavioral and Brain Sciences, 7*, 413–471.

8

Childhood Victimization and Adolescent Problem Behaviors

Cathy Spatz Widom
The State University of New York at Albany

Considerable uncertainty and debate remain about the extent of early childhood victimization. Even less is known about its impact on children and adolescents. For children who have been abused or neglected, the immediate consequences may involve physical injuries or psychological trauma. However, the emotional and developmental scars that these children receive may persist into adolescence and beyond. Because many other events in the child's life may mediate the effects of child abuse or neglect, the long-term consequences of early childhood victimization have been difficult to determine.

Researchers have begun to document the role of childhood victimization as a risk factor for later problem behaviors. Much has been written about the "cycle of violence" (Widom, 1989b, 1989c), and the relationship between childhood victimization and later delinquency and violence. This chapter focuses on the potential effects of childhood victimization on children's subsequent vulnerability to and risk for the development of a variety of adolescent problem behaviors.

Unlike adults, children lack the physical, financial, or legal power to escape from an abusive home environment or to eliminate problems associated with severe neglect. One set of responses available to children, however, may be engaging in deviant acts in adolescence. Theft, for example, may represent an attempt to gain some measure of financial independence, whereas aggression may be an attempt to control the environment, and running away and substance abuse may be forms of escape (Agnew, 1985). Some children may engage in early sexual activity, or sexually promiscuous behavior, in search of relationships. And others, rather than acting out, may direct their hurt and frustration inwardly, becoming depressed and engaging in self-destructive and suicidal behaviors.

The first part of this chapter briefly defines childhood victimization and reviews a number of methodological limitations characteristic of some research in the area. I then examine the connections between childhood victimization and six kinds of adolescent problem behaviors: delinquency and violence; running away from home; sexual promiscuity and teenage pregnancy; alcohol use and abuse; illicit drug use and abuse; and self-destructive behaviors, such as depression and suicide attempts. The third part speculates on potential mechanisms linking childhood victimization to later problem behaviors, and in the fourth part I describe a number of possible protective factors that might act to buffer some children from experiencing negative consequences of victimization during childhood. Finally, I draw conclusions and suggest directions for future research, policy, and interventions.

DEFINITIONS AND METHODOLOGICAL ISSUES

In the early 1960s, child abuse was labeled the *battered child syndrome* and defined as a clinical condition experienced by children who had been injured deliberately by physical assault by a parent or caretaker (Kempe, Silverman, Steele, Droegemueller, & Silver, 1962). Gradually, the terms *child abuse*, *child abuse and neglect*, *child maltreatment*, and *childhood victimization* have been used in place of the less encompassing term *battered child syndrome*. The Federal Child Abuse Prevention and Treatment Act of 1988 defines child abuse and neglect as "the physical or mental injury, sexual abuse or exploitation, negligent treatment, or maltreatment of a child by a person who is responsible for the child's welfare, under circumstances which indicate that the child's health or welfare is harmed or threatened." Using this definition, it was estimated that 1.6 million children in the United States experienced some form of abuse or neglect in 1986 (Sedlak, 1990). Furthermore, it is estimated that more than 1,000 children die each year under circumstances suggestive of parental maltreatment (Daro & McCurdy, 1991). Although the literature on childhood victimization deals with several distinct phenomena, including physical abuse, sexual abuse, neglect, severe physical punishment, and psychological maltreatment, this chapter focuses on the first four and only indirectly deals with psychological maltreatment. In interpreting the findings described in this chapter, the following definitions may be helpful. *Physical abuse* generally refers to incidents of striking, punching, kicking, biting, throwing, or burning a child. *Sexual abuse* covers a wide variety of behaviors from relatively nonspecific charges of "assault and battery with intent to gratify sexual desires" to more specific incidents involving fondling and touching, sodomy, and incest. *Neglect* refers to behavior that represents serious omission by parents or caretakers, for example, where there is a failure to provide children with needed food, clothing, shelter, medical attention, and protection from hazardous conditions.

Methodological Issues

Methodological limitations in the existing research make interpretation of findings from some studies ambiguous. For example, most research is primarily correlational in nature, with data collected at one point in time. Unfortunately, this poses two problems. First, many studies depend on retrospective accounts of childhood victimization. Studies based on retrospective accounts of childhood experiences may be open to a number of potential biases (Widom, 1988; Yarrow, Campbell, & Burton, 1970). For example, if asked to recall early childhood events, it is possible that respondents forget or redefine their behaviors in accord with later life circumstances and their current situation. It is also possible that a person might redefine someone else's behavior in light of current knowledge. Unconscious denial (or repression of traumatic events in childhood) also may be at work in preventing the recollection of severe cases of childhood abuse.

Second, correlational studies do not permit examination of causal sequences, introducing ambiguity in the temporal nature of the events. Although the majority of research is based on the assumption that childhood victimization leads to delinquency and other adolescent problem behaviors, it is possible that delinquency or adolescent problem behavior brings on abuse. For example, some runaway delinquents may come under the control of pornographers and pimps and thus these delinquents become susceptible to physical and sexual victimization by pimps and customers (Fisher, Weisberg, & Marotta, 1982, cited in Gray, Garbarino, & Plantz, 1986).

Research on childhood victimization is also often limited because of the use of designs that lack appropriate comparison or control groups. Much childhood victimization occurs in the context of multiproblem homes, and child abuse and/or neglect may be only one of the family's problems. The general effects of other family variables, such as poverty, unemployment, parental alcoholism or drug problems, or other inadequate social and family functioning, need to be disentangled from the specific effects of childhood abuse or neglect. Control groups matched on socioeconomic status (SES) and other relevant variables become necessary and vital components of this research, in order to determine the effect of childhood victimization on later behavior, independent of family and demographic characteristics frequently found to correlate with delinquency or other problem behaviors (Widom, 1989c). Similarly, Beitchman, Zucker, Hood, DaCosta, and Akman (1991) concluded that the child sexual abuse literature "has been vague in separating effects directly attributable to sexual abuse from effects that may be due to preexisting psychopathology in the child, family dysfunction, or to the stress associated with disclosure" (p. 538). Awareness of these methodological limitations is important when attempting to evaluate the strength of these research findings and when considering their policy relevance.

CHILDHOOD VICTIMIZATION AND ADOLESCENT PROBLEM BEHAVIORS

Delinquency

Much research has examined the relationship between childhood victimization and later delinquency (Widom, 1989c, 1991b). In prospective studies that follow up adolescents who had been abused or neglected as children, the incidence of delinquency is estimated to be about 20% (Widom, 1989c). In retrospective studies, where delinquents were asked about their early backgrounds, estimates of abuse ranged from approximately 8% to 26%. In general, research suggests that the majority of abused children do not become delinquent, and that the majority of delinquents are not abused as children. In at least one study (McCord, 1983), rejected male children had higher rates of delinquency than abused, neglected, or loved children.

In 1986, I began research to address the relationship between early child abuse and neglect and later delinquent and violent criminal behavior (see Widom, 1989a, for details of the design). In this cohorts design study, children who were abused and neglected approximately 20 years before were followed up through an examination of official criminal records and compared with a matched control group of children with no official records of abuse or neglect. Results indicated that early childhood victimization significantly increased a child's risk for an arrest during adolescence by more than 50% (26% vs. 17%). Abused and neglected children, furthermore, began their official criminal activity approximately 1 year earlier than the control subjects (16.5 vs. 17.3 years) and had approximately two times the number of arrests. Within each gender, early childhood victimization was associated with increased risk of arrest as a juvenile (prior to age 18), as compared to controls. For females, the risk of juvenile arrest increased from 11% to 19% (an increase of 73% for abused and neglected girls over controls), and for males, the increase was from 22% to 33% (a 50% increase in risk).

Violence

Almost 30 years ago, Curtis (1963) expressed the concern that abused and neglected children would "become tomorrow's murderers and perpetrators of other crimes of violence, if they survive" (p. 386). Subsequently, a number of small-scale, clinical reports involving case histories of violent or homicidal offenders in clinical settings described prior abuse in the family backgrounds of adolescents who attempted or succeeded in killing their parents. Easson and Steinhilber (1961), for example, provided clinical accounts of eight boys who had committed murderous assaults. Although all the boys were from socially normal families, two had a clear history of habitual brutal beatings by their parents, and the histories of three others led the authors to wonder if brutality to the child was being hidden. In another study of nine adolescent boys who had committed homicide as teenagers, King (1975) found that as children, they were subject to more beatings than their siblings. Sendi and Blomgren (1975), furthermore, compared case histories and current behavior of three groups of adolescents boys: 10 who had committed homicide; 10 who had threatened or attempted homicide; and a control group of 10 hospitalized adolescents. They found that both homicide groups were more likely than the hospitalized control adolescents to come from "unfavorable" home environments. The results of these and similar studies stimulated other researchers to examine more systematically the relationship between brutality and abuse in the family and a child's violent behavior.

Following the lead of these earlier clinical reports, a number of larger and more systematic studies explored the relationship between child abuse, neglect, and violent behavior. Some of these involved delinquents (Alfaro, 1981; Geller & Ford-Somma, 1984; Gutierres & Reich, 1981; Hartstone & Hansen, 1984; Kratcoski, 1982) and others involved groups of patients; many of these lacked control groups. Interestingly, findings were not consistent. Some studies provided strong support for the cycle of violence (Geller & Ford-Somma, 1984; Lewis, Shanok, Pincus, & Glaser, 1979; Lewis et al., 1985), whereas in others, the abused and nonabused delinquents did not differ (Kratcoski, 1982). In at least one study, abused delinquents were less likely to engage in later aggressive crimes (Gutierres & Reich, 1981). Fagan, Hansen, and Jang (1983) found low incidences of both child abuse and parental violence among violent juvenile offenders compared with nationwide rates. In most of the studies, the majority of abused children became neither delinquent nor violent offenders.

In their telephone survey of a nationally representative sample of more than 6,000 individuals (1985 Family Violence Resurvey), Straus and Gelles (1990) asked parents whether there were any special difficulties with the child during the past 12 months. They found that children who were reported to have experienced severe violence had higher rates of behavior problems (trouble making friends, temper tantrums, failing grades in school, disciplinary problems in school and at home, physically assaultive behavior at home and outside the home, vandalism and theft, and drinking and drug use) than other children in the survey. Regardless of social class or gender, children who were both victims of parental assault and witnesses of parental assault were much more likely to assault a nonfamily member than children from nonassaultive families.

In my own research described earlier, abused and neglected children did not have significantly higher rates of arrest for violent crimes as juveniles than controls (4% vs. 3%), although there was a surprising trend for abused and/or neglected females (but not males) to be at increased risk of arrest for violent crimes during adolescence (Widom, 1991b). Based on the cycle of violence hypothesis (Widom, 1989b), one would expect that childhood victims of physical abuse would be at increased risk for becoming violent juvenile offenders. Table 8.1 presents the percentages of arrests for juvenile violent offenses by type of childhood victimization. Overall, children who were neglected had the highest arrest rates for violence. The pattern for females is different from that of the males, however. Physically abused females had the highest arrest rates for violent offenses, compared to other abused and/or neglected females and controls.

TABLE 8.1
Violent Arrest as a Juvenile as a Function of Type of Abuse (in Percent)

	Controls	Abuse/ Neglect	Sex Only	Sex Plus	Physical & Neglect	Physical Only	Neglect Only
N	667	908	125	28	70	76	609
Overall[a]	2.8	4.2	1.6	3.6	0.0	3.9	5.3
Males[b]	5.4	6.5	—	—	—	2.1	8.4
Females[c]	0.3	1.9	1.9	4.3	—	6.9	1.4

Note. [a]$\chi^2(5) = 9.92$, $p < .10$.
[b]$\chi^2(5) = 8.97$, ns.
[c]$\chi^2(5) = 12.52$, $p < .05$.

Although it is commonplace to compare gender differences in the extent and types of delinquency (e.g., Geller & Ford-Somma, 1984; Hamparian, Schuster, Dinitz, & Conrad, 1978; Strasburg, 1978), surprisingly little research has compared the consequences of abuse and neglect on males and females separately. If gender differences exist, do they parallel gender differences in socialization experiences, reflecting perhaps a basic gender difference with respect to the expression of aggression? Because males and females are not necessarily subject to the same forms of maltreatment (Adams-Tucker, 1982; Gutierres & Reich, 1981), to what extent are these factors taken into account in studying outcomes?

The few studies that examine males and females separately have produced inconsistent results. In Alfaro's (1981) 1950s sample of children referred to child protection services for suspected child abuse or neglect, a higher percentage of boys were later reported to family court as delinquent. On the other hand, this is complicated because in the other half of the Alfaro investigation—the reverse records check of juveniles reported as delinquents or ungovernable in the early 1970s—21% of the boys and 29% of the girls had been reported, when younger, as abused or neglected. The fact that the association between maltreatment and delinquency was higher in the girls may in part reflect a gender differential in processing within the juvenile justice system. A generalized tendency to be more lenient toward girls in trouble would thus result in a higher incidence of family pathology—including a history of abuse or neglect—in any sample of delinquent or ungovernable girls.

In my research, abused and neglected females tended to be at greater risk for violent juvenile offending than control females, whereas the same pattern was not found in males (Widom, 1991b). However, because these findings are based on official criminal records, it is possible that these differences represent spurious findings, or that they are related to increased surveillance of abused and neglected females by the juvenile justice system. Despite these cautions, it is important to understand the future violence potential of females as well as males. Because these results are somewhat different than those for adult arrest outcomes (Rivera & Widom, 1990; Widom, 1989a), research that covers the life span is needed to provide a picture of continuity and discontinuity in these patterns.

In summary, the results of recent research convincingly demonstrate that early childhood victimization increases risk for males and females of becoming a delinquent adolescent, but not necessarily a violent delinquent. There may also be gender differences in the pattern of consequences and life trajectories that need to be explored. The majority of abused and neglected children in these studies did not become delinquent or violent. Thus, although early abuse and neglect may place children in a negative life trajectory, the relationship between childhood victimization and later antisocial and criminal behavior is far from inevitable. Another type of adolescent problem behavior associated with childhood victimization takes the form of running away from home. In the next section, I examine the extent to which existing research supports this relationship.

Runaways

Pagelow (1984) noted that a growing number of professionals who work with status offenders or delinquents increasingly recognized that "many runaway children are not running toward something, but rather are running away from something—a home life in which they were subject to abuse, particularly sexual abuse" (p. 49). Running away may serve an adaptive function for children who are being abused at home. To what extent do current research findings indicate that being abused or neglected in childhood places one at high risk for running away as an adolescent?

Based on data from the *1975 National Statistical Survey on Runaway Youth* (Office of Youth Development, 1976), it was estimated that approximately 1.25 million youths run away each year and that about 9% to 12% of U.S. children run away from home at least once. A more recent survey (Finkelhor, Hotaling, & Sedlak, 1990) estimated that 446,700 children ran away from households and 4,000 ran from juvenile facilities in 1988.[1] Interestingly, this study did not find evidence of a higher level of running away in 1988 as compared to the results from the *1975 National Statistical Survey on Runaway Youth,* which used similar definitions and methodology. Both surveys found almost exactly the same rate of running away from households.

Only a handful of studies have attempted to describe the extent to which adolescents who run away report having been abused or report having run away because of abuse. In two studies, sexual abuse victims were found to have run away from home more often during adolescence than clinical controls (Herman, 1981; Meiselman, 1978). In the *1975 National Statistical Survey on Runaway Youth,* 5% of the runaway youths indicated that physical abuse by an adult had been a major impetus for their running away (Office of Youth Development, 1976). Among a study of 308 adolescents served by a runaway program in Connecticut, approximately 12% reported that they left home because of abuse (Gullotta, 1977, cited in Gray, 1986). In the 1988 national survey of *Missing, Abducted, Runaway, and Thrownaway Children in the United States,* approximately 3% of the runaways reported having been sexually abused and 1% physically harmed (Finkelhor et al., 1990). About 30% of the runaways from juvenile facilities were picked up by the police and some were involved in prostitution (5%), drug dealing (3%), armed robbery (3%), and other crimes. In contrast to these relatively small percents, 75% of the youths in a runaway shelter in Ohio reported having experienced physical maltreatment (McCoard, 1983).

In a New York City Police Department study (Ryan, 1987), 168 runaways from outside the New York City area were interviewed. The majority of these were female, White, and about 15–16 years old. Of 116 respondents, 35% reported that their home environment was either too strict or too overprotective, 19% reported

---

[1]These figures are based on a broad definition of *runaways* that included children who left home without permission and stayed away overnight. There were an estimated 133,500 runaways from household and juvenile facilities in 1988 using a more restricted definition (children who had run away from home and had no familiar and secure place to stay; Finkelhor et al., 1990).

that they were emotionally or physically neglected, and another 18% stated that there was continuing conflict with family members. The study found that the "most significant personal reason given for running away from home was that they could not get along with someone in the family unit" (p. 5). Of these runaways, 40% became involved in prostitution; some because they were recruited by a pimp (14%) and others in the context of panhandling as a means of survival (19%). A number of the runaways reported personal victimization—being robbed or sexually or physically abused—after they had run away.

The results of these retrospective studies suggest that there may be a link between childhood victimization and running away. Nevertheless, these study designs do not include control groups, thus we do not know the proportion of children who run away even without abusive or neglectful experiences in their homes. Using a prospective design, and tracing official criminal histories for a large sample of abused and neglected children and matched controls, I found direct support for the hypothesized relationship between early childhood victimization and adolescent running away (Widom, 1991b). Specifically, as adolescents (before age 18), male and female abused and neglected children were significantly more likely to have an arrest as a runaway than controls (5.8% vs. 2.4%). Interestingly, the percent of these abused and/or neglected children who had official contact with the system (as in arrests) was still small, and similar to the percentages in the studies of runaways who reported a history of childhood victimization.

In summary, although the evidence is not as strong as one would wish, victims of early childhood victimization appear at increased risk of running away from home and being picked up by the police. However, from national surveys in which runaways were asked about their early childhood histories, the majority of runaways do not report having been sexually or physically abused prior to their running away. Likewise, based on data from my prospective cohorts study comparing abused and neglected children with controls, one can conclude that abused and/or neglected children are at increased risk for being picked up by the police for running away. However, the majority of abused and/or neglected children were not runaways.

This research illustrates the importance of examining the consequences of childhood victimization in a temporal (and preferably longitudinal) perspective. This hypothesized linkage between early childhood victimization and later running away warrants further examination because it may shed light on at least one of the pathways to problem behaviors and on possible intervention points. In the case of children who run away, delinquent behavior seen during adolescence may represent an adaptive response to an abusive home situation. For these children, one might speculate that the long-term consequences may be different for children who do not manifest this type of acting out during adolescence. At the same time, the effects of early abusive experiences may be manifest in ways not related to delinquency or running away, but may lie in more subtle manifestations of emotional damage such as low self-esteem, depression, withdrawal, or, in the extreme, suicide. Thus, it is important to examine alternative adolescent problems that may be related to early childhood victimization. Sexual promiscuity and teenage pregnancy are examples of other possible outcomes.

Sexual Promiscuity and Teenage Pregnancy

It is generally believed by clinicians and researchers that there is a connection between childhood sexual abuse and sexually promiscuous or dysfunctional behavior in adolescence. A number of researchers have described a relationship between childhood sexual abuse and sexual dysfunction and promiscuity (Courtois, 1979; DeYoung, 1982; Finkelhor, 1979; Finkelhor, Hotaling, Lewis, & Smith, 1989; Herman & Hirschman, 1977), sex offenses (Becker, Kaplan, Cunningham-Rathner, & Kavoussi, 1986; Fehrenbach, Smith, Monastersky, & Deisher, 1986; Groth, 1979; Seghorn, Prentky, & Boucher, 1987), and prostitution (Allen, 1980; Burgess, Hartman, & McCormack, 1987; Greenwald, 1970; James & Meyerding, 1977; Silbert & Pines, 1981). However, because these studies vary in methodological rigor, empirical support for a causal relationship between sexual abuse and sexual dysfunction and promiscuity may not yet justify the widespread acceptance of this relationship. Indeed, in a review of research on the impact of child sexual abuse, Browne and Finkelhor (1986) cautioned that "Although clinical literature suggests that sexual abuse during childhood plays a role in the development of other problems ranging from anorexia nervosa to prostitution, empirical evidence about its actual effects is sparse" (p.66).

Based on past literature, one would expect that victims of childhood sexual abuse would be more likely than nonvictims to become prostitutes. For example, we have found that in comparison to victims of other types of child abuse and neglect, childhood sexual abuse victims as adolescents were not more likely to have an arrest for sex crimes, which would include prostitution (Widom & Ames, 1994). It is, however, important to note that this analysis is based on the number of arrests, which reflects only a fraction of the actual occurrences of prostitution in the United States (Sheehy, 1971). Similarly, many children run away without being picked up by the police and, even if picked up by the police, a record may or may not be made of an arrest.

Another body of research has examined general patterns of sexual behavior in relation to sexual victimization. Based on this broader literature, and despite a paucity of specific relevant research, it is generally believed that female victims of child sexual abuse are at increased risk of becoming pregnant as teenagers. Teenage pregnancy is an important outcome variable because of the supposed link between premature parenting and inadequate childrearing practices, thus, perpetuating the cycle of abuse from one generation to the next.

In a review of this literature, Bohigan (1989) concluded that existing research had not yet clearly established a relationship between child sexual abuse and adolescent pregnancy. One difficulty in interpreting this literature is that a teenager's pregnancy may have resulted from forced sexual intercourse or from promiscuity or irresponsible contraceptive protection following a history of sexual abuse (Gershenson et al., 1989). In a review of 29 studies that gathered data on fertility outcomes of maltreating families, Zuravin and Taylor (1987) concluded that neglectful families had more children than abusive families and begin bearing children at an earlier age. Zuravin (1988), for example, found that "abusive and neglectful mothers compared to control mothers space their first two children closer in years, have their first child at a younger age, and have more live births, more unplanned live births, and more children by different fathers" (p. 988).

Although there is some correlational evidence that victims of childhood abuse may have increased vulnerability to become sexually promiscuous and at increased risk for teenage pregnancy, existing research provides only minimal support. Current knowledge of the extent and nature of these relationships is ambiguous at best. In particular, research is needed to clarify and extend our knowledge about possible causal relationships between childhood victimization (particularly sexual abuse) and adolescent pregnancy, while controlling for appropriate demographic variables.

Alcohol Problems

Most of the literature relating alcohol problems to child victimization focuses on parents' alcohol abuse as a risk factor for child abuse and neglect, with a majority of studies simply noting the co-occurrence of child abuse and alcohol problems in families (Behling, 1979; Gil, 1973; Johnson & Morse, 1978; Young, 1964). Even so, reviewers of this research have concluded that there was no adequate empirical basis to support an association between family alcohol problems and child abuse (Orme & Rimmer, 1981) and that the results of these studies were contradictory (Hamilton & Collins, 1982). When estimates of alcoholism and alcohol problems in the general population were taken into account, the prevalence appeared to be almost identical in those groups to the rates found in child abusers. More recently, Famularo, Stone, Barnum, and Wharton (1986) found a significant overrepresentation of alcoholism in a maltreating parent population (mothers and fathers who had lost custody of their children by court order because of abuse and neglect) compared to parents of children in a pediatric hospital.

Similar to escaping from an abusive home environment by running away, alcohol use may serve as a coping strategy adopted by abused and neglected children to help them deal with their early childhood trauma and to distance themselves from the painful realities they experienced (Ireland & Widom, 1991). For victimized children, alcohol use may serve a number of possible functions: (a) to provide emotional and/or psychological escape from an abusive and aversive environment, (b) to serve as a form of self-medication in which the child tries to gain control over his or her negative life experiences, (c) to act as a form of self-enhancement to improve the child's self-esteem, or (d) to reduce feelings of isolation and loneliness.

Despite these plausible explanations for an hypothesized association between childhood victimization and adolescent alcohol problems, only minimal supporting evidence is available. In one study, Dembo et al. (1990) examined the relationship between alcohol use and emotional/psychological functioning in a cohort of high-risk youth (detained juveniles approximately 16 years old at first testing). Using structural equation modeling to test a number of hypothesized effects, Dembo and his colleagues found that physical abuse was significantly related to alcohol use prior to the initial interview. However, neither physical abuse nor sexual victimization was associated with the use of alcohol during the follow-up period about 1 year later.

Because much child abuse that occurs is committed by biological parents, in examining the relationship between childhood victimization and the child's subsequent risk for alcohol problems, it is important to recognize the potential contribution of familial factors. Some research suggests that children of parents with alcohol problems are generally at increased risk for the development of alcohol problems (Goodwin, Schulsinger, Hermansen, Guze, & Winokur, 1973; Goodwin, Schulsinger, Knop, Mednick, & Guze, 1977; Russell, Henderson, & Blume, 1985; Schuckit, 1986a). Thus, if parents with alcohol problems are more likely to abuse or neglect their children, then, there are multiple reasons for hypothesizing that their offspring will be at increased risk for the development of alcohol problems. This complexity is illustrated by research by Kroll, Stock, and James (1985), on a sample of adult alcoholic men, who found that the abusing parent in the childhood of the abused men was almost always the natural father (90%), who was alcoholic (83%). Given that there may be some genetic basis for alcoholism, research is needed to disentangle the effects of a genetic predisposition from the effects of an abusive or neglectful home environment.

Illicit Drug Use or Abuse

Reasons similar to those used in hypothesizing an increased vulnerability of childhood victims to alcohol use in adolescence have been used to speculate on a possible increased risk for illicit drug use or abuse in adolescence by abused and/or neglected children. If a child perceives running away as an unrealistic option, then, illicit drug use may serve as a form of emotional and/or psychological escape. Illicit drug use may also serve as a form of self-medication in which the child attempts to control sensations of aversion (Cavaiola & Schiff 1989; Harrison, Hoffmann, & Edwall 1989a; Singer, Petchers, & Hussey 1989). Or, adolescent illicit drug use may be the result of a need for self-enhancement, and may serve to make the adolescent feel better by improving his or her self-esteem (Dembo, LaVoie, Schmeidler, & Washburn, 1987; Dembo et al., 1989). Drugs may also be used to reduce feelings of isolation and loneliness, by providing the adolescent with a peer group, as he or she becomes part of the drug culture (Singer et al., 1989).

In contrast to the sparse literature on adolescent alcohol problems and childhood victimization, several studies provide empirical support for a relationship between childhood victimization and adolescent substance abuse (Benward & Densen-Gerber, 1975; Cavaiola & Schiff, 1989; Dembo et al., 1987, 1989; Gomes-Schwartz, Horowitz, & Sauzier, 1985; Harrison, Hoffmann, & Edwall, 1989a, 1989b; Lindberg & Distad, 1985; Runtz & Briere, 1986; Sansonnet-Hayden, Haley, Marriage, & Fine, 1987; Singer et al., 1989), although the results of this research are not totally consistent. For example, Goldston, Turnquist, and Knutson (1989) found that drug abuse was more common among control group girls than sexually abused girls, and that four other indices of problem behaviors did not differentiate the two groups. In another study of 444 adolescent girls admitted to chemical dependency treatment programs, Harrison et al. (1989a) found that sexually abused girls did not differ in the overall prevalence or frequency of substance use from nonvictims, although the victims were more likely to report regular use of particular drugs, and to report an earlier age of onset of drug use, more self-medication, and more drug use to escape family problems. Based on these findings with girls, Harrison et al. (1989a) suggested that the earlier entry into substance use by these sexual abuse victims supports the self-medication hypothesis, rather than motivations associated with peer pressure. In a second study with adolescent males in a chemical dependency treatment program, the same authors (Harrison et al., 1989b) found that male victims of sexual abuse used a wider variety of drugs than nonvictims and used more drugs to self-medicate. They did not find the same results with boys in regard to age of onset of drug use. These gender differences may be related to differences in socialization experiences, to age-related patterns of drug use, or to actual differences in age of onset of drug behavior (Colten & Marsh, 1984).

Most studies of the association between illicit drug use and childhood victimization have focused on sexually abused children in clinical settings or in detention facilities. With some exceptions, these studies are cross-sectional in design, include information about childhood abuse experiences based on retrospective self-reports, and do not utilize control groups. Although there may be some connections between childhood victimization and later illicit drug use, given the limitations of existing research, some caution should be used in attributing a causal connection between childhood victimization and adolescent substance use or abuse.

Self-Destructive Behavior, Depression, and Suicide Attempts

Given the pervasive acceptance of the hypothesis that violence begets violence, it is not surprising that much of the work in this area has focused on aggression and violence. However, a number of writers have suggested that severe abuse or neglect in childhood also is related to self-destructive behavior (Gutierres & Reich, 1981), withdrawal (George & Main, 1979; Kagan, 1977; Martin & Beezley, 1977), suicide (Green, 1978), and depression (Allen & Tarnowski, 1989; Kazdin, Moser, Colbus, & Bell, 1985). Thus, not only might abused and neglected children be destructive and abusive toward others, but they may also be damaging to themselves (see Widom, 1989c).

Although this body of work is not extensive, some abused and neglected children appear to engage in self-abusive and self-destructive behavior in adolescence. Green (1978), for example, found that a group of 59 physically abused children, ages 5–12, had a higher incidence of suicide attempts and self-mutilation than a group of neglected but nonabused children and a group of normal controls.

Lindberg and Distad's (1985) study of 27 adolescents with incest histories found that one third had attempted suicide.

Studies of clinic (Kazdin et al., 1985) and nonclinic (Allen & Tarnowski, 1989) samples have found that children with a history of physical abuse are more likely than other children to exhibit depressive symptomatology. Sansonnet-Hayden et al. (1987) found that depressive symptoms and schizoid/psychotic symptoms (hallucinations) significantly differentiated adolescent inpatients with a history of sexual abuse from those with no history of sexual abuse, although it was not clear whether these behaviors came before or after the abusive experiences. In a more recent investigation involving prepubescent (ages 7 to 12) maltreated children, Kaufman (1991) found that a disproportionate number of the maltreated children met the diagnostic criteria for one of the major affective disorders. Overall, 18% of the sample met the criteria for major depression, and 25% met the criteria for dysthymia.

The clinical literature in adults who report a history of childhood abuse implicate depression and suicide attempts. This small body of research also suggests that abused and neglected children exhibit depressive symptomatology and suicide attempts in childhood and early adolescence. Further research appears warranted to systematically assess the extent to which this self-destructive and negative life trajectory characterizes abused and neglected children.

Summary

Victims of child abuse and/or neglect are at increased risk for delinquency and running away. However, existing research indicates that the relationship is not inevitable, because the majority of childhood victims do not manifest these problem behaviors. Significantly less is known about connections between childhood victimization and other problem behaviors, such as teenage pregnancy, alcohol and illicit drug use and abuse, and self-destructive behavior. Current knowledge about these outcomes is sparse and only suggestive. Further research is desperately needed to document whether abused and/or neglected children are at increased risk for these adolescent problem behaviors, in comparison to control children and adolescents, and to indicate the extent or magnitude of these relationships. Despite the paucity of research, one can still speculate on some of the potential mechanisms that may link childhood victimization and adolescent problem behaviors.

POTENTIAL MECHANISMS LINKING CHILDHOOD VICTIMIZATION AND ADOLESCENT PROBLEM BEHAVIORS

Considering the variety of adolescent problem behaviors potentially linked to childhood victimization, it is very likely that there are multiple pathways by which these early stressful and abusive life experiences influence behavior and increase risk for problem behaviors. Rutter's (1983) discussion of ways in which early stressful experiences may be linked to disorders some years later provides a useful analogy and has influenced this discussion. A number of possible mechanisms linking childhood victimization with problematic or dysfunctional behaviors in adolescence are outlined here. The first four of these potential mechanisms stem from developments within the child, whereas the last two result from external influences. Child abuse and/or neglect may not directly cause problem behaviors, but rather these outcomes may be an indirect by-product of these early experiences.

1. *Childhood victimization may lead to immediate sequelae that then have an irremediable effect on the subsequent development of the child.* A child does not need to be struck on the head to sustain brain injuries. Dykes (1986) described infants who were shaken so vigorously that they sustained intracranial and intraocular bleeding with no signs of external trauma. Being abused or neglected as a child may result in brain dysfunction as a result of direct brain injury or as a result of malnutrition. These forms of physical abuse (e.g., battering) or severe neglect (e.g., dehydration, diarrhea, and failure to thrive) may lead to developmental retardation that, in turn, may affect school performance and behavior (e.g., truancy). Some empirical support is provided by a study of Barbadian children by Galler, Ramsey, Solimano, and Lowell (1983) who found that malnourished children ages 5–11 years old had significantly lower IQ scores than a matched control group. The malnourished children also exhibited more attention deficits, poorer social skills, and less emotional stability, in comparison to the controls.

2. *Experiences of early childhood victimization may lead to bodily changes that influence a child's vulnerability to certain adolescent problem behaviors.* For example, as a direct result of being beaten continually, or as a result of severe stress associated with the abuse or neglect, a child might become "desensitized" to future painful or anxiety-provoking experiences. This desensitization might decrease the child's emotional and physiological responsiveness to the needs of others, or cause the child to suppress or deny, and then internalize negative feelings. Desensitization might also work to protect the individual from aversive life events in later life; however, whether desensitization occurs and serves a positive or negative function remains an unstudied empirical question.

One possible mechanism underlying this type of bodily change may be related to stress, which if occurring during critical periods of development, may give rise to abnormal brain chemistry that may lead to aggressive behavior at later points in life (Eichelman, 1990). For example, rats stressed by being immobilized for several hours a day for a period of 1 month displayed increased aggressive behavior and increased tyrosine hydroxylase in the hypothalamus long after the stress had been discontinued (Lamprecht, Eichelman, Thoa, Williams, & Kopin, 1972).

It is also possible that the link between childhood victimization and certain later behaviors are in part mediated through an effect on the serotonin system. Based on research findings from studies of nonhuman primates, Suomi, Higley, and their colleagues suggested that rearing experiences may be associated with changes in central nervous system neurotransmitter activity in both norepinephrine and serotonin monamine systems (Higley & Suomi, 1989). Research findings indicate that rearing conditions affect reactivity, and that, in turn, influences levels of both norepinephrine and serotonin (Higley, Melman, & Taub, 1991). Peer-reared monkeys (a laboratory analogue to being neglected or reared without parental figures) showed aggressive behavior and low levels of 5-HIAA (a crude indicator of serotonin turnover) and consumed significantly more alcohol than mother-reared controls (Higley, Hasert, Suomi, & Linnoila, in press). Although the extent to which findings from this work on nonhuman primates can be generalized to humans is not known, this research with nonhuman primates holds promise for understanding individual differences in reactivity and behavior. This research may be particularly useful to examine mechanisms by which childhood victimization leads to later dysfunctional behavior given the ethical constraints of research with humans.

3. *Abuse and/or neglect may encourage the development of certain styles of coping that may be maladaptive.* For example, childhood victimization might lead to the development of impulsive behavioral styles that, in turn, lead to deficiencies in problem-solving skills or inadequate school or occupational performance. Childhood victims, especially incest victims, may learn to "tune out" or dissociate during abuse experiences and may generalize this process to other relationships (Herman & Hirschman, 1977). Furthermore, adaptations that may be functional at one point in development (avoiding an abusive parent or desensitizing oneself against feelings) may later compromise the person's ability to draw upon and respond to the environment in an adaptive and flexible way. For example, early child abuse and neglect may lead directly to altered patterns of behavior that, in place in rudimentary form during early childhood, become manifest only some years later. Disordered patterns of adaptation may lay dormant, only to be manifest during times of increased stress or in conjunction with particular circumstances (Sroufe & Rutter, 1984).

In a series of studies with nonhuman primates, Suomi, Higley, and colleagues showed that differences between peer-only reared monkeys (reared for the first 30 days in neonatal nurseries with or without terry cloth surrogate mothers) and mother-reared monkeys was most dramatic under challenges such as exposure to novel sounds or the appearance of a stranger. Even as adults, peer-only reared monkeys, when exposed to novel situations, or social separation, were more likely to show behaviors characteristic of anxiety. Furthermore, under the stressor of a new baby, these at risk peer-only reared monkeys were more likely to reject or neglect their first offspring (Suomi & Ripp, 1983).

Although the extent to which one can generalize from this research with nonhuman primates to humans is questionable, the striking similarities between the concepts operationalized in the nonhuman primate literature (stress, anxiety, and rearing conditions of neglect) and the concepts of interest in the child development literature (cf. Crittendon & Ainsworth, 1989) invite serious consideration. Animal analogue studies permit control of environments and monitoring of outcomes, and experimental manipulations that are obviously not possible with humans.

4. *Early childhood victimization may alter the child's self-concept, attitudes, or attributional styles that, in turn, may influence the adolescent's response to later situations.* For example, the clinical literature has identified low self-esteem as one of the major characteristics of childhood victims (Bagley & Ramsay, 1986; Courtois, 1979; Herman, 1981). Lowered self-esteem may result from childhood

victimization directly, by the child's feelings of low self-worth, derived from the idea that he or she was somehow responsible for the abuse or neglect. Low self-esteem may also be indirectly related to abuse and neglect as a by-product of lowered cognitive functioning, poor social and interpersonal skills. Although dysfunctional behaviors (such as running away) may serve as an escape mechanism for abused and neglected children, these surface solutions to problems at one stage may lead ultimately to other more deeply entrenched problems at later ages.

In a similar way, other researchers have argued that the experience of physical abuse leads to chronic aggressive behavior by having an impact on the development of social information-processing patterns (Dodge et al., 1990). Essentially, these authors argue that the experience of severe physical harm is associated with later violent behavior through the "acquisition of a set of biased and deficient patterns of processing social provocative information" (p. 1679). Dodge et al. (1990) found that physically harmed 4-year-old children showed deviant patterns of processing social information at age 5 and that these patterns were related to aggressive behavior. The physically harmed children (relative to nonphysically harmed children) were significantly less attentive to relevant social cues, more biased toward attributing hostile intent, and less likely to generate competent solutions to personal problems.

5. *Child abuse and/or neglect may lead to changed environments or family conditions that, in turn, may increase risk for delinquency or other problem behaviors.* In this way, adolescent problem behaviors may result not so much from the victimization experience per se, but instead as a result of a chain of events occurring subsequent to the victimization. For example, being taken away from one's biological parents, subsequent to the abuse and neglect incident(s), and placed in foster care can be associated with deleterious effects (Bohman & Sigvardsson, 1980; Bryce & Ehlert, 1977; Canning, 1974; Frank, 1980; Littner, 1974).

6. *The observed relationship between early childhood victimization and problem behaviors in adolescence may be in part a function of juvenile justice system practices that disproportionately label and adjudicate maltreatment victims as juvenile offenders (Smith, Berkman, & Fraser, 1980).* In reviewing the literature on the relationship between child maltreatment and delinquency, Garbarino and Plantz (1986) suggested that delinquency may be one eventual consequence of maltreatment because some of the behavioral responses to maltreatment are officially defined as delinquent. As an example, they cited the child who becomes estranged from his or her parents or from prosocial peers and who then develops friendships with antisocial friends. In turn, this association with delinquent friends leads to the adoption of a highly visible delinquent lifestyle.

In summary, the processes linking childhood victimization with later negative consequences may have an immediate impact or a delayed outcome, manifest only some time later. Childhood victimization very likely interacts with aspects of the child's environment to determine outcomes. Thus, it is possible that only in conjunction with characteristics associated with abusive and/or neglectful families (poverty, unemployment, stress, or alcohol and drug problems) do adolescent problem behaviors occur. Research is needed to disentangle some of these undoubtedly complex relationships.

Although less is known than we would wish about the long-term consequences of childhood victimization and the processes linking child abuse and neglect with later problem behaviors, one of the emerging findings is that a substantial portion of abused and/or neglected children do not appear to manifest negative outcomes. It would be premature to conclude that the majority of abused and/or neglected children do not show problem behaviors in adolescence on the basis of the existing literature; however, given some of the findings, it certainly seems appropriate to speculate on what might make a difference for some of these children. Some ways of handling or responding to potentially traumatic experiences of child abuse or neglect might lead to better outcomes for that child. The next section discusses possible mediating variables (attributes and experiences) that may act to buffer abused and neglected children from the dysfunctional outcomes that characterize many of these children.

POTENTIAL PROTECTIVE FACTORS

Abused and neglected children appear at risk of manifesting a variety of adolescent problem behaviors. It is becoming increasingly recognized, however, that not all abused and neglected children grow up to become delinquents or violent adolescents, or to have alcohol or drug problems, or to become prostitutes or pregnant as teenagers. Whereas some children follow a direct pathway between childhood victimization and adolescent problem behaviors, others do not. Garmezy (1981) called attention to the role of protective factors—those dispositional attributes, environmental conditions, biological predispositions, and positive events that can act to mitigate against early negative experiences. In the previous section, I speculated on a number of mechanisms that might explain why childhood victims may be vulnerable to adolescent problem behaviors. In this section, I discuss potential protective factors (characteristics of the child or life experiences) that may act as buffers against long-term negative consequences.

Intelligence

High intelligence and good scholastic attainment may exert a protective effect in the context of an abusive environment. Intelligence may play a direct role or it may operate as a protective influence mediating such other factors as school performance, problem-solving skills (Shure & Spivack, 1979), or levels of self-esteem, which may then be related to levels of involvement in problem behaviors. There is evidence to suggest that lower levels of intelligence are related to higher rates of delinquency (Wilson & Herrnstein, 1985). Some interpret this increased risk as an example of the problems faced by children from educationally deprived backgrounds. However, Moffit, Gabrielli, Mednick, and Schulsinger (1981) found a negative relationship between IQ and delinquency, while controlling for socioeconomic status. They suggest that "low IQ children may be likely to engage in delinquent behavior because their poor verbal abilities limit their opportunities to obtain rewards in the school environment" (p. 152). In their longitudinal study of nearly 700 children in Hawaii, followed from birth to age 18, Werner and Smith (1982; Werner, 1983) found that low intelligence was among the most important precursors of offending.

Frodi and Smetana (1984) found that controlling for IQ eliminates differences between maltreated and nonmaltreated children in their ability to discriminate emotions. Furthermore, high IQ children have been found to maintain good achievement test performance at both low and high levels of stress, whereas low IQ children show a drop in performance under high stress (Garmezy, Masten, & Tellegen, 1984). This research suggests that the relationship between childhood victimization and IQ may be direct, and that other problem behaviors may be by-products of decreased cognitive and intellectual functioning (cf. Dodge, Bates, & Pettit, 1990), that is, indirect effects of childhood victimization. One can also speculate that children with high intelligence may be perceived as more appealing to teachers in school, receive more attention from the teacher, and develop close relationships. In turn, these bonds with teachers might serve to minimize proclivities toward truancy and dropping out of school, both of which are early precursors of delinquency. Unfortunately, the role of intelligence as a mediator between childhood victimization and adolescent problem behaviors is not well understood at present.

Temperament

Despite problems with the concept and measurement of temperament (Bates, 1980), there is evidence that infants and young children with different temperaments may elicit different parental behaviors (Bates, 1989). In some cases, temperament may protect the child; whereas in others, temperament may place the child at risk by virtue of its negative effects on parent–child interactions (Dunn, 1980; Keogh & Pullis, 1980). There is some support for the notion that children with difficult temperaments are singled out for abuse (e.g., Friedrich & Boriskin, 1976). For example, Herrenkohl and Herrenkohl (1981) found that victims of physical abuse tend to be described by their mothers as being "difficult" children. However, other researchers have not found this to be the case (e.g., Dodge et al., 1990; Silver, Dublin, & Lourie, 1969).

Findings from the Cambridge Study in Delinquent Development (Farrington, Gallagher, Morley, St. Ledger, & West, 1988) are of relevance here, although the boys in this study were not abused or neglected. Of the 411 London males in this prospective longitudinal study, Farrington et al. defined a "vulnerable" group of 63 boys from criminogenic backgrounds on the basis of nonbehavior predictors of delinquency at ages 8–10. Following these males to age 32, Farrington and his colleagues found that temperament (neurotic at age 10) was one of the characteristics predictive of the more successful men (absence of convictions and other deviant behavior; good adjustment and employment history). These findings are consistent with those of Olweus (1980) who found that one of the four factors that explained a considerable amount of variance in his sample of Norwegian boys' habitual levels of aggression was temperament. Furthermore, the more negative childhood conditions boys were exposed to and the more active and hotheaded their temperaments, the more likely they were to exhibit aggressive behavior in adolescence.

Temperament most likely interacts with early childhood experiences to exacerbate in some cases, or to minimize in other cases, a child's level of risk for the development of adolescent problem behaviors. In an analysis of characteristics associated with the avoidance of delinquency in abused and neglected children, Widom (1991a) found that a small group of children ($n = 51$, 6.6%) who had indications of early behavior problems in their records,[2] were more likely to have extensive criminal histories as adolescents than other abused and/or neglected children. In contrast to the abused and neglected children with no mention of behavior problems in childhood, children with a history of behavior problems were over eight times as likely to be arrested.

Cognitive Appraisal of Events

One might assume that child abuse and/or neglect are straightforward, objectively definable events amenable to empirical investigation without consideration of the meaning of the event to the individual. However, research suggests that a person's cognitive appraisal of life events strongly influences his or her response to those particular events (Lazarus & Launier, 1978). The same event may be perceived by different individuals as irrelevant, benign, positive, or threatening and harmful. In considering the effects of childhood victimization, it is especially likely that the child's cognitive appraisal of events will determine at least in part whether they are experienced as neutral, negative or harmful. This appraisal might reflect the child's perception of the experience, or an appraisal substantially influenced by external responses (from family, friends, neighbors, teachers, and officials) to the abusive or neglectful experience.

Herzberger, Potts, and Dillon (1981) stressed the importance of obtaining the child's perspective of his or her social environment, suggesting that studying the perceptions of children may contribute to understanding the long-term consequences of abuse.

> Seeing abuse as an indicator of parental rejection may have more harmful effects than perceiving abuse as being caused by the parent's externally imposed frustrations. Furthermore, perceiving abuse as a legitimate means of resolving conflicts may increase the likelihood that the child will model parental aggression. (p. 89)

---

[2]Behavior problems refer to notations in the juvenile probation department records or in the original case material that the child had engaged in chronic fighting, fire setting, destructiveness, or defiance of authority or had severe temper tantrums, uncontrolled anger, sadistic tendencies (as in aggressiveness toward weaker children), or was extremely difficult to control.

There is sparse research on the extent to which abused and neglected children's cognitive appraisal of the events mediates the development of negative behaviors in adolescence. As part of a larger 14-year longitudinal study of 2,000 families, Zimrin (1986) identified 35 families with abused children, and from that group, a small group of abused children ($n = 9$) who had survived the trauma of their childhood and grew up to be well-adjusted individuals. Variables that appeared to distinguish the survivors from the other children (those who showed a high degree of psychosocial pathology) were: fatalism, self-esteem, cognitive abilities, self-destructiveness, hope and fantasy, behavior patterns, and external support. Zimrin's interpretation of these results was that it was the child's cognitive appraisal or perception of their good personal resources, intellectual potential, good self-image and hope, coupled with relatively sound external resources, that protected the survivor children.

Brown and Harris (1978) suggested that vulnerability factors operate by creating feelings of low self-esteem and lack of mastery. This feeling of hopelessness, of believing that you are unable to control your fate, makes a person less able to deal with stressful life events. The role of cognitive sets and attributional styles lead some to postulate a "learned helplessness" model (Seligman, 1975) on the part of abused and/or neglected children. Earlier, the acquisition of certain attributional styles or coping strategies was discussed as one of the potential mechanisms linking childhood victimization to later dysfunctional behavior. The flip side of this coin is that different attributional styles and coping strategies may lead to more positive outcomes. Although challenging from a research design perspective, worthwhile future research would investigate cognitive sets and attributional styles that may mediate children's responses to abuse and/or neglect.

Relationship With a Significant Person

Clinicians and child protection service workers have recognized the importance of significant persons in the lives of abused and neglected children, yet minimal systematic evidence exists of their role in protecting victimized children from long-term negative consequences. In the literature on children's response to the stress of hospital admissions, for example, a supportive relationship with a consistently present nurse reduced emotional disturbance during hospitalization (Visintainer & Wolfer, 1975). For individuals with a history of childhood victimization, the experience of having one biological parent, or foster parent, who provided support and love while growing up was associated with better outcomes in adulthood (Egeland & Jacobvitz, 1984). Despite the fact that Farber and Egeland (1987) found few competent "survivors" among their sample of physically or emotionally neglected children, children who were more likely to be competent were those children whose mothers showed some interest in them and were able to respond to them emotionally.

Among sexually abused children, the presence of a supportive, positive relationship with a nonabusive parent or sibling has been considered a positive mediating variable (Conte & Schuerman, 1988). In her review of research on the effects of sexual abuse in childhood, Berliner (1991) noted that a number of studies had indicated that the level of impact of child sexual abuse was related to whether the child was believed and supported by his or her nonabusive family members (Everson, Hunter, Runyan, Edelsohn, & Coulter, 1989; Gomes-Schwartz, Horowitz, & Cardarelli, 1990; Morrow & Sorell, 1989). Furthermore, in an examination of the prevalence of depressive disorder among a sample of 56 maltreated children, Kaufman (1991) found that the quality of social support affected the likelihood of abused children developing depressive disorder. Abused children with more positive supports and fewer conflictual relationships were less likely to be depressed than the other maltreated children in the study. The nondepressed maltreated children were also more likely to report that they felt more cared about by their supports than the depressed children.

Developing a relationship with a significant person in one's life sometimes appears naturally. For other children, such as those who are severely abused or neglected, there may be significant barriers to this happening. Research is needed to assess the extent to which this is an important omission in the lives of abused and neglected children and the extent to which having a significant person mediates long-term negative consequences.

Placement Experiences and Foster Care

Although controversial, another potential factor that may act to protect abused and neglected children from more serious long-term consequences is placement outside the home. Proponents of out-of-home placements such as foster care point to the potential for serious future harm in leaving these children in the home. They acknowledge that although some children are injured by foster parents, the rate of reported abuse by foster parents is lower than that of the general population, and far lower than the rate of re-abuse by abusive parents (Bolton, Lanier, & Gia, 1981). Furthermore, they point to the potential benefits of foster care as compared to the relatively poor results of parent treatment programs (cf. Cohn & Collignon, 1979; Herrenkohl, Herrenkohl, Seech, & Egolf, 1980; Magura, 1981). Studies of adults who grew up in foster homes found no evidence of more problem behaviors, delinquency, criminality, mental illness, or marital failure than in the general population (see Widom, 1991c). Kent (1976), for example, examined case records of a large group of court-supervised abused and neglected children in Los Angeles and found that children who had been in foster care at least 1 year were rated by their social workers as being better off (physically and socially) than at the time they entered foster care. After a 6-month period in foster care, Fanshel and Shinn (1978) found that the well-being of the majority of the children had improved in terms of physical development, IQ, and school performance. They did not find that the longer a child spent in foster care, the more likely the child was to show signs of deterioration, and most of the children maintained the improvement over the 5-year period of the study.

On the other hand, it has frequently been asserted that social intervention strategies in cases of child abuse and neglect are, at best, ineffective and destructive and, at worst, harmful to the child. Critics of foster placement outside the home stress the need to maintain biological family ties and to minimize government interference in family life, the concern over the financial cost of placement, and the concern that foster care may actually be worse for children than leaving them in the home, even taking into account the potential risk for continued abuse (Hubbell, 1981; Wald, 1976). Some examinations of foster care experiences have described the inadequacy, failures, and high costs of the system (Gruber, 1978; Schor, 1982), whereas others have reported a high rate of behavior problems (Bohman & Sigvardsson, 1980; Bryce & Ehlert, 1977; Frank, 1980; Littner, 1974) and school problems (Canning, 1974) among foster children. However, none of these studies compared rates of such behaviors in nonfoster care children or presented information about these children prior to their placement.

In discussing the policy dilemma associated with whether to utilize foster care or not, Wald, Carlsmith, and Leiderman (1988) concluded that if the major goal is to protect children from further physical harm, then this is most likely accomplished through foster care. If, however, one is concerned with emotional harm, they argue that the conclusion may need to be changed.

Although out-of-home placements may act to exacerbate already heightened levels of stress in children from abusive and neglectful households, recent evidence suggests that out-of-home placements for some abused and neglected children may not be detrimental, at least, in terms of criminal consequences. Using a matched historical cohort design with children who had been maltreated, Runyan and Gould (1985) studied the impact of foster care on the subsequent development of delinquency, comparing 114 foster children (ages 11–18 years old) who had been in foster care for 3 or more years with a (demographically matched) comparison group of 106 victims of child maltreatment who had remained in their family home. These authors concluded that "Overall, there appears to be no support for the idea that foster care is responsible for a significant portion of later problems encountered by victims of maltreatment" (p. 562).

Widom (1991c) described placement experiences for a large sample of juvenile court cases of child abuse and neglect from approximately 20 years ago, and examined the role of these placement experiences in relation to delinquency and violence. These abused and/or neglected children in foster care and other out-of-home placement experiences, who typically came from multiproblem families, are a particularly vulnerable group in that they have experienced both a disturbed family situation and separation from their natural parents. In this research, under certain circumstances, out-of-home placements did not necessarily lead to higher risk of arrest for delinquency and violence.

One of the factors examined was amount of time in first placement. The assumption was that the longer the time spent in first placement, the better off the child would be. This is based on the notion that, in the context of a stable caretaking relationship, the child would have the opportunity to develop attachments and thus a stronger sense of self and self-esteem. Children who spent more than 10 years in their first placement had the lowest overall rates of arrests as an adolescent for delinquency and for violence. Age at first placement was also examined. The percent of children later arrested for delinquency and for violent crimes increased with age at first placement. Few of the children placed before the age of 1 year had arrest records (15%) and none had arrests for violent crimes, whereas children placed initially at ages 4–6 years old, for example, had higher rates of delinquency (30%) and arrests for violence (10%). Some children may actually benefit from out-of-home placements. The challenge for social workers and therapists is to recognize and to act upon the different needs of these children and their families.

Summary

Individual characteristics, such as high intelligence and certain kinds of temperament, and cognitive appraisal and experiences, such as developing a relationship with a significant person or some out-of-home placement experiences, may serve as buffers for some childhood victims growing up. For most of these characteristics and experiences, one can only speculate about ways in which they might protect abused and neglected children. For some, there is conflicting or indirect evidence. A major gap exists in our knowledge about what makes a difference in the lives of abused and neglected children. It is evident that there is much to be learned about the effects of protective factors and individual characteristics such as these, and even more to be discovered about how they operate to increase or decrease vulnerability for problem behaviors.

CONCLUSIONS AND DIRECTIONS FOR THE FUTURE

Increased Risk for Childhood Victims: Need for Systematic Evidence

Childhood victimization appears to increase risk for the development of a range of problems in adolescence, including delinquency and violence, running away, sexual promiscuity and teenage pregnancy, and alcohol and drug use and abuse. However, although there are extensive clinical accounts and speculations about the prevalence of these problem behaviors among adolescents who were abused or neglected in childhood, there is scant systematic evidence concerning the extent of these associations, the increased risk relative to control children, and the underlying causal mechanisms. Current knowledge is limited in quantity and type, compromised by methodological problems, almost exclusively limited to bivariate relationships, and often characterized by conflicting findings.

Many of the relationships between childhood victimization and adolescent problem behaviors reviewed here have received correlational support. However, relatively little is known about the temporal sequencing of these relationships. Childhood victims have been characterized as having low self-esteem, and low self-esteem may be an antecedent to the use of alcohol or illicit drugs. On the other hand, the use of alcohol and other drugs may serve as a coping mechanism for the abused or neglected child and may have as its consequence the lowering of that child's self-esteem. Further research to investigate the directionality of these potential linkages should be encouraged.

Co-Occurrence of Problem Behaviors

One of the difficulties in assessing risk for abused and neglected children is the co-occurrence of other problems (or co-morbidity) in the children and their parents. Although certain forms of childhood victimization may be perceived as acute stressors, child abuse and/or neglect often occur against a background of more chronic adversity. The question arises as to whether the presence or absence of certain characteristics or other adverse events influence a child's response to childhood victimization. Other research has found that adverse effects interacts with one another, so that the combined effects of the two may be greater than the sum of the two considered separately (Rutter, 1979). Whether this interaction effect applies to childhood victimization is not known, although it is highly likely.

Evaluating relationships between childhood victimization and adolescent problem behaviors is also made difficult because some of the behaviors of interest (e.g., alcohol and illicit drug use) are illegal for teenagers, creating a natural confounding of alcohol or substance use with delinquency. Unfortunately, few studies of abused and neglected children have used methods of assessment and diagnostic criteria that permit simultaneous examination of multiple characteristics and consequences. Furthermore, research in the area of childhood victimization has generally not been undertaken to examine the interrelationships among problem behaviors and symptoms of dysfunction in other spheres of living. Because childhood victims may be at risk for the development of multiple problem behaviors, an examination of the co-occurrence of problems may provide a fruitful direction for future research. For example, the co-occurrence of alcoholism, antisocial personality disorder, and substance use has been noted among male jail detainees (Abram, 1990). Alcoholics often attempt destructive behaviors, including suicide attempts (Schuckit, 1986b), and diagnoses of alcoholism are complicated by the presence of antisocial personality disorder, which in turn, includes components of criminal behavior and sexual promiscuity. Engaging in any one of these behaviors, then, might increase the likelihood of involvement in other at-risk behaviors.

Generalized or Specific Risk for Adolescent Problem Behaviors

Early childhood victimization may increase a person's risk of exhibiting a syndrome of problem behaviors. Some researchers believe that various manifestations of problem behaviors should be considered in terms of a single underlying tendency, often referred to as a *problem behavior syndrome* (Jessor, 1987; Kaplan, 1980; Robins, 1978; Robins & Wish, 1977). Others believe that different sets of problem behaviors represent fundamentally different etiologies (Elliott, Huizinga, & Menard, 1989; Kandel & Andrews, 1987; Kandel, Kessler, & Margulies, 1978;

McCord, 1990). To what extent are victims of early child abuse and/or neglect at risk for the development of general adolescent problem behaviors versus risk for specific outcomes strongly associated with childhood victimization?

If there is a syndrome of problem behaviors, and abused and neglected children are at increased generalized risk, then, it is more likely that they will engage in many of these forms of problem behaviors. On the other hand, if problem behaviors represent discrete behaviors with different etiologies, then the consequences of childhood victimization may be confined to more limited domains of dysfunction. These contrasting models also have different implications for intervention strategies. Researchers who emphasize syndromes believe that reducing problem behaviors depends on prevention or intervention to influence a common underlying trait. If specific problem behaviors represent specific etiologies, then a single general strategy might fail to reduce the problems of most individuals.

If there is a group of abused and neglected children who concurrently manifest multiple problem behaviors (the syndrome), then, a related question is whether this group accounts for the differences noted across a number of studies (the problem behavior variance). At the same time, there is a separate and perhaps larger group who have few or no problems. These children should be targeted for future study as well. What are the protective factors or interventions that have occurred in the lives of the functioning abused and/or neglected children that may have led to the more positive outcomes? Studies are needed with sample sizes large enough to examine multiple outcomes, while simultaneously controlling for relevant demographic characteristics.

Gender Differences in Vulnerability to and Manifestation of Adolescent Problem Behaviors

At least with prepubertal children, gender differences in response to most kinds of stressful events seem to operate in the same direction. Boys appear to be more vulnerable than girls (Eme, 1984; Hetherington, 1980; Rutter, 1982; Wallerstein, 1983; Wallerstein & Kelly, 1980). Do boys and girls respond in similar ways to the experiences of early abuse and neglect?

For a number of reasons, few studies have directly compared the consequences of child abuse and neglect in males and females. For example, the early clinical reports of violence primarily describe violent male adolescents. Studies of sexual promiscuity and teenage pregnancy have utilized samples of females, and primarily females who were sexually abused. For each of these gender-linked outcomes (violence:male and sexuality:female), studying the nonstereotypic sex may yield important insights. Abused and neglected females in Widom's (1991b) delinquency analysis had higher rates of arrests for violence than controls, and this pattern was not in evidence for the males. Finkelhor (1990) called attention to the need to study males who have been sexually abused in childhood, at the same time that we continue to attend to the research and treatment needs of female childhood sexual abuse. It may also be instructive to examine the extent to which sexually abused males are sexually promiscuous and involved in paternity as a teenager (even if they are not responsible for the care of the child). For alcohol, illicit drug use, and self-destructive behaviors, not enough published research exists to permit the disentanglement of differences associated with gender. Large scale studies assessing the consequences of child abuse and neglect for male and female children are necessary to systematically compare outcomes. Perhaps the consortium of studies funded through the National Center for Child Abuse and Neglect will provide answers to some of these questions.

Characteristics of the Abuse Incident

Researchers have begun to examine the relationship between characteristics of the abuse incident(s) and outcome. For example, some researchers have examined whether types of abusive or neglectful experiences place children at higher risk for the development of later problem behaviors.

The current examination of abused and neglected children's risk for adolescent problem behaviors reinforces the need to consider separately the effects of different types of child maltreatment. Most of the past research has focused on physical and sexual abuse, with relatively little attention paid to neglect. Some recent findings suggest that neglect by itself may have serious long-term negative consequences (Bousha & Twentyman, 1984; McCord, 1983; Widom, 1989b, 1989c, 1991b). Indeed, the large group of neglected children in Widom's research had the highest rates of arrest for violence as juveniles. It may be that the accumulation of stressful experiences associated with chronic neglect produces consequences for young children that are similar to those produced through direct victimization by physical abuse. Given that the number of cases of child neglect far outweigh those for physical abuse in national statistics (Westat, 1988), these findings on neglect may be of great relevance to forecasts of future violent behavior. Theories and prevention strategies need to incorporate neglected children's increased risk, in addition to physical and sexual child abuse victims. In terms of research, the common practice of treating abused and neglected children together, or eliminating one type of maltreatment from study, may reveal only a partial portrait of childhood victims' risk for adolescent problem behaviors.

If the child is viewed as a developing organism and not simply a static one, then we must ask how outcomes differ depending on the age of the child when the abuse occurs. The form of children's response to childhood victimization may be influenced by their age and level of development at the time. However, relatively little is known about age-related effects of child abuse and neglect.

In speculating about age-related effects of abuse and neglect, it is useful to consider the developmental literature on children's responses to other forms of stressful life events. For example, Yarrow and Goodwin (1973) found that a child moved from a foster home to a permanent adoptive home before the age of 6 months tended to show only transitory distress. By contrast, in somewhat older children (between age 7–12 months) such a change involved more pervasive disturbances. Similarly, according to Rutter (1983), the age period of greatest risk for the stress of hospital admission is between 6 months and 4 years of age. Children below the age of 6–7 months are relatively immune because they have not yet developed selective attachments and are therefore not able to experience separation anxiety. Children above the age of 4 years or so are less vulnerable, probably because they have the cognitive skills necessary to understand the situation. Children's responses to parental divorce (Wallerstein, 1983; Wallerstein & Kelly, 1980) and bereavement (Rutter, 1966) also varied by age and level of development.

There has been some speculation in the literature that the older the child at the time of the abuse incident, the greater the subsequent disturbances (Tsai, Feldman-Summers, & Edgar, 1979). Some studies of children and adolescents have reported greater disturbances associated with abuse during the preteen and teenage years, compared to abuse at younger ages (Adams-Tucker, 1982; Peters, 1976; Sedney & Brooks, 1984; Sirles, Smith, & Kusama, 1989). On the other hand, Kinard (1980) suggested that the older the child when the abuse occurred, the less likely the child would be to exhibit aggressive behavior. Studies have reported that abuse at younger ages was associated with greater trauma (Courtois, 1979; Finkelhor, 1979; Meiselman, 1978; Russell, 1986; Wolfe, Gentile, & Wolfe, 1989). In her review of the effects of child sexual abuse, Berliner (1991) concluded that age of onset of abuse has not been consistently associated with the severity of impact. Similarly, Beitchman et al. (1991) concluded that "findings regarding the relation between age of onset and severity of outcome are inconclusive" (p.547).

Unfortunately, the dimension of time makes discussion of risk factors for adolescent problem behaviors complicated. Beitchman et al. (1991) suggested two possible explanations for the inconsistencies in findings. First, if victims are assessed as children, the full extent of the consequences may not be manifest. As children grow and develop, new symptoms associated with their abuse may emerge. Prospective longitudinal studies would permit the examination of this hypothesis. Second, it is possible that age of onset is related to the duration and type of abuse experience and this might be confounded with outcomes. Young children may not have suffered the abuse for a long period of time and may not have experienced the use of force and threats that may be more common aspects of sexual abuse with older children and adolescents (Gomes-Schwartz et al., 1985; Peters, 1976).

Concluding Comment

Not all children who grow up in abusive or neglectful households necessarily become problem adolescents. Certainly there are a wide variety of environmental stresses, potential triggering mechanisms, and other factors in the developmental process. It is possible that certain problem behaviors manifest in adolescence may change as an individual ages. Upon a person's transition to adulthood, he or she may perceive their victimization in a different context and may manifest the consequences differently than at earlier points in their lives. It is also possible that some individuals have not processed their experiences during adolescence and that the unresolved childhood victimization effects may emerge only subsequently. And, life experiences subsequent to the early childhood victimization experiences may have an important impact on ultimate development.

The study of childhood victimization has been developing rapidly, with increased sensitivity to the limitations of designs based exclusively on retrospective self-reports and increased recognition of the need for more sophisticated research designs with large sample sizes, carefully defined abuse and neglect cases, and incorporation of matched control groups. The results of an increasing number of studies indicate the need for multidimensional transactional models of the relationship between childhood victimization and development, incorporating some combination of internal and external factors, and explicitly recognizing that behavior (prosocial and deviant) occurs in a social context. There are clues in the literature about potential protective factors that have implications for the development of intervention strategies. Although we need to know more about the specific ways in which childhood victimization leads to increased risk for adolescent problem behaviors, future efforts also need to be directed at preventing the development of dysfunctional outcomes in adolescence and beyond.

ACKNOWLEDGMENTS

Special appreciation is extended to Timothy Ireland for his helpful comments on an earlier draft of this chapter. This research was supported by grants from the National Institute of Justice (86-IJ-CX-0033, 89-IJ-CX-0007), Indiana University Biomedical Research Committee (SO7 RRO731), and the Talley Foundation (Harvard University). Points of view are those of the author and do not necessarily represent the position of the United States Department of Justice.

REFERENCES

Abram, K. (1990). The problem of co-occurring disorders among jail detainees: Anti-social disorder, alcoholism, drug abuse, and depression. *Law and Human Behavior, 14,* 333–345.

Adams-Tucker, C. (1982). Proximate effects of sexual abuse in childhood: A report on 28 children. *American Journal of Psychiatry, 139,* 1252–1256.

Agnew, R. (1985). A revised strain theory of delinquency. *Social Forces, 64,* 151–167.

Alfaro, J. D. (1981). Report on the relationship between child abuse and neglect and later socially deviant behavior. In R. J. Hunner & Y. E. Walker (Eds.), *Exploring the relationship between child abuse and delinquency* (pp. 175–219). Montclair, NJ: Allanheld, Osmun.

Allen, D. M. (1980). Young male prostitutes: A psychosocial study. *Archives of Sexual Behavior, 9,* 399–426.

Allen, D., & Tarnowski, K. (1989). Depressive characteristics of physically abused children. *Journal of Abnormal Child Psychology, 17,* 1–11.

Bagley, C., & Ramsay, R. (1986). Sexual abuse in childhood: Psychosocial outcomes and implications for social work practice. *Journal of Social Work and Human Sexuality, 4,* 1– 2, 33–47.

Bates, J. E. (1980). The concept of difficult temperament. *Merrill-Palmer Quarterly, 26,* 299–319.

Bates, J. E. (1989). In G. A., Kohnstamm, J. E. Bates, & M. K. Rothbart (Eds.), *Temperament in childhood* (pp. 321–355). Chichester, England: Wiley.

Becker, J., Kaplan, M., Cunningham-Rathner, J., & Kavoussi, R. (1986). Characteristics of adolescent incest sexual perpetrators: Preliminary findings. *Journal of Family Violence, 1*, 1.

Behling, D. (1979). Alcohol abuse encountered in 51 instances of reported child abuse. *Clinical Pediatrics, 18*, 87–91.

Beitchman, J. H., Zucker, K. J., Hood, J. E., DaCosta, G. A., & Akman, D. (1991). A review of the short-term effects of child sexual abuse. *Child Abuse and Neglect, 15*, 537–566.

Benward, J., & Densen-Gerber, J. (1975). Incest as a causative factor in antisocial behavior. *Contemporary Drug Problems, 4*, 323–340.

Berliner, L. (1991, June). Effects of sexual abuse on children. *Violence Update*, pp. 1, 8, 10–11.

Bohigan, G. M. (1989, April). *Recognition of childhood sexual abuse as a factor in adolescent health issues*. Informational report of the Council on Scientific Affairs, American Medical Association.

Bohman, M., & Sigvardsson, S. (1980). Negative social heritage. *Adoption and Fostering, 3*, 25–34.

Bolton, F. G., Lanier, R. H., & Gia, D. S. (1981). For better or worse? Foster parents and foster children in an officially reported child maltreatment population. *Children and Youth Services Review, 3*, 37–53.

Bousha, D. M., & Twentyman, C. T. (1984). Mother–child interactional style in abuse, neglect, and control groups: Naturalistic observations in the home. *Journal of Abnormal Psychology, 93*, 106–114.

Brown, G. W., & Harris, T. (1978). *Social origins of depression: A study of psychiatric disorder in women*. London: Tavistock.

Browne, A., & Finkelhor, D. (1986). Impact of sexual abuse: A review of the research. *Psychological Bulletin, 99*, 66–77.

Bryce, M. E., & Ehlert, R. C. (1977). 144 foster children. *Child Welfare, 50*, 499–503.

Burgess, A., Hartman, C., & McCormack, A. (1987). Abused to abuser: Antecedents of socially deviant behaviors. *American Journal of Orthopsychiatry, 144*, 1431–1436.

Canning, R. (1974). School experiences of foster children. *Child Welfare, 53*, 582–587.

Cavaiola, A. S., & Schiff, M. (1989). Self-esteem in abused, chemically dependent adolescents. *Child Abuse and Neglect, 13*, 327–334.

Cohn, A. H., & Collignon, F. C. (1979). *NCHSR Research Report Series. Vols. I and II: Evaluation of child abuse and neglect demonstration projects, 1974–1977* (DHEW Publication number PHS 79-3217). Washington, DC: U.S. Government Printing Office.

Colten, M. E., & Marsh, J. (1984). A sex-roles perspective on drug and alcohol use by women. In C. S. Widom (Ed.), *Sex roles and psychopathology* (pp. 219–248). New York: Plenum.

Conte, J. R., & Schuerman, J. R. (1988). The effects of sexual abuse on children. *Journal of Interpersonal Violence, 2*, 380–390.

Courtois, C. A. (1979). The incest experience and its aftermath. *Victimology, 4*, 337–347.

Crittendon, P. M., & Ainsworth, M. D. S. (1989). In D. Cicchetti & V. Carlson (Eds.), *Child maltreatment* (pp. 432–463). New York: Cambridge University Press.

Curtis, G. C. (1963). Violence breeds violence—perhaps? *American Journal of Psychiatry, 120*, 386–387.

Daro, D., & McCurdy, K. (1991). *Current trends in child abuse reporting and fatalities: The results of the 1990 annual 50 state survey*. Chicago: National Committee for Prevention of Child Abuse.

Dembo, R., LaVoie, L., Schmeidler, J., & Washburn, M. (1987). The nature and correlates of psychological/emotional functioning among a sample of detained youths. *Criminal Justice and Behavior, 14*, 311–334.

Dembo, R., Williams, L., LaVoie, L., Berry, E., Getreu, A., Wish, E., Schmeidler, J., & Washburn, M. (1989). Physical abuse, sexual victimization,, and illicit drug use: Replication of a structural analysis among a new sample of high-risk youths. *Violence and Victims, 4*, 121–137.

Dembo, R., Williams, L., LaVoie, L., Schmeidler, J., Kern, J., Getreu, A., Berry, E., Genung, L., & Wish, E.D. (1990). A longitudinal study of the relationship among alcohol use, marijuana/hashish use, cocaine use, and emotional/psychological functioning problems in a cohort of high-risk youths. *The International Journal of the Addictions, 25*, 1341–1382.

DeYoung, M. (1982). *The sexual victimization of children.* Jefferson, NC: McFarland Press.

Dodge, K. A., Bates, J. E., & Pettit, G. S. (1990). Mechanisms in the cycle of violence. *Science, 250*, 1678–1683.

Dunn, J. (1980). Individual differences in temperament. In M. Rutter (Ed.), *Scientific foundations of developmental psychiatry* (pp.101–109). London: Heinemann Medical.

Dykes, L. (1986). The whiplash shaken infant syndrome: What has been learned? *Child Abuse and Neglect, 10*, 211–221.

Easson, W. M., & Steinhilber, R. M. (1961). Murderous aggression by children and adolescents. *Archives of General Psychiatry, 4*, 27–35.

Egeland, B., & Jacobvitz, D. (1984) *Intergenerational continuity of parental abuse: Causes and consequences.* Paper presented at the Conference on Biosocial Perspectives on Abuse, York, ME.

Eichelman, B. (1990). Neurochemical and psychopharmacologic aspects of aggressive behavior. *Annual Review of Medicine, 41*, 149–158.

Elliott, D. S., Huizinga, D., & Menard, S. (1989). *Multiple-problem youth: Delinquency, substance use, and mental health problems.* New York: Springer-Verlag.

Eme, R. F. (1984). Sex-related differences in the epidemiology of child psychopathology. In C. S. Widom (Ed.), *Sex roles and psychopathology* (pp. 279–316). New York: Plenum.

Everson, M. D., Hunter, W. M., Runyan, D. K., Edelsohn, G. A., & Coulter, M. L. (1989). Maternal support following disclosure of incest. *American Journal of Orthopsychiatry, 59*, 198–207.

Fagan, J., Hansen, K. V., & Jang, M. (1983). Profiles of chronically violent delinquents: Empirical test of an integrated theory. In J. Kleugel (Ed.), *Evaluating juvenile justice* (pp. 91–119). Beverly Hills, CA: Sage.

Famularo, R., Stone, K., Barnum, R., & Wharton, R. (1986). Alcoholism and severe child maltreatment. *American Journal of Orthopsychiatry, 56*, 481–485.

Fanshel, D., & Shinn, E. B. (1978). *Children in foster care: A longitudinal investigation.* New York: Columbia University Press.

Farber, E. A., & Egeland, B. (1987). Invulnerability among abused and neglected children. In E. J. Anthony & B. Cohler (Eds.), *The invulnerable child* (pp. 253–288). New York: Guilford Press.

Farrington, D. P., Gallagher, B., Morley, L., St. Ledger, R. J., & West, D. J. (1988). Are there any successful men from criminogenic backgrounds? *Psychiatry, 51*, 116–130.

Fehrenbach, P., Smith, W., Monastersky, C., & Deisher, R. W. (1986). Adolescent sexual offenders: Offender and offense characteristics. *American Journal of Orthopsychiatry, 56*, 225–233.

Finkelhor, D. (1979). *Sexually victimized children.* New York: The Free Press.

Finkelhor, D. (1990). Early and long-term effects of child sexual abuse: An update. *Professional Psychology: Research and Practice, 21*, 325–330.

Finkelhor, D., Hotaling, G., Lewis, I., & Smith, C. (1989). Sexual abuse and its relationship to later sexual satisfaction, marital status, religion, and attitudes. *Journal of Interpersonal Violence, 4*, 379–399.

Finkelhor, D., Hotaling, G., & Sedlak, A. (1990). *Missing, abducted, runaway, and thrownaway children in America* (Executive Summary. First report: Numbers and characteristics National Incidence Studies). Washington, DC: U.S. Department of Justice.

Frank, G. L. (1980). Treatment needs of children in foster care. *American Journal of Orthopsychiatry, 50*, 256–263.

Friedrich, W. H., & Boriskin, J. A. (1976). The role of the child in abuse: A review of the literature. *American Journal of Orthopsychiatry, 46*, 580–590.

Frodi, A., & Smetana, J. (1984). Abused, neglected, and nonmaltreated preschoolers' ability to discriminate emotions in others: The effects of IQ. *Child Abuse and Neglect, 8*, 459–465.

Galler, J. R., Ramsey, F., Solimano, G., & Lowell, W. E. (1983). The influence of malnutrition on subsequent behavioral development. II. Classroom behavior. *Journal of the American Academy of Child Psychiatry, 24*, 16–22.

Garbarino, J., & Plantz, M. (1986). Part I review of the literature. In E. Gray (1986), *Child abuse: Prelude to delinquency?* (pp. 5–18). Washington, DC: U.S. Department of Justice, Office of Juvenile Justice and Delinquency Prevention.

Garmezy, N. (1981). Children under stress: Perspectives on antecedents and correlates of vulnerability and resistance to psychopathology. In A. I. Rabin, J. Aronoff, A. M. Barclay, & R. A. Zucker (Eds.), *Further explorations in personality*. New York: Wiley.

Garmezy, N., Masten, A. S., & Tellegen, A. (1984). The study of stress and competence in children: A building block for developmental psychopathology. *Child Development, 55*, 97–111.

Geller, M., & Ford-Somma, L. (1984). *Violent homes, violent children. A study of violence in the families of juvenile offenders* (New Jersey State Department of Corrections, Trenton, Division of Juvenile Services). Paper prepared for National Center on Child Abuse and Neglect, Washington, DC.

George, C., & Main, M. (1979). Social interactions of young abused children: approach, avoidance, and aggression. *Child Development, 50*, 306–318.

Gershenson, H. P., Musick, J. S., Ruch-Ross, H. S., Magee, V., Rubino, K. K., & Rosenberg, D. (1989). The prevalence of coercive sexual experience among teenage mothers. *Journal of Interpersonal Violence, 4*, 204–219.

Gil, D. (1973). *Violence against children: Physical child abuse in the United States.* Cambridge, MA: Harvard University Press.

Goldston, D. B., Turnquist, D. C., & Knutson, J. F. (1989). Presenting symptoms of sexually abused girls receiving psychiatric services. *Journal of Abnormal Psychology, 98*, 314–317.

Gomes-Schwartz, B., Horowitz, J., & Cardarelli, A. (1990). *Child sexual abuse: The initial effects.* Newbury Park, CA: Sage.

Gomes-Schwartz, B., Horowitz, J. M., & Sauzier, M. (1985). Severity of emotional distress among sexually abused preschool, school-age, and adolescent children. *Hospital and Community Psychiatry, 36*, 503–508.

Goodwin, D. W., Schulsinger, F., Hermansen, L., Guze, S. B., & Winokur, G. (1973). Alcohol problems in adoptees raised apart from alcoholic biological parents. *Archives of General Psychiatry, 28*, 238–243.

Goodwin, D. W., Schulsinger, F., Knop, J., Mednick, S., & Guze, S.B. (1977). Alcoholism and depression in adopted-out daughters of alcoholics. *Archives of General Psychiatry, 34,* 751–755.

Gray, E. Garbarino, J., & Plantz, M. (1986). *Child abuse: Prelude to delinquency.* Washington, DC: U.S. Department of Justice, Office of Juvenile Justice and Delinquency Prevention.

Green, A. H. (1978) Self-destructive behavior in battered children. *American Journal of Psychiatry, 135,* 579–582.

Greenwald, H. (1970). *The elegant prostitute.* New York: Ballantine.

Groth, A. (1979). Sexual trauma in the life histories of sex offenders. *Victimology, 4,* 6–10.

Gruber, A. R. (1978). *Children in foster care.* New York: Human Sciences Press.

Gutierres, S., & Reich, J. A. (1981). A developmental perspective on runaway behavior: Its relationship to child abuse. *Child Welfare, 60,* 89–94.

Hamilton, C. J., & Collins, J. J. (1982). The role of alcohol in wife beating and child abuse: A review of the literature. In J. J. Collins (Ed.), *Drinking and crime: Perspectives on the relationships between alcohol consumption and criminal behavior* (pp.253–287). London: Guilford Press.

Hamparian, D. M., Schuster, R., Dinitz, S., & Conrad, J.P. (1978). *The violent few: A study of dangerous juvenile offenders.* Lexington, MA: D.C. Heath.

Harrison, P. A., Hoffmann, N. G., & Edwall, G. E. (1989a). Differential drug use patterns among abused adolescent girls in treatment for chemical dependency. *The International Journal of the Addictions, 24,* 499–514.

Harrison, P. A., Hoffmann, N. G., & Edwall, G. E. (1989b). Sexual abuse correlates: Similarities between male and female adolescents in chemical dependency treatment. *Journal of Adolescent Research, 4,* 385–399.

Hartstone, E., & Hansen, K. (1984). The violent juvenile offender: An empirical portrait. In R. Mathias, P. DeMuro, & R. S. Allison (Eds.), *Violent juvenile offenders: An anthology* (pp.82–112). San Francisco, CA: National Council on Crime and Delinquency.

Herman, J. (1981). *Father–daughter incest.* Cambridge, MA: Harvard University Press.

Herman, J., & Hirschman, K. (1977). Father–daughter incest: A feminist theoretical perspective. *Signs: Journal of Women in Culture and Society, 2,* 735–756.

Herrenkohl, R. C., & Herrenkohl, E. C. (1981). Some antecedents and developmental consequences of child maltreatment. In R. Rizley & D. Cicchetti (Eds.), *Developmental perspectives on child maltreatment, 11,* 57–76.

Herzberger, S. D., Potts, D. A., & Dillon, M. (1981). Perceptions of abused and non-abused children toward their parents. *Journal of Consulting and Clinical Psychology, 49,* 81–90.

Hetherington, E. M. (1980) Children and divorce. In R. Henderson (Ed.), *Parent–child interaction: Theory, research, and prospect.* New York: Academic Press.

Higley, J. D., Hasert, M. F., Suomi, S. F., & Linnoila, M. (in press). *A nonhuman primate model of alcohol abuse: Effects of early experience, personality and stress on alcohol consumption.* Proceedings of the National Academy of Sciences USA.

Higley, J. D., Melman, P., & Taub, D. (1991). CSF monoamine and adrenal correlates of aggression in feral living rhesus monkeys. *Biological Psychiatry, 29*(50A), 16.

Higley, J. D., & Suomi, S. J. (1989). Temperamental reactivity in non-human primates. In G. A. Kohnstamm, J. E. Bates, & M. K. Rothbart (Eds.), *Temperament in childhood* (pp. 153–167). New York: Wiley.

Hubbell, R. (1981). *Foster care and families: Conflicting values and policies.* Philadelphia: Temple University Press.

Ireland, T. O., & Widom, C. S. (1991, November). *Childhood victimization and risk for alcohol and drug arrests: Preliminary findings.* Paper presented at the American Society of Criminology meetings, San Francisco, CA.

James, J., & Meyerding, J. (1977). Early sexual experience and prostitution. *American Journal of Psychiatry, 134,* 1382–1385.

Jessor, R. (1987). Problem-behavior theory, psychosocial development, and adolescent problem drinking. *British Journal of Addictions, 82,* 331–342.

Johnson, B., & Morse, H. A. (1978). Injured children and their parents. *Children, 15,* 147–152.

Kagan, J. (1977). The child in the family. *Daedalus: Journal of the American Academy of Arts and Sciences, 106,* 33–56.

Kandel, D. B., & Andrews, K. (1987). Process of adolescent socialization by parents and peers. *International Journal of the Addictions, 22,* 319–342.

Kandel, D. B., Kessler, R. C., & Margulies, R. Z. (1978). Antecedents of adolescent initiation into stages of drug use: A developmental analysis. In D. B. Kandel (Ed.), *Longitudinal research on drug use* (pp.73–99). New York: Wiley.

Kaplan, H. B. (1980). *Deviant behavior in defense of self.* New York: Academic Press.

Kaufman, J. (1991). Depressive disorders in maltreated children. *Journal of the American Academy of Child and Adolescent Psychiatry, 30,* 257–265.

Kazdin, A., Moser, J., Colbus, D., & Bell, R. (1985). Depressive symptoms among physically abused and psychiatrically disturbed children. *Journal of Abnormal Psychology, 94,* 298–307.

Kempe, C. H., Silverman, F. N., Steele, B. F., Droegemueller, W., & Silver, H. K. (1962). The battered-child syndrome. *Journal of the American Medical Association, 181,* 17–24.

Kent, J. T. (1976). A follow-up study of abused children. *Journal of Pediatric Psychology, 1,* 25–31.

Keogh, B. K., & Pullis, M. E. (1980). Temperamental influences on the development of exceptional children. *Advances in Special Education, 1,* 239–276.

Kinard, E. M. (1980). Emotional development in physically abused children. *American Journal of Orthopsychiatry, 50,* 686–696.

King, C. H. (1975). The ego and the integration of violence in homicidal youth. *American Journal of Orthopsychiatry, 45,* 134–145.

Kratcoski, P. C. (1982). Child abuse and violence against the family. *Child Welfare, 61,* 435–444.

Kroll, P. D., Stock, D. F., & James, M. E. (1985). The behavior of adult alcoholic men abused as children. *Journal of Nervous and Mental Disease, 173,* 689–693.

Lamprecht, F., Eichelman, B., Thoa, N. B., Williams, R. B., & Kopin, I. J. (1972). Rat fighting behavior: Serum dopamine-beta hydroxylase and hypothalalamic tyrosine hydroxylase. *Science, 177,* 1214–1215.

Lazarus, R. S., & Launier, R. (1978). Stress-related transactions between person and environment. In L. A. Pervin & M. Lewis (Eds.), *Perspectives in interactional psychology.* New York: Plenum.

Lewis, D. O., Shanok, S. S., Pincus, J. H., & Glaser, G. H. (1979). Violent juvenile delinquents: Psychiatric, neurological, psychological, and abuse factors. *Journal of the American Academy of Child Psychiatry, 18,* 307–319.

Lewis, D. O., Moy, E., Jackson, L. D., Aaronson, R., Restifo, N., Serra, S., & Simos, A. (1985). Biopsychological characteristics of children who later murder: A prospective study. *American Journal of Psychiatry, 142,* 1161–1167.

Lindberg, F. H., & Distad, L. J. (1985). Survival responses to incest: Adolescents in crisis. *Child Abuse and Neglect, 9,* 521–526.

Littner, N. (1974). *Some traumatic effects of separation and placement.* New York: Child Welfare League of America.

Magura, S. (1981). Are services to prevent foster care effective? *Child and Youth Services Review, 3,* 193–212.

Martin, H.P., & Beezley, P. (1977). Behavioral observations of abused children. *Developmental Medicine and Child Neurology, 19,* 373–387.

McCoard, W.D. (1983). Ohio project uncovers abuse/runaway links. *Midwest Parent–Child Review,* 8–9.

McCord, J. (1983). A forty-year perspective on effects of child abuse and neglect. *Child Abuse and Neglect, 7,* 265–270.

McCord, J. (1990). Problem behaviors. In S. S. Feldman & G. R. Elliott (Eds.), *At the threshold: The developing adolescent* (pp. 414–430, 602–614). Cambridge, MA: Harvard University Press.

Meiselman, K. (1978). *Incest.* San Francisco: Jossey-Bass.

Moffit, T.E., Gabrielli, W.F., Mednick, S.A., & Schulsinger, F. (1981). Socioeconomic status, IQ, and delinquency. *Journal of Abnormal Psychology, 90,* 152–156.

Morrow, K. B., & Sorell, G. T. (1989). Factors affecting self-esteem, depression, and negative behaviors in sexually abused female adolescents. *Journal of Marriage and the Family, 51,* 677–786.

Office of Youth Development. (1976). *National statistical survey of runaway youth parts I and II* (DHHS Publication No. HHS 105, 75-2105). Washington, DC: U.S. Government Printing Office.

Olweus, D. (1980). Familial and temperamental determinants of aggressive behavior in adolescent boys: A causal analysis. *Developmental Psychology, 16,* 644–660.

Orme, T. C., & Rimmer, J. (1981). Alcoholism and child abuse. *Journal of Studies on Alcohol, 42,* 273–287.

Pagelow, M. D. (1984). *Family violence.* New York: Praeger.

Peters, J. J. (1976). Children who are victims of sexual assault and the psychology of offenders. *American Journal of Psychotherapy, 30,* 398–421.

Rivera, B., & Widom, C. S. (1990). Childhood victimization and violent offending. *Violence and Victims, 5,* 19–34.

Robins, L. N. (1978). Sturdy predictors of adult antisocial behavior: Replications from longitudinal studies. *Psychological Medicine, 8,* 611–622.

Robins, L. N., & Wish, E. (1977). Childhood deviance as a developmental process: A study of 223 urban black men from birth to 18. *Social Forces, 56,* 448–473.

Runtz, M., & Briere, J. (1986). Adolescent "acting-out" and childhood history of sexual abuse. *Journal of Interpersonal Violence, 1,* 326–334.

Runyan, D. K., & Gould, C. L. (1985). Foster care for child maltreatment: Impact on delinquent behavior. *Pediatrics, 75,* 562–568.

Russell, D. E. H. (1986). *The secret trauma: Incest in the lives of girls and women.* New York: Basic Books.

Russell, M., Henderson, C., & Blume, S. B. (1985). *Children of alcoholics: A review of the literature.* New York: Children of Alcoholics Foundation, Inc.

Rutter, M. (1966). *Children of sick parents: An environmental and psychiatric study* (Institute of Psychiatry Maudsley Monographs No. 16). London: Oxford University Press.

Rutter, M. (1979). Protective factors in children's responses to stress and disadvantage. In M. W. Kent & J. E. Rolf (Eds.), *Primary prevention of psychopathology: Social competence in children* (Vol.3). Hanover: University Press of New England.

Rutter, M. (1982). Epidemiological-longitudinal approaches to the study of development. In W. A. Collins (Ed.), *The concept of development: Minnesota symposia on child psychology* (Vol. 15). Hillsdale, NJ: Lawrence Erlbaum Associates.

Rutter, M. (1983). Stress, coping, and development: Some issues and some questions. In N. Garmezy & M. Rutter (Eds.), *Stress, coping, and development in children* (pp. 1–41). New York: McGraw-Hill.

Ryan, J.F. (1987). The plight of our modern Huckleberry Finns—the runaways. *Missing/Abused, 3,* 3–6.

Sansonnet-Hayden, H., Haley, G., Marriage, K., & Fine, S. (1987). Sexual abuse and psychopathology in hospitalized adolescents. *Journal of the American Academy of Child and Adolescent Psychiatry, 26,* 753–757.

Schor, E.L. (1982). The foster care system and health status of foster children. *Pediatrics, 69,* 521–528.

Schuckit, M.A. (1986a). Alcohol and alcoholism. In R. E. Petersdorf, R.D. Adams, E. Braunwald, K. J. Isselbacher, J. B.Martin, & J. D. Wilson (Eds.), *Harrison's Principles of Internal Medicine* (pp. 2106–2111). New York: McGraw-Hill.

Schuckit, M. A. (1986b). Primary men alcoholics with a history of suicide attempts. *Journal of Studies in Alcohol, 47,* 78–81.

Sedlak, A. J. (1990). *Technical amendments to the study findings—national incidence and prevalence of child abuse and neglect* (NIS 2).

Sedney, M. A., & Brooks, B. (1984) Factors associated with a history of childhood sexual experience in a nonclinical female population. *Journal of the American Academy of Child and Adolescent Psychiatry, 23,* 215–218.

Seghorn, T., Prentky, R., & Boucher, R. (1987). Childhood sexual abuse in the lives of sexually aggressive offenders. *Journal of the American Academy of Child and Adolescent Psychiatry, 26,* 262–267.

Seligman, M. E. P. (1975). *Helplessness: On depression, development and death.* San Francisco: Freeman.

Sendi, I. B., & Blomgren, P. G. (1975). A comparative study of predictive criteria in the predisposition of homicidal adolescents. *American Journal of Psychiatry, 132,* 423–427.

Sheehy, G. (1971). *Hustling.* New York: Dell.

Shure, M. B., & Spivack, G. (1979). Interpersonal problem-solving, thinking, and adjustment in the mother–child dyad. In M. W. Kent & J. E. Rolf (Eds.), *Primary prevention of psychopathology: Social competence in children* (Vol.3, pp. 201–209). Hanover, NH: University Press of New England.

Silbert, M., & Pines, A. (1981). Sexual child abuse as an antecedent to prostitution. *Child Abuse and Neglect, 5,* 407–411.

Silver, L. R., Dublin, C. C., & Lourie, R. S. (1969). Does violence breed violence? Contributions from a study of the child abuse syndrome. *American Journal of Psychiatry, 126,* 152–155.

Singer, M. I., Petchers, M. K., & Hussey, D. (1989). The relationship between sexual abuse and substance abuse among psychiatrically hospitalized adolescents. *Child Abuse and Neglect, 13,* 319–325.

Sirles, E. A., Smith, J. A., & Kusama, H. (1989). Psychiatric status of intrafamilial child sexual abuse victims. *Journal of the American Academy of Child and Adolescent Psychiatry, 28,* 225–229.

Smith, C. P., Berkman, D. J., & Fraser, W. M. (1980). *A preliminary national assessment of child abuse and neglect and the juvenile justice system: The shadows of distress.* Washington, DC: Office of Juvenile Justice and Delinquency Prevention.

Sroufe, L. A., & Rutter, M. (1984). The domain of developmental psychopathology. *Child Development, 55,* 17–29.

Strasburg, P. A. (1978). *Violent delinquents: A report to the Ford Foundation.* New York: Monarch.

Straus, M. A., & Gelles, R. J. (1990). *Physical violence in American families.* New Brunswick, NJ: Transaction.

Suomi, S. J., & Ripp, C. (1983). A history of motherless mother monkeys mothering at the University of Wisconsin primate laboratory. In M. Reite & N. Caine (Eds.), *Child abuse: The nonhuman primate data* (pp.50–78). New York: Alan R. Liss.

Tsai, M., Feldman-Summers, S., & Edgar, M. (1979). Childhood molestation: Variables related to differential impact of psychosexual functioning in adult women. *Journal of Abnormal Psychology, 88,* 407–417.

Visintainer, M. A., & Wolfer, J. A. (1975). Psychological preparation for surgical pediatric patients: The effects on children's and parents' stress responses and adjustment. *Pediatrics, 56,* 187–202.

Wald, M. S. (1976). State intervention on behalf of neglected children: Standards for removal of children from their homes, monitoring the status of children in foster care, and termination of parental rights. *Stanford Law Review, 28,* 625–706.

Wald, M. S., Carlsmith, J. M., & Leiderman, P. H. (1988). *Protecting abused and neglected children.* Stanford, CA.: Stanford University Press.

Wallerstein, J. S. (1983). Children of divorce: Stress and developmental tasks. In N. Garmezy & M. Rutter (Eds.), *Stress, coping, and development in children* (pp. 265–302). New York: McGraw-Hill.

Wallerstein, J. S., & Kelly, J. B. (1980). *Surviving the break up: How children and parents cope with divorce.* New York: Basic Books.

Werner, E. E. (1983). *Vulnerability and resiliency among children at risk for delinquency.* Paper presented at the annual meeting of the American Society of Criminology, Denver, CO.

Werner, E. E., & Smith, R. S. (1982). *Vulnerable but invincible: A longitudinal study of resilient children and youth.* New York: McGraw-Hill.

Widom, C. S. (1988). Sampling biases and implications for child abuse research. *American Journal of Orthopsychiatry, 58,* 260–270.

Widom, C. S. (1989a). Child abuse, neglect, and adult criminal behavior: Research design and findings on criminality, violence, and child abuse. *American Journal of Orthopsychiatry, 59,* 355–367.

Widom, C. S. (1989b). The cycle of violence. *Science, 244,* 160–166.

Widom, C. S. (1989c). Does violence breed violence? A critical examination of the literature. *Psychological Bulletin, 106,* 3–28.

Widom, C. S. (1991a). Avoidance of criminality in abused and neglected children. *Psychiatry, 54,* 162–174.

Widom, C. S. (1991b). Childhood victimization: Risk factor for delinquency. In M. E. Colten & S. Gore (Eds.), *Adolescent stress: Causes and consequences* (pp. 201–221). New York: Aldine deGruyter.

Widom, C. S. (1991c). The role of placement experiences in mediating the criminal consequences of early childhood victimization. *American Journal of Orthopsychiatry, 6,* 195–209.

Widom, C. S., & Ames, M. E. (1994). Criminal consequences of childhood sexual abuse. *Child Abuse and Neglect, 18,* 303–318.

Wilson, J. Q., & Herrnstein, R. J. (1985). *Crime and human nature.* New York: Simon Schuster.

Wolfe, V. V., Gentile, C., & Wolfe, D. A. (1989). The impact of sexual abuse on children: A PTSD formulation. *Behavior Therapy, 20*, 215–228.

Yarrow, M. R., Campbell, J. D., & Burton, R. V. (1970). Recollections of childhood: A study of the retrospective method. *Monographs of the Society for Research in Child Development, 135*(5), (Serial No. 138).

Yarrow, M. R., & Goodwin, M. S. (1973). The immediate impact of separation: Reactions of infants to a change in mother figures. In L. J. Stone, H. T. Smith, & L. B. Murphy (Eds.), *The competent infant: Research and commentary.* New York: Basic Books.

Young, L. (1964). *Wednesday's child: A study of child neglect and abuse.* New York: McGraw- Hill.

Zimrin, H. (1986). A profile of survival. *Child Abuse and Neglect, 10*, 339–349.

Zuravin, S. (1988). Fertility patterns: Their relationship to child physical abuse and child neglect. *Journal of Marriage and the Family, 50*, 983–993.

Zuravin, S., & Taylor, R. (1987). *Family planning behaviors and child care adequacy.* Final report submitted to the U.S. Department of Health and Human Services, Office of Population Affairs (Grant FPR 0000028-01-0).

9

Problem Behaviors and Masculinity Ideology in Adolescent Males

Joseph H. Pleck
Wellesley College
Freya L. Sonenstein
Leighton C. Ku
Urban Institute

The objective of this chapter is to call attention to the potential role of masculinity ideology—beliefs about what men are like and how they should act—as a factor in the etiology and maintenance of problem behaviors in adolescent males. The notion that male problem behaviors have something to do with "masculinity" has been formulated in various ways over recent decades. It has recently been expressed at the highest policy levels, as illustrated by former Department of Health and Human Services (DHHS) Secretary Louis Sullivan's (1991) call for action to address "a generation whose manhood is measured by the caliber of the gun he carries or the number of children he has fathered" (p. 1). Likewise, Virginia Governor Douglas Wilder (1991) urged the policy community to get across the message that "contrary to what many of today's young people think, making babies is no act of manhood" (p. A14).

However, the potential linkage between masculinity and adolescent male problem behaviors has been conceptualized and empirically investigated in several different ways. Further, the role of masculinity in problem behaviors has received relatively little attention in recent research. Using data from the 1988 National Survey of Adolescent Males, this study reports an exploratory analysis of the association between one aspect of masculinity, termed here *masculinity ideology*, and problem behaviors in four areas: school problems, substance use, delinquency, and sexual activity.

One reason for thinking that masculinity is related to adolescent problem behaviors is that, to varying degrees, their rates are higher and/or their ages of onset are lower in males than in females. This pattern raises the possibility that biogenetic factors related to being male are involved in etiology (Rowe, this volume; Udry, 1988, this volume). This chapter, however, focuses on the potential influence on problem behaviors of masculinity viewed as a sociopsychological dynamic. In the remainder of the chapter, we first develop the social constructionist perspective on masculinity, from which the concept of masculinity ideology is derived, in the context of prior theoretical views of the male gender role. The possible application of these approaches to adolescent females is considered. The study hypothesizes that among adolescent males, holding traditional masculinity ideology is associated with school problems, substance use, delinquency, and sexual activity. The results of the study suggest that masculinity ideology is indeed a risk factor for these problem behaviors.

THEORETICAL BACKGROUND: THREE CONCEPTUALIZATIONS OF THE MALE ROLE

Formulating the impact of masculinity on adolescent male problem behaviors presupposes a broader theoretical perspective on the male role and its development. Prior research has conceptualized the male role in three different ways, each with different implications for the understanding of problem behaviors in males. The first two conceptualizations, termed here *male sex role identity* and *trait masculinity*, are interrelated. The third interpretation, the *social role analysis* of masculinity, adopts a quite different approach.

Male Sex Role Identity

The earliest theoretical interpretation of the male role is the "theory of male sex role identity" (Pleck, 1981, 1983). (In the theory's heyday from the late 1940s to the early 1970s, the term *sex role* was used rather than *gender role*.) During the three postwar decades, male identity theory was expounded by leading scholars in U. S. developmental, personality, and social psychology as well as sociology (e.g., Biller, 1972; Kagan, 1964a; Lynn, 1969; Parsons, 1959). It was a central component of the structural–functionalist theory of the family (Parsons & Bales, 1955) underlying much of the research conducted in human development and family studies during the postwar era. It was also the theoretical basis of some of the most influential works in the social sciences in this period, from Adorno, Frankel-Brunswick, Levinson, and Sanford's (1950) *The Authoritarian Personality* to the so-called *Moynihan Report* (Moynihan, 1967).

The theory's fundamental idea is that persons have an intrinsic developmental need or imperative to develop gender role identity, which according to this theory is directly expressed through possession of the traits, attitudes, and interests typical for one's sex. For males, however, the acquisition of gender role identity is thwarted by the relative absence of male models and by other factors such as feminized environments in schools and women's changing roles. Therefore, male identity theory posits that males are at considerable risk of having insecure gender role identity. The theory includes specific arguments about the etiology of two problem behaviors in males, delinquency and school difficulties, as expressions of this insecurity.

First, the theory posits that one potential response to insecurity in male identity is to "defend" against it through "hypermasculine" behavior such as delinquency (see Miller, 1958; Parsons, 1947; Toby, 1966, for classic statements). In Toby's words, "structural features of contemporary societies create a problem of masculine identification....Much of the exaggerated roughness and toughness of preadolescent and adolescent boys should be understood...as the result of unconscious needs to repudiate a natural identification with their mothers" (p. 20). The most common research design used to test this hypothetical link was to relate delinquency to the factor most thought to lead to insecure identity, father absence, rather than relating delinquency directly to measures of male identity. This aspect of male identity theory was frequently applied to Black adolescents, so that delinquency, for example, was interpreted as a consequence of the sex role identity problems resulting from the high rates of father absence in Black males.

The male identity perspective also had an interpretation of why boys have problems in school, and why they exhibit school difficulties more frequently than girls. Specifically, the predominance of female teachers and other ways in which schools are "feminized" environments promote insecurity in male identity (see Kagan, 1964b; Sexton, 1970).

> Though run at the top by men, schools are essentially feminine institutions, from nursery school through graduate school....The feminized school simply bores many boys but it pulls some in one of two opposite directions. If the boy absorbs school values, he may become feminized himself. If he resists, he is pushed toward failure and rebellion. (Sexton, 1970, pp. 25, 33)

Although the relationship between family structure and delinquency is still investigated today, and gender dynamics in the schools also continue to be studied, the theory of male sex role identity has fallen into disuse as the perspective guiding such research. Money and Ehrhardt's (1972) alternative interpretation of gender identity and gender role development has been generally accepted in its place. In their alternate view, gender *identity* (knowledge of being male or female) and gender *role* (personality traits and social role behaviors culturally defined as masculine or feminine) are viewed as quite distinct—in contrast to the male identity theory's postulate that the latter is the direct expression of the former. In Money and Ehrhardt's interpretation, gender identity is acquired with no difficulty for all but the tiniest minority—in contrast to the earlier premise that insecure male identity is quite common. According to Money and Ehrhardt, once gender identity is attained, individuals may develop gender roles culturally perceived as inappropriate for their biological sex; although this may cause various other difficulties, it does not reflect or cause a problem in gender identity.

Further, the father absence studies that were interpreted as confirming the insecure male identity explanation of delinquency are now seen as having serious limitations and as subject to a variety of other interpretations (Adams, Milner, & Schrepf, 1984; Pleck, 1981; Stevenson, 1991; Stevenson & Black, 1988). Investigations of the consequences of having male teachers on boys' performance and behavior in elementary school, which the male identity perspective implies should be positive, actually find few differences (Gold & Reis, 1982; Pleck, 1981).

In spite of these disconfirmations, "insecurity in male sex role identity" was the leading interpretation of at least two of the major adolescent male problem behaviors through the late 1970s (Pleck, 1981). Some theorists attempted to extend identity theory to explain female development as well, although not focussing on problem behaviors (Lynn, 1969). Had alcohol and drug abuse been recognized as prevalent among adolescents as they are now, these behaviors would no doubt have also been interpreted as defenses against insecure gender role identity. Although this interpretation has fallen into general disuse in research, it undoubtedly continues to be applied in clinical work with adolescent males. The broader theory of male sex role identity also remains widely accepted by the lay public because it provides a simply understood theoretical justification for urging fathers to be more involved with their children, especially sons—"boys need male models." Although this popular recommendation can be justified on other grounds, many view male identity theory as its only possible rationale.

Trait Masculinity

A second theoretical approach to the male role evident in recent research views it as a constellation of traits that are more frequent or occur at higher levels in males. This "trait masculinity" approach is conceptually intertwined with the male identity perspective, and the two theories in fact share a common intellectual progenitor, the line of research on masculinity–femininity (M–F) initiated by Terman and Miles (1936). In brief, M–F scales were first developed during the 1930s on a relatively atheoretical basis. In the postwar period, the theory of male sex role identity became the dominant basis for interpreting them (see Pleck, 1983, for more detailed analysis). M–F measures were commonly understood as indicators of gender identity, within the male identity framework: Scoring high on a masculinity–femininity scale meant that a male had successfully acquired male gender role identity.

As part of the demise of male identity theory in the mid-1970s, M–F measures began to be interpreted and used differently, in two ways. First, researchers now interpreted M–F scales as assessing the personality component of gender role in Money and Ehrhardt's sense, instead of underlying gender identity. (Money and Ehrhardt used the term *gender role*—perhaps confusingly—to mean both the role behavior and personality traits culturally defined as masculine and feminine.) Although the second, more purely psychometric development described next received more attention, this first shift represented a far more significant theoretical event.

Second, M–F research took a well-known psychometric turn. Whereas earlier research had viewed M and F as opposite ends of a single bipolar continuum (masculinity–femininity), the new paradigm held that they are separate, orthogonal, unipolar dimensions (Bem, 1974; Spence & Helmreich, 1978). Research within this new perspective posited that individuals could be simultaneously high (or low) on both dimensions, and hypothesized that being high on both M and F was psychologically optimal. The latter claim has not been consistently validated, however (see Lenney, 1979). Although news of the dual, unipolar conception of M–F probably remained restricted to a narrow group within personality psychology, the basic idea became quite well-known and popular to the lay public under the term *androgyny*.

Most of the earlier research using the new kind of M and F measures—most often the Bem Sex Role Inventory (BSRI), and Spence and Helmreich's Personal Attributes Questionnaire (PAQ)—focused on testing the hypothesis that being high on both M and F was associated with positive correlates such as self-esteem. However, the new conceptualization of trait masculinity (M) as distinct from trait femininity (F), and the discarding of the theoretical assumption that among males, being high in M by itself denoted "secure" male gender identity, also laid the groundwork for a new kind of critical analysis of the correlates of trait masculinity. If, as various theoretical analyses argued, the "traditional" male role could have negative consequences for men themselves as well as for women (Pleck, 1976), then M should be correlated with indicators of these negative consequences. Thus, the "trait masculinity" model of the male role afforded a new way of understanding problem behaviors in adolescent and older males.

Only a few studies took advantage of this theoretical opportunity, however. The most notable is Horwitz and White's (1987) important longitudinal study of 1,308 New Jersey adolescents tested at ages 12, 15, and 18, using the M and F scales from the PAQ. Contrary to the investigators' hypothesis, M was associated with lower rates of self-reported alcohol and drug problems among older males, and had no consistent association with substance use among younger males. M was, as predicted, associated with higher rates of delinquency, but in only one of several comparisons. These analyses did not appear to control for sociodemographic background factors. Undoubtedly, similar studies are rare because both Bem and Spence and Helmreich at first theoretically formulated M and F as including only the socially desirable, and thus socially positive, components of masculinity. Thus, it was unlikely that researchers would hypothesize that M had negative correlates.

In a subsequent stage of this line of research, however, Spence and Helmreich's group distinguished positive and negative components within M and F. This shift is far less widely known than the initial differentiation of masculinity and femininity as distinct unipolar dimensions. In a revision of the PAQ, the Extended Personal Attributes Questionnaire (EPAQ), components of masculinity labeled M+ (achieving, responsible, etc.) and M– (aggressive, exploitative, etc.) were thus differentiated. With this revised conception of trait masculinity, problem behaviors among males could be interpreted as a result of elevations in a "negative masculinity" trait.

Following unpublished work noted in Spence and Helmreich (1978), Spence, Helmreich, and Holahan (1979) observed in a large college sample that M– was positively correlated with an index of acting out (a composite of current alcohol and drug use, and current and past misdemeanors, verbal and physical fights, and school misbehavior) in both males and females. Snell, Belk, and Hawkins (1987) also reported a correlation between M– and use of both alcohol and mind-altering drugs in a similar college sample, again in both sexes. This approach to masculinity and problem behaviors is intuitively plausible and empirically promising, but it has not been pursued in other studies. Perhaps the reason it has not been more widely used is that the principal available measure for positive and negative components within M and F, the EPAQ, is so complex: besides M+, M–, and F+, it distinguishes two different kinds of F– (formulated as "unmitigated communion" and verbal passive–aggressiveness), as well as a separate bipolar M–F scale.

Social Role Analysis and Masculinity Ideology

The third general theoretical approach to the masculinity can be termed *social role analysis* (Pleck, 1981). This approach is compatible with Kimmel and Messner's (1989) and Brod's (1987) social constructionist perspective. The basic notion is that cultures hold definitions of masculinity that are socially constructed. Inherent in the cultural definition of masculinity in many Western societies, it is argued, is engaging in certain behaviors that, although officially disapproved, are culturally defined as validating masculinity. Indeed, the social disapproval of these behaviors is in many instances fundamental to what makes them so masculinity-validating. As applied to adolescent problem behaviors, this perspective implies that premarital sex, alcohol and drug use, and illegal activities are an inherent part of how adolescent masculinity is socially defined in Western societies.

Fine (1987) elegantly used the social role model in qualitative research among preadolescent White males. Fine documented in detail how boys' definitions of masculinity contain negative elements such as engaging in violent and sexy talk, minor delinquency, and racist behavior that run counter to—and have greater formative effect than—adults' values in the socialization of boys. In Fine's analysis, boys participate in a "vast subcultural network stretching through his community and throughout American society" (p. 3) that positively sanctions these behaviors. This "vast subcultural network" is, in effect, male culture (Pleck, 1987).

The social role approach has not been widely used in quantitative research, however. To apply it, social expectations and male culture require translation into a concept that describes the individual male's acceptance of the definition of masculinity, and his internalization of the male culture, of his society. We propose *masculinity ideology* as the necessary linking construct. The social role approach views masculinity not as a dimension of personality in the trait sense, but as an ideology, that is, as a set of beliefs and expectations about what men are like and should do. To illustrate further, a "traditional" male, viewed in terms of traits, is a male who actually has traditional male characteristics; viewed in terms of masculinity ideology, he is a male who believes that men should have these characteristics. As applied to problem behavior, the idea is that males exhibit problem behaviors not because they are high in the trait of negative masculinity, but because they believe in a particular (traditional) conception of masculinity.

Operationally, masculinity ideology is measured by endorsement of traditional attitudes toward male roles. Here, it is important to distinguish attitudes toward men from attitudes toward women (or gender). To assess attitudes toward male roles, statements must refer to the importance or value of a man conforming to male role standards or expectations (e.g., "A young man should be physically tough, even if he's not big"). Specifically, items should refer only to men, and not to comparisons or relationships between the sexes. If items do the latter (e.g., "Men are less emotional than women"), one cannot justifiably say they refer to attitudes about men as distinct from attitudes about women. This is a weakness in some scales intended to assess attitudes specifically toward men or the male role (e.g., Fiebert, 1983). In addition, it is also important that items not concern the respondent's own behaviors (e.g., "I try to be physically tough"), because such items assess masculinity as a trait, instead of attitudes about men in general.

The assessment of male role attitudes with such scales does not make the assumption that all social groups, cultures or subcultures, or periods have the same conception of the male role. Different subcultures in the United States undoubtedly emphasize somewhat different attributes as defining masculinity. Brannon (1976), for example, argued that male role expectations include several different dimensions whose relative salience may vary among individuals and social groups. It is assumed, however, that items included in these scales reasonably represent the range of characteristics potentially included in definitions of masculinity in major U.S. subcultures, although different subcultures will emphasize some characteristics more than others. Indeed, these measures can be used to identify how conceptions of appropriate male behavior vary in different social groups, by comparing groups' average responses to individual items. Although assessing each male's masculinity attitudes with a scale developed for his specific subculture may be an ideal, and the development of subculture-specific measures should be undertaken, the currently available measures are practical approximations.

Three previous studies provide results relevant to this third approach to masculinity as a factor in socially negative behaviors. In a sample of college men, Mosher and Sirkin's (1984) Hypermasculinity Inventory was significantly correlated with self-reported recent drug use, aggressiveness, driving after drinking, and delinquent behavior during high school. However, the Hypermasculinity Inventory included some trait masculinity items in addition to male role attitude items. Also, many items specifically concerned aggressive and risky behaviors, so that correlation between this scale and other self-report measures of such behaviors are not surprising. In another study with college students, Thompson (1990) found a significant association between attitudes toward masculinity and the use of psychological (although not physical) violence in dating relationships, in discriminant function analyses controlling for age, gender orientation, acceptance of courtship violence, and seriousness of relationship. In a study examining other attitudinal correlates of beliefs about men, Bunting and Reeves (1983) found an association between attitudes toward male roles and endorsement of myths about rape. Also relevant to this general approach is Anderson's (1989) recent ethnographic work on the "sex codes" of poor inner-city male youth, which he interpreted as fundamentally concerning how males should act to assert masculinity in the context of limited or nonexistent job opportunities.

Thus, previous research has examined the link between masculinity adolescent problem behaviors in varying ways. The "male sex role identity" model of male problem behaviors has fallen into disuse. The "trait masculinity" perspective shows promise, but has not been empirically pursued, perhaps due to the complexity of the measures required. Several recent studies employing the "masculinity ideology" approach suggest that adolescent males' attitudes about masculinity (as distinct from their degree of masculinity, viewed as either an identity or a trait) may be involved in problem behaviors. The present study develops this third approach further, investigating the link between masculinity and problem behaviors in adolescent males in a more systematic way and with a more representative sample than has been used in prior research. Employing national survey data originally collected for other purposes, the study examines the association between attitudes toward the male role and problem behaviors concerning schooling, alcohol and drug use, delinquency, and sexual activity, controlling for sociodemographic factors found to be related to problem behaviors in other studies.

Parallel Approaches to Problem Behaviors in Adolescent Females

Before proceeding, the application of these three theoretical approaches to adolescent females should be briefly discussed. As described earlier, sex role identity theory primarily focused on the causes and consequences of males' hypothesized greater difficulty in acquiring secure gender role identity. For females, it could be argued that nonsexual acting-out behaviors of various kinds represent gender identity conflicts revolving around "rejection" of feminine identity; sexual acting out might signify other kinds of gender identity conflicts leading to a need to establish attractiveness to males. The first author's experiences in clinical training during the 1970s suggest that such interpretations were indeed popular in the mental health field. Hetherington (1972) found that daughters of divorced fathers show inappropriately high levels of attention-seeking from males, a result frequently interpreted in terms of gender identity conflicts resulting from fathers' hypothesized role in promoting daughter's feminine identities. However, Stevenson (1991) pointed out that although Hetherington's study frequently appears in psychology textbooks, at least six other investigations have failed to replicate it in key respects.

Paralleling the trait masculinity approach, it can be hypothesized that excessive levels of trait femininity, especially negative femininity, lead to certain dysfunctional behaviors in females such as remaining in abusive relationships. However, the adolescent problem behaviors most often studied have not been investigated among women from this perspective. The three studies cited earlier as illustrating the trait masculinity approach also include analyses of the association of trait femininity (and masculinity) to problem behaviors in females. Taken together, they suggest that negative femininity has a less consistent association with problem behaviors in women than negative masculinity does in men. Negative masculinity is most consistently associated with problem behaviors in both sexes (Snell et al., 1987; Spence et al., 1979).

As noted earlier, attitudes toward women's roles and toward gender relations have been studied far more frequently than attitudes specifically toward masculinity. In both female and male samples, conservative attitudes toward women's role have often been found associated with limited educational and occupational aspirations, being married, and higher number of children (Lipman-Blumen, 1972; Pleck, 1978). However, these attitudes have not generally been examined as factors in adolescent female problem behaviors.

In light of current concerns about the exclusion or underrepresentation of women as subjects in health-related research (Ritt, 1991), some may question the present study's focus on the dynamics of problem behaviors only among males. Two distinctions will help make our rationale clear. First, the male-only research that has rightfully aroused objections is comprised of studies that investigate processes hypothetically occurring in both sexes (e.g., the role of diet in heart disease), but arbitrarily select only a male sample to do so. The hypothetical dynamic investigated in the present study—that problem behaviors in adolescent males are related to masculinity—is one that logically applies only to males. A parallel argument for adolescent females has been developed for premarital sex, in Fox's (1977) analysis of the "nice girl dilemma" in adolescent female contraception. Second, in the male-only studies receiving criticism, males are not explicitly studied or conceptualized *as males* (i.e., understood to be only one of two genders whose life experience differs in systematic ways). In our research, however, the concept of masculinity is central to the investigation.

METHOD

Sample

The National Survey of Adolescent Males (NSAM) interviewed 1,880 never married males aged 15–19 between April and November 1988.[1] Its sample represents the noninstitutionalized never-married male population ages 15–19 in the contiguous United States. The sample was stratified to overrepresent Black and Hispanic respondents, and in-person interviews were completed with 676 young Black men, 386 young Hispanic men, and 755 young White, non-Hispanic men, and 63 respondents in other racial groupings. The response rate for those eligible to be interviewed was 73.9%. For other information on the sample, see Sonenstein, Pleck, and Ku (1989).

---

[1]The data are available from Sociometrics, Inc., Palo Alto, CA. A follow-up survey was conducted in 1990–1991.

Sample weights are available so that distributional results can be estimated for all noninstitutionalized never married 15- to 19-year-old males. Analyses of distributions for problem behaviors and attitudes about masculinity use the full sample, and are weighted. Multivariate analyses use the 1,595 cases with complete data on all measures, and are unweighted.

Measures

In addition to the personal interview, the NSAM also included a short self-administered questionnaire (SAQ) for questions judged to be especially sensitive, which respondents completed and returned to the interviewer in a sealed envelope. Many of the 10 measures of problem behaviors were taken from the SAQ. In later analyses, a high score always denotes being high on the construct.

School Difficulties.   Two items from the SAQ concerning school problems were employed. Males were asked: "Have you ever repeated a grade, or been held back a grade in school?" and "Were you ever suspended from school?"

Alcohol and Drug Use.   The SAQ included parallel items for (a) drinking "beer, wine, hard liquor, or any other alcoholic beverage," (b) trying "cocaine or crack," and (c) trying "any other street drugs." For each, respondents were asked whether they had ever done the activity, and if so, how often they done it during the last 12 months ("never," " a few times," " monthly," " weekly," or "daily").

Delinquent Activity.   Males were asked in the SAQ: "Have you ever been picked up by the police for doing something wrong?" and "Have you ever done something that the police would pick you up for if they had found out?" Those answering positively were asked how often this had happened ("once or twice," "3–5 times," "6–10 times," and "11 or more times").

Sexual Activity.   Three measures of sexual activity were selected for inclusion in this analysis. Sexual activity status was assessed by the question "Have you ever had sexual intercourse with a girl (sometimes this is called 'making love,' 'having sex,' or 'going all the way')?" Current level of sexual activity was indicated by respondents' reports of the number of different sexual partners they had in the last year; for this analysis, those not sexually active in the last year were assigned a code of zero. These two measures appeared in the interviewer-administered part of the NSAM. Finally, a measure of coercive sex was taken from the SAQ: "Have you ever tricked or forced someone else to have sex with you?"

Masculinity Ideology.   Masculinity ideology was assessed by an eight-item scale for traditional male role attitudes. Seven items were adapted from Thompson and Pleck's (1986) 26-item abbreviated version of the Brannon Masculinity Scale

(Brannon, 1985), which was in turn based on a theoretical analysis of male role expectations concerning emotional self-control, achieving status, aggression, and avoidance of femininity. Items considered most relevant to an adolescent sample were selected, and wording was simplified or otherwise altered to be more appropriate for this age group. An additional item specifically about sex, a topical area omitted in Brannon's scale, was also included (Snell, Hawkins, & Belk, 1988).

A summary index was derived from the eight items, with a coefficient alpha of .56. Analyses indicated that all items contributed to the index, and that omission of items would not lead to improvement in reliability. Although this level of internal reliability is less than ideal, it was considered minimally adequate for use in further analysis. Thompson (1990) reported a coefficient alpha of .91 in a college sample for the 26-item scale from which most of the eight items used in the present study were adapted. The lower reliability found in the present study (.56) results from the smaller number of items used, and perhaps from the greater heterogeneity of the sample. A measure of this type has not previously been used in a national representative sample.

Sociodemographic and Personal Background Variables.   B e s i d e s current age, respondents reported the level of education they thought they would ever complete (collapsed to "less than high school diploma," " high school diploma," " some college or vocational school," "four years of college," " postgraduate"). Attendance at religious services at age 14 was reported in four categories: " never," " less than once a month," " one to three times a month," and "once a week or more." Race was coded as Black non-Hispanic, White non-Hispanic, Hispanic, and other race, with White non-Hispanic used as the reference category in regression analyses. Respondents estimated their family annual income in one of seven categories (in thousands: 0–10, 10–20, 20–30, 30–40, 40–50, 50–60, and 60+; coded 1–7). Region of the country was coded as the four census regions (north, midwest, west, and south), with south as the reference category.

Statistical Analyses

Logistic regression analyses were used for the problem behavior measures assessed in dichotomous form, and odds ratios are reported for predictors found to be statistically significant (Morgan & Teachman, 1988). Ordinary least-squares regression was used for the problem behaviors on continuous scales. In both sets of analyses, current age, expected level of education completed, frequency of religious attendance at age 14, race/ethnicity, current family income, and region of the country were included to control for sociodemographic and personal background factors.

RESULTS

Frequency of Problem Behaviors

Table 9.1 presents the weighted distributions for the 10 measures of problem behavior used in this analysis. Difficulties in school were relatively frequent, with more than 30% of the sample reporting repeating a grade in school, and 38% reporting suspension.

About 20% of the sample reported drinking weekly or daily during the last year. Somewhat over 6% reported using cocaine or crack in the last year. Among these, most reported cocaine use only "a few times." Use of "other street drugs" in the last year was acknowledged by 17.4%. (To a follow-up question, almost 90% reported the drug was marijuana.)

Of the sample, 28% said they had ever been "picked up" by the police. For most, this occurred only once or twice. A larger proportion, 47.6%, acknowledged ever doing something that the police would pick them up for, and 12% reported such activity six or more times.

Sixty percent of the sample were sexually active. (Sonenstein et al., 1989, provide detailed breakdowns by age and race/ethnicity.) Regarding number of different sexual partners in the last year, besides the percentage distributions for the whole sample given in Table 9.2, the proportions having each number of partners can also be calculated among the 1,133 sexually active only. Most who were sexually active reported either none or 1 partner in the last year (54.6% of the 1,133 actives) or 2 partners (24.9%). Among the 39 cases with 6 or more partners, 18 reported 10 or more; the largest number reported was 24. About 2% said they had tricked or forced someone to have sex with them.

Distributions of the Traditional Male Role Attitude Items and Index

Table 9.2 provides the means and standard deviations for the items assessing traditional male role attitudes. Item distributions may vary not only because of true differences in the rate of endorsement of one aspect of traditional male role expectations compared to another, but also because item wordings may not be precisely equivalent in intensity; because of the latter possibility, differences in means should be interpreted with caution. With this caveat in mind, this sample reported relatively strong endorsement of traditional male role expectations concerning being respected by others, self-confidence, and avoidance of overt femininity (Items 1–3, 6). By contrast, the mean levels of endorsement for the items concerning physical toughness and hypersexuality (Items 5, 8) were close to the theoretical midpoint of 2.5. These two items also showed the largest standard deviations. Finally, respondents tended on the average to disagree with the items assessing traditional male role expectations regarding not expressing weakness and not doing housework.

TABLE 9.1
Frequencies of Problem Behaviors

Measure	Weighted N	%
Ever repeated a grade?		
Yes (1)	560	30.1
No (0)	1,298	69.9
Ever suspended?		
Yes (1)	700	37.7
No (0)	1,158	62.3
Drink beer, wine, hard liquor?		
Never (0)	250	13.6
Ever, but not past year (1)	127	6.9
A few times past year (2)	803	43.8
Monthly past year (3)	270	14.7
Weekly past year (4)	360	19.6
Daily past year (5)	26	1.4
Try cocaine or crack?		
Never (0)	1,686	91.7
Ever, but not past year (1)	37	2
A few times past year (2)	104	5.7
Monthly past year (3)	5	0.3
Weekly past year (4)	5	0.3
Daily past year (5)	5	0.3
Try other street drugs?		
Never (0)	1,381	75.3
Ever, but not past year (1)	134	7.3
A few times past year (2)	232	12.6
Monthly past year (3)	40	2.2
Weekly past year (4)	39	2.1
Daily past year (5)	8	0.4
Ever picked up by police?		
Never (0)	1,323	72
Once or twice (1)	459	25
3–5 times (2)	39	2.1
6–10 times (3)	12	0.7
11 or more times (4)	5	0.3
Ever done something police would pick you up for if they found out?		
Never (0)	959	52.4
Once or twice (1)	470	25.7
3–5 times (2)	17	9.5
6–10 times (3)	92	5
11 or more times (4)	136	7.4

(Continued)

TABLE 9.1 *(Continued)*

Measure	Weighted N	%
Ever had sexual intercourse?		
Yes (1)	1,133	60.4
No (0)	742	39.5
Number of different sex partners in last year		
0	848	45.1
1	513	27.3
2	282	15
3	91	4.8
4	58	3.1
5	45	2.4
6+	39	2.1
Ever tricked or forced someone to have sex with you?		
Yes (1)	39	2.1
No (0)	1,801	97.9

TABLE 9.2

Means and Standard Deviations of Traditional Male Role Attitude Items
and Index

Item	Mean[a]	SD
1. It is essential for a guy to get respect from others.	3.23	0.80
2. A man always deserves the respect of his wife and children.	3.53	0.71
3. I admire a guy who is totally sure of himself.	3.30	0.79
4. A guy will lose respect if he talks about his problems.	1.76	0.87
5. A young man should be physically tough, even if he's not big.	2.63	1.03
6. It bothers me when a guy acts like a girl.	3.33	0.92
7. I don't think a husband should have to do housework.	1.72	0.88
8. Men are always ready for sex.	2.13	0.96
Traditional male role attitudes index	2.80	0.44

Range of weighted Ns for items = 1,868 to 1,877; Weighted N for index = 1,851.
[a]Range: 1–4; 1 = *disagree a lot,* 2 = *disagree a little,* 3 = *agree a little,* 4 = *agree a lot.*

Association Between Masculinity Ideology and Problem Behaviors

Results of the regression analyses of the association between masculinity ideology, as assessed by traditional male role attitudes, and problem behaviors are reported in Tables 9.3 and 9.4. These analyses indicate that traditional male role attitudes showed a significant independent association with 7 of the 10 problem behaviors. Specifically, traditional attitudes were associated with ever being suspended from school; drinking and use of street drugs (primarily marijuana); frequency of being picked up by the police; being sexually active, number of heterosexual partners in the last year, and tricking or forcing someone to have sex. Number of partners in

TABLE 9.3

Logistic Regression Analyses of Problem Behaviors on Masculinity Ideology and Sociodemographic Factors (N = 1,595)

Predictor	Repeated Grade		Suspended		Sexually Active		Forced Sex	
	B^a	OR^b	B	OR	B	OR	B	OR
Traditional male role attitudes	-0.03		0.40**	1.49	0.70**	2.01	0.66**	1.93
Age	-0.02		0.07		0.57***	1.77	0.21*	1.24
Expected education	-0.51**	0.57	-0.44**	0.64	-0.13***	0.88	-0.06	
Religious attendance at age 14	-0.13*	0.88	-0.14**	0.87	-0.22**	0.81	-0.33**	0.72
Black[c]	0.39**	1.48	0.79**	2.20	1.40**	4.05	1.86**	6.45
Hispanic	0.34**	1.40	0.22		0.22		1.49**	4.44
Other race	-0.18		0.13		-0.02		1.98**	7.24
Family income	-0.15**	0.86	0.02		0.03		0.15	
North[d]	0.06		0.47**	1.59	-0.08		0.39	
Midwest	-0.62**	0.54	0.46**	1.59	0.13		-0.01	
West	-0.96**	0.38	0.40**	1.50	-0.28		-0.37	
Model chi-square (11 df)	252.72		167.35		313.90		45.73	

*p < .05. **p < .01.

[a]B is standardized coefficient

[b]OR is Odds Ratio

[c]Reference category for race is White

[d]Reference category for region is South

TABLE 9.4
Multiple Regression Analyses of Problem Behaviors on Masculinity Ideology and Sociodemographic Factors (standardized regression coefficients; $N = 1,595$)

Predictor	Drink alcohol	Use cocaine	Use other drugs	Picked up by police	Police would pick up	Number partners last year
Traditional male role attitudes	0.06*	0.02	0.06*	0.09**	0.03	0.11*
Age	0.22**	0.12**	0.09**	0.08**	0.05	0.14**
Expected education	-0.04	-0.09***	-0.10***	-0.16***	0.01	0.07
Religious attendance at age 14	-0.05	-0.09***	-0.08***	-0.09***	-0.05*	-0.07***
Black[a]	-0.22**	-0.10*	-0.15***	-0.06*	-0.20**	0.22**
Hispanic	-0.08*	0.03	0.04	0.01	-0.11**	0.01
Other race	-0.06	0.02	0.01	0.01	-0.04	-0.01
Family income	0.14**	0.02	0.05	0.04	0.12**	0.08**
North[b]	0.04	0.04	0.01	0.08*	0.01	0.04
Midwest	0.06*	-0.01	0.04	0.15***	0.01	0.03
West	0.00	0.06*	0.04	0.07*	0.01	-0.02
Adjusted R^2	0.12	0.04	0.05	0.07	0.06	0.10

*$p < .05$. **$p < .01$.
[a]Reference category for race is White
[b]Reference category for region is South

the last year was also modeled among the sexually active only; the coefficient for traditional male role attitudes remained significant (beta = .079, p < .05).

Based on factor and reliability analyses not shown in detail here, an index combining the three substance use and the two illegal activities measures was created (alpha = .69), and results paralleled those for the individual problem behavior indicators. In addition, possible interactions between male role attitudes and race, age, and educational expectations were examined, to detect whether the association between traditional attitudes and problem behaviors might differ among different sample subgroups. In no case did inclusion of such interaction terms improve model fit. The problem behaviors significantly associated with male role attitudes included at least one measure from each broad area of problem behaviors investigated here.

In the ordinary least squares (OLS) regression analyses, the size of associations observed between masculinity attitudes and problem behaviors were modest, with betas ranging from .06 to .11. In the logistic regression analyses, an increment of one scale point (somewhat over 2 standard deviations) on the male role attitudes index was associated with about a 50% greater odds of being suspended from school, and about twice the odds of being sexually active and ever forcing someone to have sex.

DISCUSSION

This analysis clearly confirms that problem behaviors in adolescent males are associated with attitudes toward masculinity. Before interpreting the broader implications of this result, however, the limitations of the study and some additional results should be noted. Although the measures of problem behavior span four different areas, they are restricted in depth and are subject to self-report bias. In these cross-sectional data, problem behaviors are assessed retrospectively, whereas masculinity ideology is measured, in effect, after the behavior. Further, although the time frame for the assessment of substance use and number of sexual partners was restricted to the last year, the other problem behaviors reported (school difficulties, delinquent activity, and sexual coercion) may have occurred any time in the past. Thus, the associations observed here between male role attitudes and problem behaviors should not be interpreted as causal. In addition, the study did not comparatively test alternative ways of linking masculinity issues to problem behaviors, but focused on the masculinity ideology approach deriving from the social role analysis of the male role. Finally, we did not examine parallel dynamics in the etiology of problem behaviors in adolescent females.

The findings for other predictors of problem behaviors besides masculinity ideology are also of interest. In particular, the lower rates of alcohol and drug use reported by Blacks compared to Whites in the regression analyses parallel bivariate results in recent National Institute of Drug Abuse surveys (NIDA, 1988, 1990). Mensh and Kandel's (1988) analyses suggest that drug use may be underreported by minorities, especially among the young. The lower rate of nonapprehended delinquent activity for Blacks is consistent with other national self-report surveys of male and female youth (Bachman, Johnston, & O'Malley, 1988; Benson & Donahue, 1989; Elster, Ketterlinus, & Lamb, 1990; Ketterlinus, Nitz, Lamb, & Elster, 1992). But the present finding that Blacks report being apprehended by the police less often than Whites is inconsistent with youth arrest statistics (cited in Dryfoos, 1990). Our item concerning being "picked up by the police" is not identical with arrest, however.

As noted at the outset, the notion that masculinity plays a role in the etiology and maintenance of problem behaviors in adolescent males has been occasionally advanced in recent decades. The exact nature of this linkage, however, has been conceptualized in different ways. Recent researchers have generally neglected the role of masculinity in problem behaviors. This study's results lend credence to the notion that adolescent males' beliefs about masculinity are associated with a variety of problem behaviors. We found that, controlling for sociodemographic and personal background variables, adolescent males who reported more frequent involvement in problem behaviors held more traditional conceptions of what males are like and how they should act. Our analyses found no evidence that the strength of these associations varied among racial-ethnic groups or among subgroups defined by age or educational expectations.

Although our study did not compare the three alternate ways that masculinity has been conceptually linked to problem behaviors, it does highlight potential strengths of the masculinity ideology approach. First, this approach yields findings that are not subject to an alternative interpretation that needs to be ruled out for results generated by the earlier male identity and trait masculinity approaches. The association between, for example, being picked up by the police and indicators of male identity or negative masculinity, which often include males' self-ratings on aggression and toughness, might be interpreted as simply showing that one indicator of antisocial tendencies is correlated with another. An association between problem behaviors and beliefs about masculinity, however—for example, between illegal acts, and agreeing that males lose respect if they talk about their problems or that men should not do housework—is far less intuitively obvious. The masculinity ideology perspective hypothesizes a relationship that, from this perspective, is more theoretically ambitious than do prior approaches.

Second, our results do not appear to be an artifact of including only socially undesirable characteristics in the masculinity ideology scale. If the conception of traditional male roles implied by the scale emphasized the aspects of masculinity sometimes viewed as creating difficulties for males themselves or for others, the study's results would not be surprising. Further, the study could be criticized as defining traditional masculinity in a biased way, designed to show that its endorsement has negative correlates. However, the measure includes a balance of both negative and positive masculine attributes. One scale item does concern males being highly sexually active ("Men are always ready for sex"), but the remaining items define traditional masculinity in terms of a range of other attributes, several of which are generally viewed positively in U. S. society, as corroborated by their high level of endorsement in this sample (e.g., having the respect of others, self-confidence). Thus, our results suggest that it is not simply those traditional attitudes about masculinity viewed by some as undesirable that have negative implications for adolescent functioning. Instead, these problematic consequences are associated with a wider range of traditional attitudes about masculinity, including attitudes about expected male characteristics that are generally positively regarded by Americans.

Third, perhaps the broadest implication of our results is that traditional beliefs about masculinity are a "risk factor" for problem behaviors in adolescent males. In Jessor's (1992) conceptual scheme, traditional masculinity ideology can be interpreted as an aspect of both the personality system (as a core value) and the perceived environment (insofar as masculinity beliefs concern how others will respond to traditional male behaviors). Masculinity ideology may be significantly correlated with other personality factors that have received attention in the etiology of problem behaviors, especially low self-control (Gottfredson & Hirschi, this volume). Although we controlled for sociodemographic factors and selected personal characteristics such as educational expectations and religious attendance, we were not able to control for this personality factor. However, if the present study can be faulted on the grounds that traditional masculinity ideology should be interpreted as a specific concomitant of low self-control, it may be equally valid to argue the obverse: Research on self-control and problem behavior among adolescent males may neglect the role of traditional conceptions of manhood in fostering low self-control.

Regarding policy and practice, the results of the study suggest that interventions that directly address the role of traditional views about masculinity in problem behaviors may be of value. In another study, for example, we found that traditional beliefs about male responsibility in preventing pregnancy are associated with low consistency of condom use (Pleck, Sonenstein, & Ku, 1991). We thus argued that educational efforts directed to sexually active male youth should give greater attention to males' attitudes about their responsibility for contraception. Consistent with the pleas by former DHHS Secretary Sullivan and Virginia Governor Wilder cited at the outset of the chapter, our results imply that addressing and challenging certain traditional beliefs about masculinity may be of benefit in interventions intending to reduce problem behaviors in adolescent males. A parallel approach, focusing on beliefs about femininity, may also aid in effective interventions with adolescent females.

ACKNOWLEDGMENTS

The National Survey of Adolescent Males and work on this chapter were supported by grants from the National Institute of Child Health and Human Development and the Office of Adolescent Pregnancy Prevention Programs. The authors wish to thank the volume editors for their helpful comments.

REFERENCES

Adams, P. L., Milner, J. R., & Schrepf, N. A. (1984). *Fatherless children*. New York: Wiley-Interscience.

Adorno, T. W., Frenkel-Brunswick, E., Levinson, D. J., & Sanford, R. N. (1950). *The authoritarian personality*. New York: Wiley.

Anderson, E. (1989). Sex codes and family life among poor inner-city youths. *Annals of the American Academy of Political and Social Science, 501*, 59–78.

Bachman, J., Johnston, L. D., & O'Malley, P. (1988). *Monitoring the future: Questionnaire responses from the nation's high school seniors, 1986*. Ann Arbor, MI: Institute for Social Research.

Bem, S. L. (1974). The measurement of psychological androgyny. *Journal of Personality and Social Psychology, 42*, 155–162.

Benson, P. L., & Donahue, M. S. (1989) Ten-year trends in at-risk behavior: A national study of black Americans. *Journal of Adolescent Research, 4*, 125–139.

Biller, H. B. (1972). *Father, child, and sex role*. Lexington, MA: Heath.

Brannon, R. (1976). The male sex role: Our culture's blueprint for manhood and what it's done for us lately. In D. David & R. Brannon (Eds.), *The forty-nine percent majority: The male sex role* (pp. 1–48). Reading, MA: Addison-Wesley.

Brannon, R. (1985). A scale for measuring attitudes about masculinity. In A. G. Sargent (Ed.), *Beyond sex roles* (pp. 110–116). St. Paul, MN: West.

Brod, H. (Ed.). (1987). *The making of masculinities: The new men's studies*. Winchester, MA: Allen & Unwin.

Bunting, A. B., & Reeves, J. B. (1983). Perceived male sex orientation and beliefs about rape. *Deviant Behavior, 4*, 281–295.

Dryfoos, J. (1990). *Adolescents at risk: Prevalence and prevention*. New York: Oxford University Press.

Elster, A. B., Ketterlinus, R. D., & Lamb, M. E. (1990). Association between parenthood and problem behavior in a national sample of adolescents. *Pediatrics, 85*, 1044–1050.

Fiebert, M. S. (1983). Measuring traditional and liberated males' attitudes. *Perceptual and Motor Skills, 56*, 83–86.

Fine, G. T. (1987). *With the boys: Little league baseball and preadolescent culture*. Chicago: University of Chicago Press.

Fox, G. L. (1977). "Nice girl": Social control of woman through a value construct. *Signs, 2*, 805–817.

Gold, D., & Reis, M. (1982). Male teacher effects on young children: A theoretical and empirical consideration. *Sex Roles, 8*, 493–513.

Hetherington, E. M. (1972). Effects of father absence on personality development in adolescent daughters. *Developmental Psychology, 7*, 313–326.

Horwitz, A. V., & White, H. R. (1987). Gender role orientation and styles of pathology among adolescents. *Journal of Health and Social Behavior, 28*, 158–170.

Kagan, J. L. (1964a). Acquisition and significance of sex typing and sex-role identity. In M. L. Hoffman & L. W. Hoffman (Eds.), *Review of child development research* (Vol. 1, pp. 137–168). New York: Russell Sage Foundation.

Kagan, J. L. (1964b). The child's sex role classification of school objects. *Child Development, 35*, 1051–1056.

Ketterlinus, R. D., Nitz, K., Lamb, M. E., & Elster, A. B. (1992). Adolescent nonsexual and sex-related problem behaviors. *Journal of Adolescent Research, 7*, 431–456.

Kimmel, M. S., & Messner, M. A. (1989). Introduction. In M. S. Kimmel & M. A. Messner (Eds.), *Men's lives* (pp. 1–15). New York: Macmillan.

Jessor, R. (1992). Risk behavior in adolescence: A psychosocial framework for understanding and action. *Developmental Review, 12*, 374–390.

Lenney, E. (Ed.). (1979). Androgyny. *Sex Roles, 5*(6), 703–840 (entire issue).

Lipman-Blumen, J. (1972). How ideology shapes women's lives. *Scientific American, 226*(1), 34–62.

Lynn, D. B. (1969). *Parental and sex role identification: A theoretical analysis.* Berkeley, CA: McCutchan.

Mensh, B. S., & Kandel, D. B. (1988). Underreporting of substance use in a national longitudinal youth cohort: Individual and interviewer effects. *Public Opinion Quarterly, 52*, 100–124.

Miller, W. B. (1958). Lower-class culture as a generating milieu for gang delinquency. *Journal of Social Issues, 14*, 5–19.

Money, J., & Ehrhardt, A. (1972). *Man and woman, boy and girl.* Baltimore, MD: Johns Hopkins University Press.

Morgan, S. P., & Teachman, J. D. (1988) Logistic regression: Description, examples, and comparisons. *Journal of Marriage and the Family, 50*, 929–936.

Mosher, D. L., & Sirkin, M. (1984). Measuring a macho personality constellation. *Journal of Research in Personality, 18*, 150–163.

Moynihan, D. P. (1967). The Negro family: The case for national action. In L. Rainwater & W. Yancey (Eds.), *The Moynihan report and the politics of controversy* (pp. 39–124). Cambridge, MA: MIT Press.

National Institute on Drug Abuse. (1988). *Illicit drug use, smoking, and drinking by America's high school students, college students, and young adults, 1975–1988.* Washington, DC: Author.

National Institute on Drug Abuse. (1990). *National household survey on drug abuse: Main findings 1988.* Washington, DC: Author.

Parsons, T. C. (1947). Certain primary sources and patterns of aggression in the social structure of the Western world. *Psychiatry, 10*, 167–181.

Parsons, T. C. (1959). The social structure of the family. In R. Anshen (Ed.), *The family: Its function and destiny* (pp. 16–40). New York: Harper & Row.

Parsons, T. C., & Bales, R. F. (1955). *Family socialization and interaction process.* Glencoe, IL: The Free Press.

Pleck, J. H. (1976). The male sex role: Problems, definitions, and sources of change. *Journal of Social Issues, 32*, 155–164.

Pleck, J. H. (1978). Men's traditional attitudes toward women. Conceptual issues in research. In J. Sherman & F. Denmark (Eds.), *The psychology of women: New directions in research* (pp. 619–644). New York: Psychological Dimensions.

Pleck, J. H. (1981). *The myth of masculinity.* Cambridge, MA: MIT Press.

Pleck, J. H. (1983). The theory of male sex role identity: Its rise and fall, 1936–present. In M. Lewin (Ed.), *In the shadow of the past: Psychology portrays the sexes* (pp. 205–225). New York: Columbia University Press.

Pleck, J. H. (1987). Diamonds in the rough. *Readings: A Journal of Reviews and Commentary in Mental Health, 2*(4), 13–15.

Pleck, J. H., Sonenstein, F. L., & Ku, L. C. (1991). Adolescent males' condom use: Relationships between perceived cost–benefits and consistency. *Journal of Marriage and the Family, 53*, 733–746.

Ritt, I. F. (1991). Double standard, double jeopardy: Research on health problems of adolescent women (editorial). *Journal of Adolescent Health, 12*, 361.

Sexton, P. C. (1970). *The feminized male: Classrooms, white collars, and the decline of manliness.* New York: Vintage Books.

Snell, W. E., Belk, S. S., & Hawkins, R. C. (1987). Alcohol and drug use in stressful times: The influence of the masculine role and sex-related personality attributes. *Sex Roles, 16,* 359–373.

Snell, W. E., Hawkins, R. C., & Belk, S. S. (1988). Stereotypes about male sexuality and the use of social influence strategies in intimate relationships. *Journal of Social and Clinical Psychology, 7,* 42–48.

Sonenstein, F. L., Pleck, J. H., & Ku, L. C. (1989). Sexual activity, condom use and AIDS awareness among adolescent males. *Family Planning Perspectives, 21,* 152–158.

Spence, J. T., & Helmreich, R. L. (1978). *Masculinity and femininity: Their psychological dimensions, correlates, and antecedents.* Austin: University of Texas Press.

Spence, J. T., Helmreich, R. L., & Holahan, C. T. (1979). Negative and positive components of psychological masculinity and femininity and their relationships to self-reports of neurotic and acting out behaviors. *Journal of Personality and Social Psychology, 37,* 1673–1682.

Stevenson, M. (1991). Myth, reality, and father absence. *Men's Studies Review, 8*(1), 3–8.

Stevenson, M., & Black, K. (1988). Paternal absence and sex-role development: A meta-analysis. *Child Development, 59,* 793–814.

Sullivan, L. (1991, May 25). US secretary urges TV to restrict "irresponsible sex and reckless violence." *Boston Globe,* p. 1.

Terman, L. M., & Miles, C. M. (1936). *Sex and personality.* New York: McGraw Hill.

Thompson, E. H. (1990). Courtship violence and the male role. *Men's Studies Review, 7*(3), 1, 4–13.

Thompson, E. H., & Pleck, J. H. (1986). The structure of male role norms. *American Behavioral Scientist, 29,* 531–543.

Toby, J. (1966). Violence and the masculine mystique: Some qualitative data. *Annals of the American Academy of Political and Social Science, 36*(4), 19–27.

Udry, J. R. (1988). Biological predispositions and social control and adolescent sexual behavior. *American Sociological Review, 53,* 709–722.

Wilder, D. (1991, March 28). To save the Black family, the young must abstain. *Wall Street Journal,* p. A14.

10

The Microsocial Structure Underpinnings of Adolescent Problem Behavior

David W. Andrews
Thomas J. Dishion
Oregon Social Learning Center

The etiology of problem behavior has been addressed from a variety of theoretical and methodological perspectives within this volume. Sociological, ecological, criminological, biological, and behavior–genetic explanations of problem behavior lifestyles have been explored. This chapter presents yet another approach—the social interactional perspective. Within this chapter, we explore the social interactional underpinnings of problem behavior lifestyles, focusing specifically on friendships and parent–child microsocial behavior patterns.

Microsocial behavior patterns are specific behaviors that occur within the moment-to-moment interactions with others. These behaviors are assessed by carefully observing the interactions of individuals and documenting patterns in their behavioral interactions. Behaviors such as "directives," "negative engagement," and "positive engagement" that summarize the moment-by-moment interactions with a friend are examples of specific, microsocial behaviors. Microsocial behavior can be empirically defined as rates per minute, proportion scores (unconditional probabilities), or conditional probabilities. Conditional probabilities represent the contingent relation between two interpersonal behaviors forming the basis for analyses of sequential patterns.

Problem behavior lifestyles, in contrast, describe behavioral patterns across time and settings. These are typically derived from retrospective reports taken from a variety of reporting agents. Parent ratings of their adolescent's antisocial behavior or teacher reports of the number of peer conflicts at school are empirical definitions of traits or dispositions.

The context of interactions is the overall environment in which particular microsocial interactions occur. Three major contextual variations are explored in this chapter. Social contexts can be evaluated in terms of the *interactants* (e.g., parents with adolescents, adolescents with their friends), the *site of the interaction* (e.g., home, school, or laboratory) and the *developmental time frame* in which the interaction occurred. These definitions are used in conjunction with specific theoretical assumptions to explain the role of microsocial behavior patterns, across a variety of contexts, in the emergence of a problem behavior lifestyle.

The evidence presented here subscribes to the following theoretical positions that frame our approach to the study of adolescent problem behavior. First, the social behaviors we seek to explain are learned behaviors. Contrary to Rowe's position, expressed in this volume, we emphasize the role of social interaction in the acquisition of behavioral dispositions. Individuals adapt to the outcome of their moment-to-moment exchanges with their social environment, noted by insidious shifts in future moment-to-moment exchanges (e.g., Snyder, Dishion, & Patterson, 1986). The social interactional approach is an applied approach (Dishion, Reid, & Patterson, 1988; Patterson, Reid, & Dishion, in press). We assume that improved understanding of the microsocial underpinnings of problem behavior lifestyles provides a manual for change. It is at the microsocial level that our interventions are aimed to produce change. For example, parent training interventions aim to reduce parental use of aversive limit-setting approaches and are replaced by more systematic use of positive reinforcement, problem-solving techniques, and sane, effective disciplining (Patterson, Chamberlain, & Reid, 1982). The social interactional approach arises from the behavioral tradition and has a well-documented place in the literature (Bandura & Walters, 1959; Miller & Dollard, 1958; Skinner, 1953). Later in this chapter, our focus turns to elaborating the coercion model (Patterson, 1982) in respect to the issue of children's development of problem behavior.

Second, problem behavior lifestyles are composite indices of numerous microsocial behaviors exhibited across a wide range of contexts. From this perspective, larger behaviors are a reflection of numerous microsocial exchanges as well as attributional biases of the raters. Problem behavior lifestyles are evident when the outcome of microsocial exchanges leads to general behavior patterns that are demonstrated across different contexts and can be assessed by global measurements taken from a variety of reporting agents (teachers, parents, adolescents, and court records). A topographical map of microsocial behavior, generated across several contexts, results in a profile of an individual's behavior that is labeled and ascribed as an intra-individual characteristic.

Researchers (Jessor, this volume; Ketterlinus & Lamb, 1993) often refer to these traits as *lifestyles*. Others might label this acquired consistency in behavioral exchange as a *trait, personality,* or *interactional style*. Considering the covariation in a variety of developmentally compromising behaviors in adolescence—behaviors such as delinquency, substance use, antisocial behavior, and precocious sexual activity—there is support for attention to this overall construct of deviant or problem behavior lifestyles (Dryfoos, 1990; Elliott, in press; Osgood, 1993). The final position of this chapter and the focus of our research is derived from the first two premises. That is, the learned microsocial exchanges of individuals are the underlying source of problem behavior lifestyles. The strength of the relationship between microsocial behavior patterns and problem behavior lifestyles is a function of the contextual similarities in which microsocial behaviors are performed. The context in which interactions occur is very important in determining the degree to which microsocial behaviors are consistently exhibited and begin to form patterns of behavior that persist across setting.

The remainder of this chapter explores the theoretical implications and methodological demands for understanding the microsocial, and contextual dimensions of problem behavior lifestyles. Specific attention is given to the role of context in the relations between microsocial behaviors. Examples from projects underway at the Oregon Social Learning Center (OSLC), along with other literature, provide illustrative examples.

A SOCIAL INTERACTIONAL PERSPECTIVE

Microsocial data reflecting moment-to-moment exchanges need to be explored across a wide range of contexts to fully understand their impact on problem behavior lifestyles. Microsocial behaviors, observed across more than one context and systematically coded into meaningful units, provide the basic information necessary to predict the organization of problem behavior lifestyles. These microsocial data can be used in different ways to untangle the etiology and maintenance of problem behavior lifestyles. First, microsocial data can be used to generate rates or frequencies of behavior that characterize an individual or a group of individuals. These rates can be generated from, and compared across, a number of different contexts. Comparisons can be made by assessing whether or not a specific behavior displayed by a group of subjects in one context occurs at similar mean rates in another context.

These data can also be used to assess the interrelatedness of individual behavior across and within contexts. One might be interested in knowing whether positive behavior rates in parent–child interactions are correlated with positive behavior rates in child–peer interactions. Or, in reference to a specific interaction, frequency counts of behavior could be used to relate the behavior rate of one individual to the behavior rate of their partner. Such comparisons yield a descriptive index of general behaviors that might cumulatively contribute to dispositional patterns that persist through adolescence.

Analyzing descriptive information on behavior rates is a useful first step in understanding the power of relationship contexts and settings on the topography of interpersonal behavior. One gets the immediate (if not obvious) sense that parent–child relationships are more conflictual than friendships in adolescence by simply comparing the rate-per-minute of "negative engagement." The same is true when comparing the rate-per-minute of laughter across parents and friends. These descriptive counts provide an empirical basis for defining the qualitative charac-teristics of relationship contexts.

This type of frequency count, however, offers little information on the etiology or maintenance of such microsocial behaviors. Frequency counts of behavior do not account for the interrelatedness of behavior on a moment-to-moment basis, and consequently these frequencies—which summarize behaviors across time—do not lead to information about likely patterns of behavior that might be consistent across different contexts. Attending to the sequencing of microsocial data is essential when attempting to determine the process of interpersonal behavior that influences and maintains a problem behavior lifestyle.

Within a given context, the degree to which microsocial behaviors are organized and predictable can be assessed by observing the proportion of behaviors and the specific microsocial sequences within the interaction. Organization and predict-ability of behavior depends on the degree of association between specific stimuli or environmental cues (antecedents, A) and the behavior (response, R) that they elicit. The consequences (C) that have followed the behavior in response to a given antecedent determine the predictability of this A–R–C chain in future interactions. Behaviors occurring within social interactions are responses (R) to social cues (serving as antecedents, A), with the predictability of any social response deter-mined by the strength of the A–R chain. The consequences of behavior demon-strated in response to a given antecedent serve to strengthen or weaken the association between specific antecedents and responses. There are, unfortunately, very few studies that empirically demonstrate the antecedent–response–conse-quence patterns of stimulus control in human interactions. Patterson (1974) re-ported an empirical approach to defining specific microsocial behaviors into "response classes" based on similarities in function. That is, behaviors that tend to follow the same antecedent and produce similar consequences were said to be members of the same response class. As demonstrated by Patterson's (1974) data, the process of identifying empirically validated response classes is laborious, precluding widespread efforts in this area.

At another level, patterns underlying adolescent problem behavior are straight-forward. Consider John and his friend Lew. John is in the store with Lew; John points at an item on the shelf and nudges Lew suggesting that he pocket (shoplift) the item. Lew puts the item in his pocket. After leaving the store, John showers Lew with praise and lets him know how impressed he is with his performance. In this example, John created a stimulus (suggestion for shoplifting), to which Lew responded (took the item), and immediately received recognition for his good work (praise).

It is important to reiterate that the consequence of an act influences the behavior only to the extent that it is elicited by a given antecedent. This is a simple distinction in behavioristic terms but often discounted by pure reinforcement theory (Schoenfeld, 1978). It is the strength of the A–R chains of behavior that are influenced by consequences, not simple responses regardless of the antecedent behavior.

A variety of methodological and analytical techniques have been proposed to address sequential data (Cairns, 1979; Gottman & Roy, 1990; Wampold & Margolin, 1982). One of the simplest procedures and a good starting point is to determine the unconditional and conditional probabilities of targeted behaviors. Unconditional probabilities represent the probability of a behavior occurring taking into account the rate of all other behaviors being exhibited. Conditional probabilities represent the likelihood of one behavior leading to the occurrence of a second behavior. Conditional probabilities generate an estimate of the degree to which a specific antecedent elicits a given response, and when used in combination with rates and proportion assessments can determine the strength of a given pattern (antecedent–response connection) of behavior. Rates of behavior, sequential patterns of responding, and context are all subject to variation in complex social interactions. The degree of covariation among these complex elements of social interaction determines the degree to which microsocial behaviors can be labeled *behavioral lifestyles.*

Microsocial behaviors are influenced by the context in which they occur. Different contexts provide different rates of antecedents and contingencies for consequences that influence the rates and patterns of given responses. Likewise, microsocial behavior patterns impact the array of contexts to which adolescents might be exposed. Patterns that become organized and predictable in one context may influence the availability of other social contexts within which an individual can find social interaction opportunities. Consider the teenager who escalates to name calling given a conflict with a popular peer. The likelihood of his or her receiving positive initiations will shift immediately downward. Uncorrected, this interpersonal pattern would lead to virtual exclusion from certain peer contexts that could potentially contribute to further development of relationship skills. Microsocial behavior patterns that are predictable across settings can enhance or inhibit opportunities for social interaction. This phenomena might be best illustrated with the social interactions of preschool children. The early age (preschool) at which consistent social rejection occurs can be partially accounted for by the cross-context consistency in inappropriate behaviors combined with the restrictions on social interaction that follow. A young child who refuses to share or cooperate with other children across a number of preschool contexts, for example, has a high probability of being rejected by other children as a preferred playmate (Eisenberg, 1982). Rejected status, which results from microsocial exchanges, then limits future interaction opportunities that in turn further impact the trajectory of social development.

Similar social conditions exist across the life span. Consider Sue's predicament. Sue had a group of friends who routinely coaxed her into arguments. When she responded by getting angry and demanding that everyone see her point of view, the group reinforced her behavior by giving in and doing things Sue's way. Sue changed schools and met some new friends (different context) who did not have the same reinforcement contingencies. Sue did not feel welcome in this context for two reasons: (a) the group was rarely interested in arguing with Sue; and (b) when there were arguments and Sue responded by getting angry, the group walked away and left Sue talking to herself. Sue's response pattern that was learned in one group (context) did not serve her well in her initial exposure to a new group (context). Sue's success in the new group depends on her ability to adapt her repertoire to the group's interaction styles (or there is a change in the group's willingness to reinforce her behavior). If she is unable to change behavior patterns, her exposure to a new context for behavior (new group of peers) will be limited.

Dishion and Paterson (in press) described a confluence model for the influence of peer relationships on social development in middle childhood through adolescence. There is a general tendency for children with similar social characteristics to become friends (Kandel, 1978). Discrepancies in behavior do exist in all relationships. It is hypothesized that maintenance of the relationship is predicated on the merging of behavior characteristics within the relationship (Kandel, 1978), whereby members of the dyad or clique become more similar over time. Within this model, relationships do not always have a salubrious impact on social development. Two deviant individuals may actually become more deviant as a function of their relationship. On the other hand, a child with problem behavior tendencies may become less deviant in the context of a prosocial friendship, or more frequently, in a prosocial clique.

Aversive behaviors that are demonstrated by individuals in exchanges with other individuals seem to be particularly salient markers of microsocial processes that demarcate development of problem behavior lifestyles. The indirect influences of negative microsocial behavior has been addressed in detail elsewhere (Coie & Dodge, 1983; Patterson, 1982) and therefore, are not explored in this chapter. The following section represents illustrative examples of direct influences of negative behavior demonstrated in a variety of social interactions. Cross-contextual similarities and differences in microsocial negative exchanges and their relationship to problem behavior lifestyles are presented.

AVERSIVE EXCHANGES AND THE COERCIVE PROCESS

Aggressive, negative, and coercive behaviors that emerge early in life have been shown to be the most stable and rigorous predictors of delinquency, substance use, school failure, and occurrence of psychiatric disorders (Dishion & Loeber, 1985; Hall & Cairns, 1984; Patterson, 1982). Due to the predictive value of negative and aversive exchanges, it is useful to focus on the consistency of these behaviors across contexts attending to both frequencies of response and sequential patterns.

Many studies have found moderate behavioral consistency in rates of specific social behaviors when assessed across different contexts. However, little has been done to assess similarities in sequential patterns of interaction across different settings. This information is critical to untangling the contributions of microsocial responses to problem behavior lifestyles. Despite the paucity of research, however, the work of Patterson (1982) has provided compelling evidence for the impact of microsocial behaviors on problem behavior lifestyles. Patterson's detailed account of coercion theory is a classic example of microsocial sequences of behavior

(A–R–C chains) occurring within a specific contextual domain and relating to broader problem behaviors. Patterson identified coercive exchanges in families by observing the microsocial structure of their interactions. He found common patterns of reciprocal negative behavior (aversiveness) in families and labeled these exchanges *coercive family processes*. Specifically, he suggested that aversive and aggressive behavior (*R*) in children are stimulated by parental cues (*A*), and the probability of an aversive response following a specific antecedent behavior (*p* $A{\rightarrow}R$) is the result of the behavior immediately following the $A{\rightarrow}R$ chain of events. A prototypic coercion pattern described by Patterson is: Mother scolds (A), child whines (R), mother stops scolding (C). In this example, the mother's removal of an aversive antecedent (negative reinforcement, i.e., scolding) will increase the probability of the child whining, given the mom starts scolding again. This negative reinforcement paradigm, originally presented by Patterson (1982), is illustrated in Fig.10.1.

In this scheme, coercive patterns produced by children and parents are aversive events that elicit reciprocal aversive responses. The fact that these patterns exist in family interactions is interesting. However, they are not particularly useful in determining the etiology of problem behaviors in adolescence. Subsequent work by Patterson and his colleagues at the OSLC, established the predictive and concurrent validity of these coercive exchanges. They found that family interactions characterized by high rates of coercive exchanges are likely to socialize children into problem behavior lifestyles. During 25 years of research, OSLC staff have consistently related coercive family process to boys' antisocial and problem behavior throughout their adolescence (Patterson et al., in press). For example, Loeber and Dishion (1984) found that boys identified as physically aggressive at home and school came from families who experienced more extreme levels of

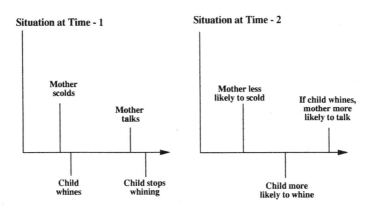

FIG. 10.1. Coercion as a negative reinforcement paradigm (from Patterson, 1982).

coercive exchanges. Furthermore, clinical studies have provided some evidence that parent training that reduces aversive exchanges between parents and children leads to concomitant reductions in child antisocial behavior (Dishion, Patterson, & Kavanagh, in press; Forgatch, 1991; Patterson, 1982).

The early role of families in socializing children and the strength of coercion as a process that contributes to problem behavior lifestyles generates two major questions: Do children whose interactions with their parents are negative, aversive, or coercive demonstrate similar types of behavior in other contexts? Do patterns of negative and coercive behavior demonstrated across a variety of contexts relate to broader problem behavior lifestyles in adolescence?

These questions are addressed in the remainder of this chapter to illustrate the multiple influences of microsocial behavior on the emergence of problem behavior lifestyles.

THE OREGON YOUTH STUDY

Three types of data are necessary to fully address cross-context consistency in microsocial behavior and its relationship to problem behavior lifestyles. First, specific and detailed information sampling of the moment-to-moment behavior of individuals in multiple contexts is necessary. Second, information on problem behavior lifestyles is necessary. And third, information is needed that characterizes the specific context in which microsocial behaviors occur. These types of data are available in the Oregon Youth Study (OYS) and are used to address the questions of direct microsocial behavior influences on problem behavior lifestyles.

The OYS has followed approximately 200 boys through 7 years of development beginning with the recruitment of two cohorts of boys between 1983 and 1985. The OYS was designed to assess the origins and consequences of antisocial behavior in adolescent boys (Patterson, 1986; Patterson & Bank, 1987; Patterson et al., in press). The exclusive use of boys in the OYS restricts the generalizability of the results presented. Implications for future research directed at replicating these results with a sample of girls are presented in a later section. The boys were 9- or 10-years-old when selected from elementary schools located in neighborhoods with a high density of delinquency. Data from parents, teachers, target children, their peers, and court records have been recorded annually on each child and their family since the first cohort was recruited in 1983. The data were generated by questionnaires, face-to-face interviews, telephone interviews, observations of laboratory tasks, home observations, and reviews of cohort records.

Microsocial data on the adolescent boys interacting with parents at home and in a laboratory setting were coded using the Family Problem Solving Code (Dishion, Garner, Patterson, Reid, & Thibodeaux, 1983). In addition, microsocial data from problem-solving sessions where the boys were asked to bring a friend into a laboratory setting were coded using the Peer Process Code (Dishion et al., 1989).

The Family Process Code and the Peer Process Code are parallel versions of a code that records behavior content and affective valence of approximately 25 minutes of interactions (Dishion et al., 1989). Combined, these observational data yield microsocial data collected across four different social settings. The data represent adolescents interacting with their parents in their home (Family Home Observations) and in a laboratory setting at two different points in time (Family Lab Observations), and adolescents interacting with a friend in a laboratory setting (Peer Lab Observations).

In addition to these microsocial data, the OYS has used parent, child, and teacher reports, court records, and interviewer impressions of behavior to generate multimethod, multiagent indicators of problem behavior constructs (Capaldi & Patterson, 1987). The problem behavior constructs generated include delinquency, antisocial behavior, depression, substance abuse, academic deficiencies, association with deviant peers, general peer relations, and friendship quality. In addition, several constructs have been generated as indices of family functioning, including discipline, monitoring, supervision, and parent rejection.

The combination of microsocial, multimethod, and multiagent data has produced a series of analyses that cumulatively illustrate the direct and indirect influences of microsocial progressions to problem behavior. For simplicity, we limit our discussion to aversive behaviors and behavioral exchanges as a singular example of microsocial behaviors demonstrated across different contexts. These aversive microsocial behaviors, labeled *negative engagement*, represent a combination of content and affect codes with confirmed similarity in psychometric properties (Dishion & Andrews, in press). Similarly the traits presented are limited to delinquency and association with deviant peers.

MICROSOCIAL BEHAVIOR ACROSS CONTEXTS

The role of reciprocal negative exchanges within children's interactions across multiple contexts has been posed as a primary question to be addressed. To this end, the rates, unconditional probabilities, and conditional probabilities of negative child behavior within interactions, were compared across the different contexts in which microsocial data were collected. Observations were organized such that the contextual influences of time, setting, and interactant (parent or peer) could be evaluated. Observations representing these contextual variations in families were observed in a laboratory setting at two time points (boys ages 9 or 10, and boys ages 14 or 15). The home and laboratory settings were used at Time 1, and children were observed in a laboratory condition interacting separately with parents and peers at Time 2. Four sets of observational data yielded the three contextual comparisons (see Table 10.1).

Contextual similarities in the rates, unconditional probabilities, and conditional probabilities (these indices are related, but not confounded in terms of measurement) across the three types of contextual variation are presented in Table 10.2. As can be seen from this table, the frequency (rate), proportion (unconditional

TABLE 10.1
Observational Data Yielding Three Contextual Comparisons

Context Comparison	Data Type
Setting	Home observations of parents and child compared to laboratory observations of parents and child. Both observations conducted when child was age 9–10.
Time	Laboratory observations of child interacting with parents at age 9–10 compared to laboratory observations of child interacting with parents at age 13–15.
Interactants	Laboratory observations of child interacting with friend compared to laboratory observations of child interacting with parents. Both observations conducted when child was age 9–10.

TABLE 10.2
Rates, Unconditional Probabilities, and Conditional Probabilities of Negative Engagement Across Contexts

	Rates		Unconditional Probabilities		Conditional Probabilities	
	M	SD	M	SD	M	SD
Setting						
Home	.21	.21	.10	.07	.09	.09
Laboratory	.31	.54	.06	.09	.06	.12
Interactants						
Parents	.68	.92	.14	.13	.13	.16
Peers	.08	.09	.05	.04	.07	.12
Time						
Time 1	.31	.54	.06	.09	.06	.12
Time 2	.68	.92	.14	.13	.13	.16

probability), and reciprocity (conditional probability) of negative engagement in social interactions varied as a function of specific contextual dimensions.

The most consistent behaviors are demonstrated across settings within families. Parent and child behavior showed little variation in mean frequency, proportion, and reciprocity across laboratory and home settings. However, there were significant differences in behavior across different interaction partners, and over time.

Children were significantly more negative with their parents than with their peers. The lack of significant negative engagement with peers was striking. Although these 14- or 15-year-old boys demonstrated on average one negative behavior toward their parents every minute or two, they were negative to peers on average less than once every 10 minutes. Likewise, the mean proportion of negative engagement with peers was 5% compared to 14% with parents, and children responded negatively to a parent's negative behavior 13% of the time, whereas they responded negatively to their peers only 7% of the time.

Children's negative engagement with parents also increased over time. At ages 9 or 10, the children demonstrated roughly one half of the negative behavior that they would eventually display at ages 14 or 15. This doubling in negativity was found in frequency, proportion, and reciprocity indexes.

These descriptive data suggest limited generalizability of behavior across settings. Mean differences in frequency, proportion, and reciprocity of negative engagement were evident in the time and interactant comparisons, whereas the setting comparison yielded consistent mean levels of behavior. However, although there was general inconsistency in negative engagement across contexts, there was consistency in the relationship between the indexes of negative engagement. For example, increases over time in frequency of negative engagement paralleled increases in proportion and reciprocity. The only exception to these parallel changes was found in the unconditional probabilities that varied across setting. These differences, however, were not statistically significant.

Correlational analyses can provide meaningful evidence of intraindividual consistency in terms of rank ordering. Correlational analyses relating behaviors exhibited across contextual variations are presented in Table 10.3.

These correlations again suggest that negative engagement was most consistent across setting. There were additional statistically significant relationships in intraindividual negative engagement across contexts, but none of the correlations were overwhelmingly persuasive in terms of practical significance (coefficients ranging from .14 to .28). The patterns of these interactions, however, are worth noting.

Fewer parallel findings across the different indices of negative engagement were found than when inspecting mean levels. Negative engagement in home and laboratory settings were significantly correlated in frequency, proportion, and reciprocity. This stability was not found across indices when relating parent to peer interactions and interactions over time. The proportion of negative engagement with peers was correlated with proportion of negative engagement with parents, but frequency and reciprocity indices of negative engagement were not significantly related across

TABLE 10.3
Correlations of Rates, Unconditional Probabilities, and Conditional
Probabilities of Children's Negative Engagement Across Contextual Variations

	Rate	Unconditional Probabilities	Conditional Probabilities
Setting	.28**	.23**	.14*
(Home with Lab)			
Interactants	.07	.22**	.06
(Parent–child with Peer–child)			
Time	.18**	.20**	.01
(Time 1 with Time 2)			

interactants. A relation between negativity in the behavior of 9- and 10-year-olds and their behavior at age 14 or 15 was found for frequency and proportion, but not for reciprocity.

In general, these correlations show less intraindividual consistency when considering reciprocity of negative engagement then when considering frequency or proportion. The relatively weak correlations, together with the inconsistency in mean levels demonstrated across different contextual variations, do not support the hypothesis that negative behaviors demonstrated to a high degree in one context are demonstrated to a similar degree in other contexts.

Instead, our data suggest that boys' negative behavior fluctuates by context. Basic behavioral tendencies, as indicated by rates and proportion of behavior, are demonstrated as appropriate to a given context. Furthermore, reciprocity as an example of an antecedent/response chain is influenced by the subtle complexities of varying contexts, as well as the overall rate of antecedent stimuli and resulting behavioral consequences elicited within a given context.

The data presented also suggest that some dimensions of contexts yield more congruent behavioral rates, proportion, and reciprocity than others. Setting and time yielded a higher pattern of correlations across context than did interactants. It may be that observing family interactions in two different settings and at two different time points provides more consistent cross-context behavior than comparing any parent–child interactions with child–friend interactions. In adolescence, parent–child relations are qualitatively different than child–peer relations; therefore, the most dramatic differences in context logically lead to the most dramatic differences in behavior across those two contexts. Children self-select their friends and the peers with whom they interact regularly, and interactions with a specific peer tend to be maintained only as long as the friendship is viewed as mutually beneficial. In contrast, parent–child relations are not this temporary and are not self-selected. High rates, proportion, and reciprocal negative behavior for many children signal an end to the mutual benefits derived from an interaction with a specific peer, and serve to terminate the relationship. Fortunately, parent–child relations are not formally terminated as a result of these negative engagements.

This is a potent example of contextual differences that influence behavior. It is not surprising that parent–child interactions yield different rates of negative engagement than child–peer interactions. The antecedents and consequences of a given behavior can vary dramatically or subtly across contexts. According to a social interaction perspective, rates, proportions, and reciprocity (or any other conditional behavior) should be similar across contexts only to the degree that there is function similarity of antecedent and consequence behaviors.

MICROSOCIAL BEHAVIOR AND PROBLEM BEHAVIOR LIFESTYLES

Next, we address the question of the extent to which microsocial behaviors relate to other indices of problem behavior lifestyles. Results already presented indicate that the majority of boys did not have high cross-context similarity in negative engagement. However, the results presented here do not reflect the fact that some of the boys demonstrated substantial negative behavior across the contextual dimensions. Based on the theoretical premise presented in an earlier section, we predicted that boys who demonstrated cross-context consistency in negative engagement should have high rates of problem behavior. Additional analyses were conducted, therefore, to determine the degree of association between negative engagement demonstrated in multiple contexts with multiagent reports of delinquency and association with deviant peers. Delinquency and association with deviant peers were selected as examples of problem behavior outcome variables based on their stability and concurrent validity with other problems such as substance abuse, antisocial behavior, and academic performance.

An inspection of the correlations of total negative engagement (using the frequency, proportion, and reciprocity indexes) suggests a positive relationship between amounts of negative engagement and problem behavior (see Table 10.4).

These data do not reflect the number of contexts in which negative behaviors were exhibited. In fact, these correlations are most influenced by high correlations of negative behavior in the home observations with the problem behavior indicators. An analysis of the number of contexts in which negative engagement occurred

TABLE 10.4
Correlations of Microsocial Indices of Social Interaction With
Problem Behaviors

	Antisocial	Deviant Peers	Delinquency
Family in Home Time 1			
Frequency	.28***	.20**	.13*
Proportion	.24**	.23**	.26**
Reciprocity	.15*	.17*	.23***
Family in Lab Time 1			
Frequency	.21**	.15*	.08
Proportion	.14	.13	.06
Reciprocity	.06	.09	.10
Family in Lab Time 2			
Frequency	.07	.07	.06
Proportion	.17*	.11	.14
Reciprocity	.08	.12*	.07
Child/Peer in Lab Time 2			
Frequency	.12*	.09	.17**
Proportion	.12	.16*	.10
Reciprocity	.14*	.18**	.18**
Sum of Negative Engagement			
Frequency	.29**	.16*	.19**
Proportion	.25**	.23**	.22**
Reciprocity	.18**	.18*	.21**

$*$ = p < .05. $**$ = p < .001.

was conducted to determine the relationship of cross-context consistency of negative engagement with delinquency and association with deviant peers.

Boys were considered "negative" in a given context if at least 10% of their behaviors were coded as negative engagement. This dichotomous definition of negativity was applied separately to both proportion (unconditional probabilities greater than .10) and reciprocity (conditional probabilities greater than .10). Table 10.5 presents differences in mean rates of delinquency and association with deviant peers according to the number of contexts in which the subjects demonstrated negative behavior.

The result presented in Table 10.5 demonstrates that, in terms of both proportion and reciprocity, delinquency and association with deviant peers were directly related to the number of settings in which the subjects demonstrated negative engagement. Children who exhibited negative engagement in multiple settings had higher scores on multiagent reports of delinquency and association with deviant peers than did children who either exhibited negative engagement in one setting, or who did not exhibit any negative engagement. Microsocial negativity demonstrated in more than one context was predictive of higher levels of problem behavior when more than one reporting agent is providing more global information about these problem behaviors, a finding that is not surprising. Congruence between multiagent macrolevel data and multicontext microlevel data is important in defining a problem as an index of multiple-context microsocial behaviors.

Next, a more detailed analysis was conducted to assess the presence or absence of negativity across specific contextual dimensions, and whether or not this distinction was predictive of problem behaviors. The contextual variations defined

TABLE 10.5
The Relationship Between Microsocial Negative Engagement in Multiples Settings and Problem Behavior

	Number of Contexts	Delinquency		Association With Deviant Peers		
		M	SD	M	SD	N
	0	−.25	.54	−.29	.71	63
Unconditional	1	.11	.90	.02	.91	64
Probabilities	2	.11	.69	.23	.75	75
		$F = 7.0$		$F = 7.7$		
		$p < .001$		$p < .001$		
	0	−.21	.49	−.36	.70	50
Conditional	1	−.11	.59	−.02	.85	63
Probabilities	2	.19	.81	.21	.79	89
		$F = 4.7$		$F = 6.14$		
		$p < .01$		$p < .003$		

TABLE 10.6
The Relationship Between Microsocial Negative Engagement in Parent and Peer Interactions and Problem Behavior

	Number of contexts	Delinquency		Association With Deviant Peers		N
		M	SD	M	SD	
	0	−.05	.78	−.10	.78	100
Unconditional	1	.04	.73	.09	.68	84
Probabilities	2	.08	.54	.16	.87	17
		F = .46		F = 1.2		
		ns		ns		
	0	−.09	.75	−.14	.76	77
Conditional	1	−.06	.68	−.02	.88	89
Probabilities	2	.43	1.08	.13	.76	30
		F = 5.4		F = 2.5		
		p < .005		p < .023		

in earlier analyses were used to assess consistency in negative engagement across time, setting, and interactants.

The analyses of consistency in negativity across interactants (parents vs. peers) yielded the most interesting findings. The most dramatic differences in both association with deviant peers and delinquency were found when children were conditionally negative with both peers and parents. Boys who reciprocated negative engagement with both parents and peers had significantly higher scores on the problem behavior indicators. These findings were found for reciprocity, but not for proportion (see Table 10.6). Comparisons across the contextual dimensions of time and setting did not yield similar results.

The differential impact of the category of interactant contributed most to the findings presented earlier on the total number of contexts in which children interacted. Negative reciprocity, consistently demonstrated with parents and peers, appears related to delinquency and association with deviant peers. These findings, taken in conjunction with the lack of differences in unconditional negativity, lend some support to a social interactional model of the influence of microsocial negative behaviors and problem behaviors and are consistent with Patterson's (1982) coercion theory.

CONCLUSIONS

The results presented in this chapter demonstrating direct influences of microsocial behavior on problem behavior lifestyles supplement other findings on the relation between negative behavior patterns and the development of behavior problems. For example, aversive exchanges between parents and their children, regardless of negativity in other contexts, have been related to antisocial behavior patterns and delinquency (Dishion et al., in press; Patterson, Reid, & Dishion, 1992). Furthermore, negative and aggressive behavior in peer relations have been found to be related to peer rejection and degree of association with deviant peers (Asher & Dodge, 1986; Dishion, Patterson, Stoolmiller, & Skinner, 1991). Until now, little effort has been made to determine how these behaviors relate to microsocial behavior across parent and peer relationship contexts.

A common scenario of indirect microsocial influences on the etiology of a problem behavior lifestyle is as follows. Negative interactions with parents lead to socially unskilled children (Patterson, 1982), who are rejected by their general peer group early in life (Coie & Dodge, 1983). Early rejection by peers, in turn, contributes to the child drifting into increased association with a deviant, socially unskilled group of peers (Dishion et al., 1991). The unskilled, undersocialized group of children (now young adolescents) in the OYS, engage in a number of problem behaviors, and their association with one another in homogeneous groups serves as the primary influence in the maintenance of problem behaviors (Kandel & Andrews, 1987).

The results presented in this chapter suggest that there may be more direct methods of assessing the influence of microsocial data on problem behavior lifestyles. Although the statistically significant coefficients reported here are in some cases of marginal practical significance, the pattern of results cumulatively represent important information on the cross-context consistency of behavior.

The finding of a lack of congruence in negative interactions is consistent with a reinforcement model of behavioral development. In general, environmental influences are conceptualized by interacting agents, settings, and time. These contextual variations are associated with entirely different learning histories. The varied meaning of a behavior is defined by context, for example, raising one's hand to speak is considered a conventionally positive antecedent to responses in classroom settings and is probably reinforced by teachers. Raising one's hand to speak when talking to parents is at best atypical, and may even be considered as an aversive stimulus in some families. From a reinforcement perspective, the function of any given behavior is necessarily determined by context in which it occurs, whereas a biologically based theory of behavioral traits would suggest less contextual variation in behavior. The magnitude of cross-setting consistency in negative engagement across contexts, in these data, is insufficient to support the underlying trait notion.

Contexts for social interaction are complex and varied. Stimuli for a given behavior and contingencies for the consequences of that behavior vary across virtually every context. It is the degree to which behaviors are consistent across multiple contexts that determine whether or not they are the underlying source of a problem behavior lifestyle. The results presented here suggest that cross-context negativity, especially reciprocal negative behavior demonstrated with families and with peers, may be related to a problem behavior lifestyle.

Future research in this area should concentrate on identifying stable antecedents/behavior chains, the consequences that support the association between the antecedent and the behavior, and the number of contexts that elicit specific chains of behavior. The optimal design to answer these questions involves naturalistic research that takes into account a multitude of contexts and many hours of observation. There are, however, very few extant data sets that represent purely naturalistic contexts for interaction. One problem is that many types of behavior sequences that underlie problem behavior lifestyles have low base rates, although they tend to exhibit highly consistent patterns across time or situation. An associated problem is that a given antecedent behavior may be consistently associated with a behavioral response that is consistently reinforced, but the occurrence of such an A–R sequence may be rare. Among some groups of adolescents, violent acts are a good example of a low base-rate behavior that is consistent in response to given antecedents, and that may be negatively reinforced by the victim and positively reinforced by the peer group. This type of behavior sequence is not likely to be captured in contrived contexts with limited observation time. However, they are most likely very salient and predictable sequences that can be captured through sustained naturalistic observations.

One hypothesis concerning the etiology of problem behavior lifestyles is that it emerges in adolescence as a product of years of microsocial interactions. Unravelling the history of these microsocial exchanges as exhibited in a variety of contexts is critical to a thorough understanding of the emergence of this behavior.

The data presented in this chapter were collected from an all-boy sample. We have no direct evidence that the findings and conclusions presented here for boys would be equally applicable to girls. Future research needs to investigate the generalizability of these findings to the etiology of problem behavior lifestyles in girls. We assume that although there should be major gender differences in the patterns of microsocial behavior, these patterns would show similar variations across different contexts among both boys and girls.

POLICY IMPLICATIONS

Bronfrenbrenner's (1979, 1986) ecological model of development can be of considerable utility when attempting to place social interaction model of problem behaviors in perspective. In Bronfrenbrenner's model, spheres of influence over children's development range from general cultural influences (i.e., macrosystem models) to specific face-to-face (i.e., microsystem models) interactions. For the purposes of this discussion, we oversimplify Bronfrenbrenner's elaborate theory in order to discuss the implications of our results for policies that would lead to programs which could influence that nature of microsocial (face-to-face) interactions of children with significant agents of socialization (e.g., peers, teachers, parents), as well as programs that could help determine the kinds and characteristics of ecologies (i.e., settings) in which children develop.

Microsocial Interactions

The way adults behave with children is generally left to chance by policymakers. Aside from outlawing blatantly abusive parenting or educational practices, there have been few systematic efforts to promote childrearing practices that are bereft of coercion at the community level (Biglan, Glasgow, & Singer, in press). Research on successful interventions designed for children with conduct disorders indicates that the technology is available to reduce child negative behavior via modeling and training of constructive and positive parenting practices (e.g., Webster-Stratton, 1984). For example, there is strong evidence that many parents' childrearing practices are improved subsequent to their viewing videotapes that model a full range of positive parenting practices (Webster-Stratton, Kolpacoff, & Hollinsworth, 1988).

The coercion model (Patterson, 1982) does an excellent job of identifying maladaptive parent–child interaction patterns underlying extremely aggressive behavior in children. More recently, this model has been extended to consider how the child's negative interpersonal adaption would disrupt the development of academic achievement and friendship with prosocial peers (Patterson et al., in press). Furthermore, as suggested by Biglan et al. (in press), we may possess enough knowledge to develop policies that promote the production and viewing of educational videotapes that model, at the mass population level, constructive, effective, and enjoyable styles of interacting with children.

The results presented here and elsewhere (Andrews & Dishion, 1991; Andrews, Dishion, & Patterson, 1993; Dishion & Patterson, in press) have implications for making adjustments to existing social skills training packages. For example, our findings suggest that antisocial children have ample numbers of friends, and that these children's interactions with friends are rarely negative; in fact, they are often quite positive. These results suggest the possibly that it is use of rarely occurring negative behaviors in peer relationships that carries the most weight in predicting which children enter, and continue, problem behavior lifestyle trajectories. The implication is that interventions focusing on improving how children behave with peers might best focus on simply reducing negative peer behaviors (Bierman, 1990).

Context

Social policy may have its most profound impact on the type and nature of ecologies in which children spend time. The easiest area of access for intervention is, of course, the school. Much is known about which characteristics of school environments promote children's development (Linney & Seidman, 1987), and eventually, education policies take into account this knowledge by focusing on promoting these characteristics.

There are specific contextual interventions in schools that might reduce the level of adolescent problem behavior. For example, ability tracking, the policy of grouping educationally at-risk children in the same classroom, develops groups of learners with homogeneous skills and abilities to whom educational material can be presented at one level. Unfortunately, many children with academic deficits are exhibiting social skills deficits with peers (who often exhibit antisocial behavior) and are familiar with coercion tactics at home (Dishion, 1990; Patterson et al., in press). Ability tracking may provide the formative interpersonal experiences for the development of deviant peer groups that seem to emerge as early as the fourth grade (Kellam, 1990). The skills and behaviors learned in these early interpersonal experiences, furthermore, show considerable stability through early adolescence, even in suburban areas (Dishion et al., 1991). The extremely high correlation between involvement with deviant peers and adolescent problem behavior (e.g., Elliott, Huizinga, & Ageton, 1985) suggests the need for policies that actively engineer environments that reduce or eliminate massive homogeneous groupings of at-risk youth.

REFERENCES

Andrews, D. W., & Dishion, T. J. (1991). *Cross-context similarities in microsocial behavior patterns as predictors of delinquency*. Unpublished manuscript, Oregon Social Learning Center, Eugene, OR.

Andrews, D. W., Dishion, T. J., & Patterson, G. R. (1993). *The differential predictive validity of peer acceptance and friendship to problem behavior in adolescent boys*. Manuscript submitted for publication.

Asher, S. R., & Dodge, K. A. (1986). Identifying children who are rejected by their peers. *Developmental Psychology, 22,* 444–449.

Bandura, A., & Walters, R. H. (1959). *Adolescent aggression*. New York: Ronald Press Co.

Bierman, K. (1990). Improving the peer relations of rejected children. In B. B. Lahey & A. E. Kazdin (Eds.), *Advances in clinical child psychology* (pp. 131–149). New York: Plenum.

Biglan, A., Glasgow, R. E., & Singer, G. (in press). The need for a science of larger social units: A contextual approach. *Behavior Therapy*.

Bronfenbrenner, U. (Ed.). (1979). *The ecology of human development: Experiments by nature and by design*. Cambridge, MA: Harvard University Press.

Bronfenbrenner, U. (1986). Ecology of the family as a context for human development. *Developmental Psychology, 22,* 723–742.

Cairns, R. B. (Ed.). (1979). *The analysis of social interaction: Methods, issues, and illustrations*. Hillsdale, NJ: Lawrence Erlbaum Associates.

Capaldi, D. M., & Patterson, G. R. (1987). An approach to the problem of recruitment and retention rates for longitudinal research. *Behavioral Assessment, 9*(2), 169–177.

Coie, J. D., & Dodge, K. A. (1983). Continuities and change in children's social status: A five-year longitudinal study. *Merrill-Palmer Quarterly, 29,* 261–282.

Dishion, T. J. (1990). The family ecology of boys' peer relations in middle childhood. *Child Development, 61,* 874–892.

Dishion, T. J., & Andrews, D. W. (in press). Adolescent boys and their friends: Dyadic interactions related to antisocial behavior. *Child Development*.

Dishion, T. J., Crosby, L., Rusby, J. C., Shane, D., Petterson, G. R., & Baker, J. (1989). *Peer process code: Multidimensional system for observing adolescent peer interaction*. Unpublished training manual, Oregon Social Learning Center, Eugene, OR.

Dishion, T. J., Gardner, K., Patterson, G. R., Reid, J. B., Spyrou, S., & Thibodeaux, S. (1983). *The family process code: A multidimensional system for observing family interaction*. (Tech. Rep.). Eugene, OR: Oregon Social Learning Center.

Dishion, T. J., & Loeber, R. (1985). Male adolescent marijuana and alcohol use: The role of parents and peers revisited. *American Journal of Drug and Alcohol Abuse, 11,* 11–25.

Dishion, T. J., Patterson, G. R., & Griesler, P. (in press). A trait confluence model for the influence of peers on the trajectory of child antisocial behavior. In L. R. Huesmann (Ed.), *Current perspectives on aggressive behavior*. New York: Plenum Press.

Dishion, T. J., Patterson, G. R., & Kavanagh, K. (in press). An experimental test of the coercion model: Linking theory, measurement, and intervention. In J. McCord & R. Trembley (Eds.), *The interaction of theory and practice: Experimental studies of interventions.* New York: Guilford Press.

Dishion, T. J., Patterson, G. R., Stoolmiller, M., & Skinner, M.S. (1991). Family, school and behavioral antecedents to early adolescent involvement with antisocial peers. *Developmental Psychology, 2,* 172–180.

Dishion, T. J., Reid, J. B., & Patterson, G. R. (1988). Empirical guidelines for a family intervention for adolescent drug use. *Journal of Chemical Dependency Treatment, 1,* 189–214.

Dryfoos, J. G. (1990). *Adolescents at risk: Prevalence and prevention.* New York: Oxford University Press.

Eisenberg, N. (1982). *The development of prosocial behavior.* New York: Academic Press.

Elliott, D. S., Huizinga, D., & Ageton, S. S. (1985). *Explaining delinquency and drug use.* Beverly Hills, CA: Sage.

Forgatch, M. S. (1991). The clinical science vortex: A developing a theory of antisocial behavior. In D. J. Pepler & K. Rubin (Eds.), *The development and treatment of childhood aggression* (pp. 291–315). Hillsdale, NJ: Lawrence Erlbaum Associates.

Gottman, J. M., & Roy, A. K. (1990). *Sequential analysis: A guide for behavioral researchers.* New York: Cambridge University Press.

Hall, W. M., & Cairns, R. B. (1984). Aggressive behavior in children: An outcome of modeling or reciprocity? *Developmental Psychology, 20,* 739–745.

Kandel, D. B. (1978). Homophily, selection, and socialization in adolescent friendships. *American Journal of Sociology, 84,* 427–436.

Kandel, D. B., & Andrews, D. A. (1987). Process of adolescent socialization by parents and peers. *International Journal of the Addictions, 22,* 319–342.

Kellam, S. (1990). Developmental epidemiological framework for family research on depression and aggression. In G.R. Patterson (Ed.), *Depression and aggression in family interaction* (pp. 11–48). Hillsdale, NJ: Lawrence Erlbaum Associates.

Ketterlinus, R. D., & Lamb, M. E. (1993). *Problem behavior lifestyles of virgins and sexually experienced males.* Manuscript submitted for publication.

Linney, J. A., & Seidman, E. (1987). The future of schooling. *American Psychologist, 44,* 336–340.

Loeber, R., & Dishion, T. J. (1984). Boys who fight at home and school: Family conditions influencing cross-setting consistency. *Journal of Consulting and Clinical Psychology, 52,* 759–768.

Miller, N. E., & Dollard, J. (1958). *Social learning and imitation.* New Haven, CT: Yale University Press.

Osgood, D. W. (1993). *Covariation among problem behaviors.* Manuscript submitted for publication.

Patterson, G. R. (1974). Interventions for boys with conduct problems: Multiple settings, treatments, and criteria. *Journal of Consulting and Clinical Psychology, 42,* 471–481.

Patterson, G. R. (1982). *Coercive family process.* Eugene, OR: Castalia.

Patterson, G. R. (1986). Performance models for antisocial boys. *American Psychologist, 41,* 432–444.

Patterson, G. R., & Bank, L. (1987). When is a nomological network a construct? In D. R. Peterson & D. B. Fishman (Eds.), *Assessment for decision* (pp. 249–279). New Brunswick, NJ: Rutgers University Press.

Patterson, G. R., Chamberlain, P., & Reid, J. R. (1982). A comparative evaluation of parent training procedures. *Behavior Therapy, 3,* 638–650.

Patterson, G. R., Reid, J. B., & Dishion, T. J. (1992). *A social learning approach: IV. Antisocial boys*. Eugene, OR: Castalia.

Schoenfeld, W. N. (1978). "Reinforcement" in behavior theory. *Pavlovian Journal, 13*, 135–144.

Skinner, B. F. (1953). *Science and human behavior*. New York: Macmillan.

Snyder, J. J., Dishion, T. J., & Patterson, G. R. (1986). Determinants and consequences of associating with deviant peers during preadolescence and adolescence. *Journal of Early Adolescence, 6*, 20–43.

Wampold, B. E., & Margolin, G. (1982). Nonparametric strategies to test the independence of behavioral states in sequential data. *Psychological Bulletin, 92*, 755–765.

Webster-Stratton, C. (1984). Randomized trail of two parent-training programs for families with conduct-disordered children. *Journal of Consulting and Clinical Psychology, 52*, 666–678.

Webster-Stratton, C., Kolpacoff, M., & Hollinsworth, T. (1988). Self-administered videotape therapy for families with conduct problem children: Comparison with two cost-effective treatments and a control group. *Journal of Consulting and Clinical Psychology, 56*, 558–566.

11

A Research Agenda for Adolescent Problems and Risk-Taking Behaviors

Evan G. Pattishall, Jr.
The Pennsylvania State University

Research on adolescence has reached the stage of development that now requires a review of the many productive disciplinary findings and an integration of these pursuits and findings into a complex and interactive biobehavioral system. The Berkeley Springs conference, with a wide diversity of perspectives, was an exciting beginning of that effort.

This chapter attempts to reflect the content, context, and process experienced at the conference, as well as to introduce additional considerations stimulated by the discussions and conversations.

The conference provided a unique opportunity to bring together a broad array of different disciplines to focus on the problems and the behaviors emanating from and within the world of the adolescent. Thus, the group was able to focus on adolescent problem behaviors and subsequent risk-taking behaviors without being locked into the narrowly focused categorical diseases or pathologies of traditional biomedical research and policy, as Ketterlinus and Lamb (Introduction, this volume; Ketterlinus, Lamb, & Nitz, chapter 2) observed. It was also enriched by the inclusion of issues that related to gender difference because the literature is heavily biased with research on male behaviors.

Presentations and discussions benefited from exploring various aspects of theory, basic and applied research continua, data and experiences from clinical practice, implications of policy and administration, and strategies for intervention. Perhaps most significant was the attempt to look at biological and psychosocial factors, linkages, and interactions within the context of the adolescent's actions, fantasies, and reactions to environment and existence.

NEED FOR MULTIDISCIPLINARY BIOBEHAVIORAL RESEARCH

Unfortunately, most of our attempts to understand the problems and high-risk behaviors of adolescents have involved studies from a single discipline or others using a single variable approach. This may secure elaborate data on the levels of testosterone, the social pressures for smoking, the psychological sequences in adolescent development, the influence of peer pressure, accident proneness, the origins of aggression and violence, and so on, but most often we have neglected to study each of these risk factors from a collaborative or multidisciplinary perspective. Nor have we attempted to integrate individual variables into the complex whole of the biobehavioral organism over time as proposed by Udry (chapter 6); Jessor (1992); Magnusson, Klinteberg, and Stattin (chapter 5); and others.

My colleague and fellow conference participant, Scheidt, suggested that the array of psychosocial and biological variables needed to be studied in adolescence are so great, so intertwined, and so interacting that the time is ripe for the establishment of a "Behavioral Framingham" that would provide the same multi-disciplinary and longitudinal research effort that was organized to study risk factors and reduce cardiovascular disease. This could be accomplished through a joint effort between federal research agencies and private foundations.

One of the major stumbling blocks of reductionist biomedical enquiry is the failure to re-insert what we have learned about molecular, cellular, neurological, or organ functions, back into the total dynamic human organism, and to study our specific findings within the context of the whole. Although our reductionist approach has produced much basic knowledge, further progress and future application is often thwarted by this scientific blindness. Ignoring the important interactions of behavior with genetic, molecular, and cellular components is a costly scientific and philosophical error that will delay our understanding of both biomedical and behavioral considerations.

As an example, in the past, traditional biomedical research on the immune system occurred within the context of the immune system as essentially an autonomous homeostatic system, with little or no attention paid to behavior or even the central nervous system as an important variable. Now, in the past 15 years our understanding of and subsequent research on the immune system has had to be reworked, and to some extent redone, because we now know that behavioral factors such as stress or depression and the central nervous system (CNS) and the cortex have both direct and indirect effects on the immune system. In addition, certain immune functions can even be behaviorally conditioned, and through multidisciplinary research efforts, we are now attempting to identify and document the specific mechanisms involved.

Similarly, biomedical and molecular biology research has attempted to ignore the bidirectional nature of biology. The assumption is that if we can understand the actions and mechanisms of the molecules at the most basic level, we will be able to explain most of the subsequent biological and behavioral actions or reactions. This unidirectional orientation does not recognize the bidirectional aspects of biology, whereby other components of the whole organism can influence and modulate the molecular components. Genetics is a relevant example, in that it is now known that the pathways of gene expression are bidirectional, and that behavior and environment can alter or modulate some gene expressions.

WE CANNOT ESCAPE OUR HISTORY

With regard to adolescent problems and risk-taking behavior, we were eloquently reminded by Moran and Vinovskis (chapter 1) that throughout history, especially since the 16th century, adolescents were frequently described as being rebellious, troubled, sensuous, uncontrolled, lacking moral fiber, antisocial, and as a direct threat to puritanism and religious conversion. We also received documentation that, at least for the past few centuries, many adolescents were attempting to survive and grow up in conditions similar to today's environment of poverty, unemployment, urban concentrations, social dislocations, orphans or separation from parents, servitude, vulnerability to diseases, and lack of education.

This historical perspective added a new dimension to the understanding of today's adolescent as a developing person who is trying to cope and to learn, and whose life and behavior consists of acting on and interacting with an environment of psychosocial, biological, and multicultural events that are often perceived as void of meaningful and enduring relationships. The ramifications of the subsequent cycle of violence and links between childhood victimization and adolescent high risk behaviors, as proposed by Widom (chapter 8), are especially relevant here. This should compel us to also consider the adolescent within the context of an evolutionary or cyclical process immeshed in societal and worldly disorder.

THE POWER OF GENETICS

The potential role of polygene transmission was proposed by Rowe (chapter 7) as an important dimension, especially in attempting to understand high-risk behavior. Behavioral genetics has found that it is possible for some psychological traits to be transmitted from one generation to the next by polygene transmission, just as parental modeling and shaping can transmit behavioral and cognitive patterns. The potential for multidisciplinary collaboration is great, especially to explore the interactions and linkages between the genetic, psychosocial, biobehavioral, physiological, and environmental components.

We must bear in mind, however, that even the genetic components of a known disorder such as schizophrenia can account for only about 30%–40% of the variance, leaving us with an important 60% that must be accounted for by other factors, such as environment, social, and cultural influences. Similar factors are undoubtedly interacting in the development and expression of high-risk behavior, and we must be able to integrate such interactions into our own understanding of adolescent problems and risk-taking behavior.

SOCIALIZING EPIDEMIOLOGY

Epidemiologists recognize behavior as one of the most important risk factors in the etiology of illness and behavioral disturbances. We must bear in mind however, that identifying and even quantifying a risk factor, does not answer the question of causality. Nor does the identification of risk factors and predictors identify the individuals who will be affected, or the specific biobehavioral mechanisms involved.

Epidemiologists and demographers naturally avoid extending their data into speculative conclusions. However, they also know a great deal about the subject being investigated and they could greatly facilitate the study of human behavior and the biomedical sciences if they would begin to collaborate with biobehavioral scientists, at least in the generation of hypotheses related to causality and interventions.

LEARNING BEHAVIORAL LIFESTYLE

The role of learning, particularly social learning theory, was promoted by Andrews and Dishion (chapter 10) as they analyzed the microsocial bases of adolescent problem behaviors. They postulated that specific problem behaviors are learned through what they called *microsocial exchanges* throughout one's lifetime, but especially during earlier stages of development. Problem behavior lifestyle was then appropriately defined as a composite of these microsocial behaviors (see also chapter 2, and Jessor, 1992). Such a conceptualization can play a crucial role in the design of intervention strategies.

Even though the psychological and biological interactions are often given the same emphasis as social factors, the role of learning is of primary importance. Certainly the interactions of cognitive, emotional, hormonal, and prior experience factors play a major role, along with the social contexts, as particular patterns of behavior are learned, practiced, rewarded, and reinforced. Social learning theory is very relevant to the establishment of problem behaviors and high risk behaviors.

Although no one argues against the importance of the learning process, we need to broaden our concepts of learning to include the interactions and interlinking of biobehavioral components. As one example, the role of endorphins should be explored, especially within the context of the endorphins' ability to generate what amounts to a "behavioral high," which then becomes a reinforcer for adolescent problem behaviors and high-risk behaviors. Overcoming such a powerful reinforcer would be much more difficult than teaching and practicing a new behavior. It would be more similar to overcoming the biobehavioral addiction of nicotine acquired through smoking.

Behavior change strategies are seriously understudied. A broad psychosocial and biobehavioral approach could yield significant advances for this critical research need, but learning theory, including reinforcement, addiction, conditioning and deconditioning deserve much more research attention than they presently receive. Yet, when integrated within a biobehavioral context, they are at the core of behavior change and behavior prevention and rehabilitation.